D1457305

Ethnoburb

Ethnoburb

The New Ethnic Community in Urban America

Wei Li

University of Hawai'i Press
Honolulu

Library of Congress Cataloging-in-Publication Data
Li, Wei.
  Ethnoburb : the new ethnic community in urban America / Wei Li.
    p.   cm.
  Includes bibliographical references and index.
  ISBN 978-0-8248-3065-6 (hard cover : alk. paper)
  1. Suburbs—North America.   2. Ethnic neighborhoods—North America.
3. Cultural pluralism—North America.   4. Ethnic neighborhoods—California—
Los Angeles Metropolitan Area—Case studies.   5. Chinese Americans—
California—Monterey Park—Case studies.   I. Title.

  HT352.N7L5 2009
  307.76097—dc22   2008038194

University of Hawai'i Press books are printed on acid-free
paper and meet the guidelines for permanence and durability
of the Council on Library Resources.

Designed by University of Hawai'i Press production staff
Printed by The Maple-Vail Book Manufacturing Group

In memory of my late parents,
   Li Linmo and Chen Chan,
   for their infinite love and sacrifice;
   To all those who love me and whom I love, and
   To my homeland and adopted homeland

Contents

Preface   ix
Acknowledgments   xiii

Introduction   1

PART 1: Exploring the Ethnic Suburb

    1. Ethnicity and Space   11
    2. Ethnoburb: An Alternative Ethnic Settlement   29

PART 2: The Los Angeles Chinese Ethnoburb

    3. Changing Chinese Settlement   53
    4. Building Ethnoburbia   79
    5. From Ethnic Service Center to Global Economic Outpost   100
    6. Anatomy of an Ethnoburb   118
    7. Portraits of Ethnoburban Chinese   150

PART 3: Ethnoburbs of North America

    8. Opportunities and Challenges for Ethnoburbs   171

Notes   185
References   193
Index   209

Preface

The inspiration for this book can be traced to a conversation I had in Washington, DC, in 1991 with a Euro-American professor from the University of Southern California. The conversation took place on the eve of my departure for Los Angeles, where I was going to do graduate work in geography at USC:

"So," said the professor, "you have never been to LA before? I would be very happy to answer any questions you might have."

"Great," I said. "First and foremost, where can I find a relatively decent area with reasonable rent to live around USC?"

The professor looked at me about thirty seconds, then said "You are Chinese, right? Why don't you live in Monterey Park, a city in the San Gabriel Valley? That's a Chinese area, you would feel very comfortable."

"But I've heard that Monterey Park is quite far from the school," I protested.

"Not at all," the professor replied, "it is only a ten-minute drive east from USC."

This conversation first oriented me to the geographic location of Monterey Park and to the perception of Angelinos that Monterey Park was a "Chinese area." During my first weekend in Los Angeles, the memory of this conversation prompted me to take a bus from USC to Monterey Park, where some friends of mine lived. Transferring in downtown's Chinatown, then touring Monterey Park, I saw sharp differences between these two Chinese communities. Downtown LA Chinatown appeared to be a geographically compact tourist attraction, with Chinatown Gate dominating the streetscape. Monterey Park neighborhoods, on the other hand, were typical suburbs, with beautiful lawns and low-rise structures, but they also had an overlay of obvious Chinese elements. Chinese "signatures" appeared on business signs as well as in the residential architecture. I strolled along Garvey Avenue, seeing Chinese characters on signs, listening to people speaking Mandarin, and hearing Chinese songs emanating from nearby stores. Had it not been for the heavy automobile traffic and frequent gas stations, I could almost imagine that I was back walking in Beijing.

Nine years later I had finished my dissertation on the Chinese community in Los Angeles and was working as an assistant professor at the University of Connecticut. I began a new research project on Asian Americans in Silicon Valley, comparing them with the San Gabriel Valley community. During my research I interviewed a fourth-generation Chinese American suburbanite who had moved from San Francisco's Chinatown to the city of Cupertino more than thirty-five years ago. As soon as I mentioned Monterey Park, she exclaimed, "Monterey Park? Isn't that a Chinese ghetto in LA?!" A short time later, I received a somewhat different perspective from a Chinese American lawyer in San Francisco who told me that he and his wife had recently visited Monterey Park. "We had thought Monterey Park was an upscale area," he said. "To our surprise, it is not like that at all—it's solid middle-class neighborhoods, with congested shopping areas and strip malls." But at an academic conference about the San Gabriel Valley in late 1997, every speaker, academics and community activists alike, claimed that the San Gabriel Valley was the future of our nation for its rapid demographic transition and ethnic diversity.

What contributes to these very different understandings? Why, after three scholarly books, many research articles, and extensive media coverage, does Monterey Park still evoke contrary images and perceptions? I was puzzled by these questions as well as by the larger question as to why minority groups form ethnically distinct suburban clusters. Why have the Chinese clustered in this area? Why did they choose Monterey Park and San Gabriel Valley over Chinatown?

As I began my investigations, I frequently read and heard references to Monterey Park as the nation's first "suburban Chinatown," a designation implying that Monterey Park was the same sort of place as downtown Chinatown, only located in the suburbs. Just as Los Angeles has always been thought "atypical" of the American urban experience, so Chinese settlement in the San Gabriel Valley was considered an isolated case of urban ethnic community formation. But the more I experienced the differences between these two Chinese communities, the more uneasy I felt about such a labeling of Monterey Park. The residents of these two communities appeared to me to be distinctly different in terms of where they came from, when they came, what languages they spoke, what jobs they held, and their socioeconomic class. For instance, since I do not understand or speak Cantonese, I personally felt estranged in Chinatown but was more comfortable in the San Gabriel Valley area, where Mandarin is common. My observations of these differences made me wonder why this suburban concentration had formed in recent decades? Had such a community existed before, or elsewhere? What forces underlay its formation?

As I learned more about economic restructuring and globalization on the one hand and about LA's regional circumstances on the other, I was able to piece together the information I had gathered and link my findings to broader socioeconomic and geopolitical contexts. I became convinced that the ethnic concentration in the San Gabriel Valley does not represent a suburban China-town, but is, instead, a new form of ethnic settlement, which I call an ethnic suburb or "ethnoburb." I also realized that the processes driving ethnoburb formation are not unique to the Chinese in LA, but appear to affect other ethnic minority and immigrant groups in other localities and even other countries. My findings about the new Chinese community in San Gabriel Valley form the substance of this book.

Acknowledgments

Without input and support from the Chinese community of Greater Los Angeles, it would have been impossible for me to complete my research. I greatly appreciate the help of this community, whose spatial transformation motivated my book and whose friendliness made the research a gratifying experience. I thank all of my interviewees for the time they spent with me and the personal experiences they shared with me. In particular, I want to express my thanks to Judy Chu, Lucia Su, and Wilbur Woo, who not only provided important information, but also key assistance by acting as my bridges to the community. Henry Hwang, founder of the Far East National Bank, who passed away in 2005, provided key insights when I interviewed him during a critical moment in his professional life in 1999. This book will, I hope, help to commemorate his life. Many local Chinese and Asian American institutions and organizations have also supported me in various ways. Asian System Media, Inc. and its general manager, T. C. Wu, and Jason Chu granted me free access to their database of Chinese businesses in Southern California in the 1990s. Joss Chu, vice president of Promotions and Advertisement of Tawa Supermarket Companies, offered important information on the establishment and development of the company. I was a volunteer for Asian American Economic Development Enterprises Inc. for several years; its former executive director, Dr. Phillip Borden, and former program development director, Mercy Murphy, provided opportunities for me to work with community members in both Chinatown and San Gabriel Valley.

The completion of this book would not have been possible without support and help from many institutions and individuals. I enjoyed my years at University of Southern California as a PhD student and subsequently as a visiting scholar. I owe my greatest debt to Jennifer Wolch. Over the years she has broadened my thinking, guided me in the right direction, and provided critical advice and inspiration. More than an academic advisor, she has been a role model, mentor, and friend who has been there for me in times of personal difficulty and professional challenges. I also benefited greatly from Thomas Jablonsky, whose residency in Monterey Park and then Temple City for more than two decades allowed him to witness the dramatic ethnic transition in San Gabriel Valley communities. His tours of the area, advice, and insights into key community changes helped guide my early thinking about ethnoburb formation. I am truly grateful to Edward Park, who provided me with sociological insights into the literature of Asian American studies, and Laura Pulido, whose critical views on race and ethnicity helped to shape my understanding of the American racialization process. I also want to thank Michael Dear and Curtis Roseman of the USC Department of Geography, who helped me better ground my ideas in theory and strengthen my research design. Other people at USC also contributed to my research in various important ways: Dowell Myers of the School of Urban Planning and Development and Cynthia Crawford provided critical technical guidance in SAS programming, while Laura Lee-Chin in Development Research helped edit an earlier version of the manuscript and made important suggestions as a friend and a fellow Chinese American.

The University of Connecticut's visionary establishment of an interdisciplinary Asian American Studies Institute created my first tenure-track academic position in the United States, which also made me the nation's first jointly appointed assistant professor in Asian American Studies and Geography. Support from UConn in the form of grants and fellowships from the Chancellor's Office, the Research Foundation, and the Dean's Office of the College of Liberal Arts and Sciences, has been critical in expanding my research. The then Geography Department Head, Dean Hanink, and the Asian American Studies Institute (AASI) Director, Roger Buckley, provided guidance and supported my research agenda. My research assistant Paul Fernald did a superb job of recreating all the original maps and in creating the spatial mean maps using his extensive statistical and GIS training. My undergraduate assistants, Karen Hoang, Daniel Wright, and Zheroo Li, did superb work transcribing interviews and handling other labor-intensive tasks. Fe Delos-Santos and Janice Law Trecker read and edited an earlier version of this manuscript. My deep gratitude goes to my former colleagues in the Department of Geography for moral and intellectual support; Karen Chow and Fe Delos-Santos at AASI, and Allison Thompson at University Relations for academic camaraderie and easy friendship. Thanks also go to Rose Kaposi at Geography and Anne Theriault at AASI for handling tedious paper work and offering administrative support. Karen Chow (now at De Anza College) and I have been close professional and personal friends since 1997. We enjoyed enormously the few hours we spent together at a Borders bookstore in San Francisco in a sunny August afternoon when she edited the last few chapters of the final version of this manuscript. I have benefited a great deal from her insights growing up as a Chinese American Southern Californian in La Puente and Hacienda Heights and her family's witnessing the transformation of San Gabriel Valley.

My work has continued since I joined Arizona State University. The former director of Asian Pacific American Program, Thomas Nakayama, and its current director, Karen Leong, and the former director of the School of Geographical Sciences, Richard Aspinall, rendered much needed support and guidance to my research. The collegiality of Carol Caruss, Melinda L. de Jesús (now at the California College of Arts, and editor of a portion of this manuscript), Karen Kuo, John Rosa, and Roisan Rubio accompanied my advancement from a junior scholar to a tenured associate professor. I now benefit from the growth of the School of Geographical Sciences, under the leadership of Luc Anselin, and the collegiality of my colleagues there with my new joint appointment. Barbara Trapido-Lurie, in particular, recreated the final version of all maps in this book in timely fashion and superb quality; she was a pleasure to work with. I am also truly grateful for the invaluable assistance of Hanh Nguyen, Kedi Wang, Dan Wang, Wei Zeng, Wei Zhong, and Yun Zhou during the finalization of the manuscript.

The Asian Pacific American Studies Program at Loyola Marymount University, the Ethnic Studies Department of the University of California, Berkeley, and the Geography Department at the University of Southern California provided invaluable support for my field research during spring and summer 2001 and 2000, and the summers of 1998 and 1999 respectively. Special thanks to Edward Park of Loyola Marymount, Ling-chi Wang, Brigid Tung, and Weichi Poon of UC Berkeley, and Douglas Sherman, John Wilson, and Billy Shotlow of USC.

I am also indebted to my Ethnic Banking Project colleagues, in particular project director Gary Dymski of University of California Center Sacramento and UC Riverside, Hyeon-Hyo Ahn and Jang-Pyo Hong from Korea, Carolyn Aldana of California State University, Maria Chee of the University of Virginia, and Yu Zhou of Vassar College. This project seeks to examine the role of minority banks in economic and community development in Southern California. One objective of this project, funded by a National Science Foundation research grant (SES-00747754), is to explore the evolution of the Chinese American and Chinese foreign banking sectors in Los Angeles County, especially their role in altering commercial infrastructures and residential landscapes in the San Gabriel Valley ethnoburb area. Some of my discussions of Chinese banks are drawn from that project.

A group of American and international scholars who are interested in and working on immigrant and integration issues have served as an inspiration to me. In particular, I thank James Allen, Thomas Boswell, Cindy Fan, Susan Hardwick, Evelyn Hu-Dehart, David Kaplan, Lawrence Ma, Janice Monk, Gary Okihiro, Kavita Pandit, Christopher Smith, and Lois Takahashi in the United States; Daniel Hiebert, Audrey Kobayashi, David Ley, Peter Li, Lucia Lo, Valerie Preston, Carlos Teixeira, and Lu Wang in Canada; Kevin Dunn in Australia; Richard Bedford and Elsie Ho in New Zealand; Jane Pollard in the United Kingdom; and Zhang Jing Zhe (C. C. Chang, my M.S. advisor at Peking University) in China for their long-term mentorship and friendship.

Being an immigrant scholar and an ethnic Chinese, I have also benefited from a cohort of Chinese American and Chinese Canadian scholars who share similar professional and personal backgrounds and academic interests in globalization, transnationalism, immigration, and a changing China. Some of these individuals are long-time Southern California residents themselves. To Huping Ling, Haiming Liu, Qingfang Wang, Zuoyue Wang, Feng Gang Yang, Phillip Fei Yang, Xiaohuang Yin, Da Zheng, Xiaojian Zhao, Min Zhou, and Li Zong, my thanks for your friendship and the opportunity to learn from you.

Masako Ikeda, an editor at the University of Hawai'i Press, has recognized the potential importance and impact of the ethnoburb phenomenon for American urban landscapes and has placed her trust in my presentation of it. Her editorial vision has greatly benefited this book. We have had a pleasant working relationship since my first edited collection titled *From Urban Enclave to Ethnic Suburb: New Asian Communities in the Pacific Rim Countries.* I am also indebted greatly to the two reviewers of this book and Cheri Dunn, managing editor at the press. Margaret Black did a superb job in copyediting this book while sharing her interests of immigration and settlement with me during the process.

Last, but certainly not least, my deepest appreciation to my extended family, especially my beloved late parents. I was born to an academic family. Both my paternal great-grandfathers were among the last cohort of Chinese scholars who passed the imperial examinations. One was appointed a scholar-in-residence at the Hanlin Academy, the country's highest academy, by Emperor Guang Xu of the Qing dynasty. My father was a professor, and my mother was an administrator, at the two top universities in Beijing; all my close relatives in my parents' generation worked as university professors or high school teachers. My late aunt, who completed her college education in the early 1930s, a rare accomplishment among Chinese women during the time, was a life-long high school English teacher. She started to teach me English when I was a little girl, a pursuit interrupted by the Cultural Revolution. My extended family of aunts, uncles, cousins, nieces and nephews helped me every way they could, especially after my mother passed away when I was only fourteen years old. I remember as a kid watching my parents working late at night reading or writing. Witnessing such effort and dedication eventually led to my own desire to work as an academic. Although I can hardly remember my mom's face, I do recall that she was an intelligent, independent woman and a loving mother. She was persecuted during the Cultural Revolution and died of cancer at the age of forty-six. After my mother passed away, my father decided he would raise me by himself and never remarry. He was a mentor, a teacher, as well as a caring father to me. After I came to the United States in 1988, he lived by himself. He never let me worry about him, but encouraged me to pursue my studies toward a doctoral degree. He saw that dream come true but succumbed to illness a year after I became the first PhD in my extended family. Although my parents will never be able to hold this book in their hands and read it, I am convinced that they both look down at me from heaven with smiles and are proud that I did what they hoped for me to do. My parents' dedication to their work and society made them my role models and guided me to work hard and to respect other people and cultures. So I dedicate this book to them, to my extended family and friends who love me and whom I love, as well as to my homeland, China, and my adopted homeland, the United States of America. I sincerely hope that this book will contribute to foster mutual understanding among various ethnic groups and cultures in Los Angeles and beyond.

INTRODUCTION

This book is about the creation of a new ethnic landscape in North America and a new model of the contemporary urban ethnic community: the ethnoburb. Ethnoburbs have emerged under the influence of international geopolitical and global economic restructuring; changing national immigration and trade policies; local demographic, economic, and political contexts; and increasing transnational networks and connections. Suburban ethnic clusters of residential areas and business districts in large metropolitan areas, ethnoburbs are multiethnic communities in which one ethnic minority group has a significant concentration but does not necessarily constitute a majority. Such suburban clusters replicate some features of an ethnic enclave and some features of a suburb that lacks any specific minority identity. Ethnoburbs coexist with traditional ethnic ghettos and enclaves in inner cities in contemporary American society.

Ethnic geography, a discipline influenced by traditional theoretical frameworks developed within cultural geography, demography, ethnic studies and sociology, has sought to explain the social and spatial integration of immigrants into the fabric of mainstream American society. Recent critiques, however, argue for a greater sensitivity to the social construction of race and to the dynamics of racialization, the sociospatial structures of ethnic communities, the role of ethnic economies in ethnic community development and globalization processes, and the transnational connections of immigrants. The new cultural geography, under the influence of postmodern thought, has responded to multiculturalism in contemporary society by refocusing on those groups traditionally excluded from Western society and often related to as the "other," groups that include women and minorities. This new perspective informs the geographical understanding of the Chinese community in Los Angeles that is the focus of this book.

Los Angeles County is considered one of the most ethnically diverse places in the United States (Allen and Turner 1989, 1996, 2002). Not only is the county the most populous in the nation, but it also includes the largest number of Chinese residents. As was true of many other cities, LA's Chinese population was historically centered in a downtown Chinatown, which can be traced back to the nineteenth century. Contemporary Chinatown in Los Angeles remains a congested neighborhood and ethnic business district, as well as a tourist attraction. Ethnic Chinese comprise a majority of all residents, including an older generation of Cantonese-speaking Chinese and new immigrants from Southeast Asia. Many are poor and have limited formal education.

Since the 1960s, many upwardly mobile Chinese have moved out of Chinatown and adjacent inner-city neighborhoods to the suburbs in search for better housing, neighborhoods, and schools. Some of them dispersed spatially and became socioeconomically assimilated into the mainstream society. However, a new trend began occurring during the same time period, which saw many new immigrants with higher educational attainment, professional occupations, and financial resources settling directly into the suburbs without ever experiencing life in the inner city. This is different from prior generations of immigrants, Chinese included, who normally settled first in the inner city and moved out to the suburbs only after they moved up socioeconomically. This traditional pattern, as described by scholars of the Chicago School of Sociology in the 1920s (see Park and Miller 1921), has been widely accepted by and deeply rooted in the minds of most Americans. However, in this new immigrant influx, another form of Chinese settlement, complete with distinct economic activities, social institutions, and cultural life, has emerged in the suburbs. By 1990 there were more than 158,000 Chinese in the San Gabriel Valley,[1] making it the largest suburban Chinese concentration in the nation.

On a geographical scale, the settlement of Chinese in the San Gabriel Valley far surpasses that of the Chinatown model. It includes cities, Census Designated Places (CDPs), and unincorporated areas in the Valley. Many of the Chinese people are Mandarin-speaking recent immigrants from Taiwan, Mainland China, Southeast Asia, Hong Kong, and other parts of the world. They are a heterogeneous, highly polarized population in terms of educational, occupational, and economic status, and they have generated rapidly growing Chinese residential areas and business districts in which Chinese residents actively participate in local politics and social life.

The emergence of a suburban Chinese community in Los Angeles over the last several decades has generated a good deal of interest among scholars, the mass media, and the general public. Timothy Fong's *The First Suburban Chinatown* (1994) traces the changing demographic composition and economic structure of the City of Monterey Park; John Horton's *The Politics of Diversity* (1995), which is partially based on UCLA's Monterey Park Project, documents political changes in the city; Leland Saito's *Race and Politics* (1998) discusses the politics of racial representation and coalition-building in congressional redistricting that has resulted due to changes in the community. Other academic journal articles and dissertations from a variety of disciplines reveal the broad extent of scholarly interest in this area.[2] The mainstream media, including *The Los Angeles Times* and *Forbes,* have also carried extensive coverage of this subject.[3]

Past studies provide valuable information and insights about the San Gabriel Valley Chinese community, but it has drawbacks. Some analysts have referred to this new ethnic concentration as a "suburban Chinatown,"[4] implying a continuation of the traditional ethnic enclave in a different geographical location: the American suburbs. In the popular American imagination, "Chinatown" evokes a crowded inner-city enclave inhabited by ethnic Chinese of a lower socioeconomic profile and an ethnic economic district marked by garment shops, Chinese restaurants and stores, or touristy areas with an exotic "Oriental" flavor. While some academics and the popular media have embraced the notion of "suburban Chinatown," such a characterization appears to me to be quite inaccurate, for the San Gabriel Valley communities do not exhibit many of the characteristics of traditional Chinatowns. This conviction is shared by many community leaders and activists inside the suburban Chinese community, who consider any labeling of Monterey Park as a "suburban Chinatown" to be inappropriate and misleading.[5] Clearly there is a need for more research on the nature of new suburban ethnic settlements and the contexts and trajectories of their development. With increasing recognition of Asian suburbanization across the Pacific Rim,[6] it is time to reflect upon this process as it has occurred in the nation's first large-scale suburban Chinese community. I attempt to address the pertinent issues in this book, especially documenting the process and forces that transformed the San Gabriel Valley into multiethnic suburbs in the latter half of the twentieth century. This is particularly imperative to understand now because census data reveals that at the beginning of the twenty-first century American racial minorities, immigrants included, increasingly call American suburbs their home. Clearly, both the traditional inner-city ethnic enclaves and the multiethnic suburbs have become new immigrant gateways (Singer, Hardwick and Brettell 2008).

Based on the Chinese experience in San Gabriel Valley, I propose a new model of ethnic settlement: the ethnoburb.[7] While patterns of immigration to the United States and the formation of ethnic communities have always been shaped by socioeconomic and political contexts, the creation of an ethnoburb is perhaps more clearly shaped and propelled by changing dynamics at the international, national, and local levels. As a form of urban ethnic settlement, the ethnoburb has been forged from the interplay of economic globalization, political struggles between and within nation-states, major U.S. immigration policy shifts, and a host of local conditions.

In this book I integrate the literature on global economic restructuring, geopolitical shifts, and national immigration and social policy with the issues of racialization and the social construction of urban ethnicity, ethnic communities, and ethnic economies. Only by so doing can we fully comprehend the complexity of contemporary urban ethnic and immigrant communities and their position and function in the global economy and American society. The ethnoburb model that results from the linkages among these different literatures can serve as a spatial dimension to new theoretical explanation of race and ethnicity and contribute to our understanding of racialization processes. Just as the traditional invasion/succession and downtown versus uptown models are related to acculturation/assimilation theory, so the ethnoburb model connects newer theoretical approaches to contemporary spatial expressions of race/ethnicity.

Traditionally, ethnic settlement forms such as the ghetto and the enclave played peripheral roles in mainstream society. Seen as repositories for subaltern groups who were excluded and ignored, these areas were left to grapple with their own concerns and problems. Because circumstances at the regional, national, and global levels have shifted dramatically, traditional models of the ghetto and ethnic enclave as isolated communities can no longer fully explain the dynamics and linkages in contemporary ethnic settlements. Ethnoburbs have become part of the reality in today's urban America. They provide opportunities for ethnic minority people to resist complete assimilation into the non-Hispanic white cultural and social "norms" of American society. More importantly, the ethnoburb model challenges the dominant view that assimilation is inevitable and remains the ideal solution for immigrants and other racial/ethnic minorities who live in the United States. By maintaining their multifaceted identities and establishing distinctive communities, ethnoburban populations can nonetheless integrate into the mainstream society through economic activities, political involvement, and community life. And in doing so, these ethnic minority groups are transforming American society.

In this book I seek to do the following:

1. elaborate a new contextual model that conceptualizes the formation of new suburban ethnic settlements—ethnoburbs—as a result of contemporary global/national/local dynamics affecting ethnic community formation and

growth, place-specific processes of racialization, and the spatiality of ethnicity in complex metropolitan regions;

2. evaluate the ethnoburb model via an analysis of the spatial transformation of the Chinese community in Greater Los Angeles, from downtown Chinatown to the San Gabriel Valley ethnoburb;

3. assess the role of the ethnoburb as a global economic outpost and a complex urban ethnic mosaic in terms of its economic structure and the demographic and socioeconomic characteristics of its residents;

4. identify major differences between this emergent Chinese ethnoburb and contemporary Chinatown; and

5. identify similar ethnoburbs in other major North American cities.

My empirical process required that I first analyze the ethnoburb model contextually. I followed this with analysis of the aggregated census data at tract level to illustrate broad settlement trends and time-series firm-level business distribution data that suggests the linkages between residential and ethnic economy expansion. I then document through census microdata the sociospatial structure of the ethnoburb and its effects on the ethnoburb's role in the larger society/economy, and finally I analyze qualitatively the ethnoburb's development path, which allows me to highlight key actors, political struggles, and the processes of racialization involved in ethnoburb formation.

The contextual analysis, which is based on secondary data and existing literature, identifies in detail the role of structural factors, institutional conditions, and activities of key agents and actors in the formation and development of the San Gabriel Valley ethnoburb. Ethnoburb formation is a complex process. The underlying forces include structural factors such as global geopolitical and economic restructuring, U.S. national immigration and trade policy changes, as well as institutional conditions, such as the regulations and policies of local governments and institutions and the activities of key agents and actors. All are assessed in order to analyze how the San Gabriel Valley ethnoburb first took root and why it is sited in its particular location. This contextual analysis includes an identification of why and how global economic restructuring has changed the relationships between the United States and the immigrants' home countries, as well as continued to provide a large pool of immigrant entrepreneurs and laborers; an illustration of the correlation between immigrant influx and important global geopolitical events; an analysis of why and how major U.S. national immigration policy changes have made it possible for large waves of immigrants to settle in the United States; an examination of how local economic restructuring, demographic features, and political changes make it more likely for an ethnoburb to emerge in certain localities; and finally an explication of how the practices of key individuals, organizations, and initiatives (local officials, entrepreneurs, real estate developments, and so forth) contribute to the ethnoburb formation process. Such a multilevel contextual analysis demonstrates how combinations of factors at different levels and spatial scales enable an ethnoburb to become a reality.

Second, I compare the spatial, population, and economic structures of the ethnoburb and of downtown Chinatown. I analyze census data to show the changing distribution of the Chinese population and examine the locations of Chinese businesses and their correlation with residential patterns. The Chinese residential and firm-level business distribution information illustrates the spatial forms of the Chinese community in Los Angeles in terms of change over time and space. Historical information is gathered to trace the evolution of the Chinese community in Los Angeles. I have collected and mapped census data for Los Angeles County at the census tract level (1980, 1990, and 2000) and information about Chinese businesses (for 1982, 1996, and 2001). The maps facilitate the visualization of basic geographic patterns over time for Chinese residential areas and business districts and for the Chinese population in both the ethnoburb and Chinatown. What emerge are the broad relationships between residence and business location patterns. These maps reveal, for example, what types of ethnic economic activity are located mainly within ethnic communities and which ones are not closely associated with Chinese residential density. The resulting information allows me to illustrate the nature of ethnic economic structures in these two places and show how their respective ethnic economies are differentially connected to the global economic network. It also allows me to demonstrate how much the Chinese ethnic economy has contributed to local economic structure in terms of revenue generation and employment creation.

The ethnoburb model argues that ethnoburbs form under dynamics different from those that formed the traditional downtown Chinatowns, and thus they exhibit distinct spatial forms and internal socioeconomic structures. The task, then, is to investigate these differences. To do this, I have analyzed microdata samples from the 1990 census (the Public Use Microdata Sample [PUMS]) to identify demographic, socioeconomic, and occupational differences between the San Gabriel Valley ethnoburb and downtown LA's Chinatown. This investigation also allows me to discover similarities and differences between these two groups of Chinese people and to reveal the extent of socioeconomic polarization—with well-to-do, educated, professionals and entrepreneurs at one end and poor, less-educated, low-skilled laborers at the other—within the ethnoburb as a proxy for the complexity and heterogeneity of the ethnoburb relative to traditional Chinatown.

In order to analyze the roles of key institutions and agents involved in the spatial transformation of LA's Chinese community, and to assess the political barriers and the racial dimensions of ethnoburb formation, I conducted in-depth interviews with elected officials, business and community leaders, and Chinese bank executives (these last being part of the ethnic banking project).

I also engaged in ethnographic research, volunteering at, participating in, and observing community events. Despite the inherent problems of ethnographic research (such as representation, power relations), I had certain advantages. I am an ethnic Chinese, fluent in Mandarin. I was born and raised in Mainland China and have lived through some critical moments of change in Chinese history and thus have gained certain insights of Chinese cultural norms and values. As a first-generation adult immigrant myself, I share life experiences that are similar to those of many ethnoburban Chinese. Some of the discussion also reflects my own personal knowledge and experience and highlights my role as cultural informant. In addition, I established extensive community ties and was directly involved in community life while I was living in the LA area. These advantages clearly helped create rapport and earn the trust of my respondents (especially those who spoke Mandarin). On the other hand, as a scholar with extensive academic training, I am also an outsider who can contextualize the research from a different perspective. Being able to take both positions has benefited me greatly during the research process, for it has allowed me to comprehend the thoughts of the interviewees from their perspectives and at the same time has given me the skills to synthesize such qualitative impressions with data from other sources.

The book consists of eight chapters, which are organized around three broad themes. Part 1 introduces the ethnoburb model and its background. Drawing insights from theoretical approaches to interethnic relations, immigration, and integration, I present my conceptual model and illustrate the differences between this new form of ethnic community and traditional ghettos and ethnic enclaves. Part 2 explores the Chinese ethnoburb in Los Angeles. I focus on the dynamics underlying the changing spatial forms of Chinese concentrations; the formation of the ethnoburb and its spatial forms, socioeconomic and demographic characteristics; and the business patterns that characterize the ethnoburb and differentiate it from the downtown ethnic enclave. Part 3 explores the future of the LA ethnoburb, examines similar ethnoburbs in other major North American metropolitan areas, and addresses the opportunities and challenges posed by the emergence of ethnoburbs.

PART 1

Exploring the Ethnic Suburb

1 Ethnicity and Space

The United States is a country largely composed of immigrants from all over the world and their descendants. For this reason, the study of race and ethnicity has a long history in this country. Scholars from many social science disciplines, particularly sociologists and anthropologists, have developed theories of race and ethnicity and conducted numerous empirical analyses of different ethnic groups. Although geographical studies of race and ethnicity have been less developed compared with other disciplines, a literature focused on the "geography of minority groups" began to develop in the 1970s and matured into the fields of ethnic geography and geography of race and racism of the 1990s. During the 1980s and 1990s, geographical studies of ethnicity underwent fundamental changes through their incorporation of social theory, change foci of research projects, and the expansion of their methodologies. Ethnic geography had traditionally sought to explain the social and spatial integration of immigrants into mainstream American society; recent critiques, however, argue for a greater sensitivity to the social construction of race and the dynamics of racialization, to the socio-spatial structuration of ethnic communities, and to the role of ethnic economies in ethnic community development.

Ethnicity and Race in American Society

Many now-classic theories were developed to explain the relationships between ethnic minority groups and the "dominant group" in mainstream American society. Of these, basically two different schools can be distinguished: acculturation-assimilation and ethnicity-pluralism.

Traditional Approaches

During the mass immigration to the United States in the nineteenth and twentieth centuries, the prevailing view in both the public and academic worlds emphasized the acculturation-assimilation of immigrants. Immigrants, often poor, ill-educated, and lacking English language skills, were expected to climb the economic ladder and merge into American society. Another metaphor was the American "melting pot," in which all different ethnic groups were integrated into a whole that followed the norms set up by Anglo Americans. Anglo-conformity demands a complete renunciation of the immigrant's ancestral culture in favor of the behavior and values of the Anglo-Saxon core group: "the 'melting pot' idea envisaged a biological merger of the Anglo-Saxon peoples with other immigrant groups and a blending of their respective cultures into a new indigenous American type" (Gordon 1964, 85). Each immigrant group is expected to undergo a "race relations cycle" of "contact, competition, accommodation, and eventual assimilation" to the host society, and this cycle is seen as "progressive and irreversible" (Park 1950, 150).

In brief, the *assimilation-acculturation* model suggests that ethnic groups gradually merge into the host society and lose their distinctive identities. Attitudinal and behavioral changes, shifts in cultural referents, community structure changes, and intermarriage dissolve the value and power conflicts that initially existed with the host society. The only remaining vestige of ethnicity may be what Gans (1979) termed "symbolic ethnicity." He argues that though ethnicity may persist for generations, it is maintained only as a set of symbolic meanings, with little social or psychological content.

Developed first by the Chicago School of Sociology at the turn of the twentieth century and refined by Gordon in the mid-1960s, *assimilation* continues to be the most frequently used concept for immigrant groups' integration with American society, and it is closely monitored and often measured by academic studies using a variety of indices. Gordon's categorization of the various stages of assimilation in 1964 included cultural or behavioral (acculturation), structural, marital (amalgamation), identificational, attitude and behavior receptional, and civic assimilation (Gordon 1964, 71).

Influenced in the 1960s by independence movements internationally and the civil rights movement nationally, both the academic world and the public media in the United States have begun to value ethnicity and pluralism over acculturation or assimilation. The *ethnicity-pluralism* approach recognizes the resiliency of ethnicity, emphasizes differences among various ethnic groups, and holds that such differences will coexist over time, making American society an ethnic mosaic (Alba 1992; Gleason 1992).

Ethnicity, as defined by Handelman (1977), is the degree of conformity by members of a group with shared norms in the course of social interaction. Handelman also categorized the organizational dimensions of ethnicity as ethnic category, network, association, and community.

According to Cohen, "Pluralism refers to a society with diverse political interest groups that may or may not be ethnically defined while plural societies generally refer to ones in which ethnically diverse segments are organized into politically relevant units" (1978, 398). The ethnicity-pluralism school emphasizes the persistence of ethnicity and the importance of pluralism. For example, Horace Kallen believed that "the development of American society would reach farther if respected pluralism and ethnic groups were allowed to make contributions from what was uniquely valuable in their cultural heritages" (quoted in Alba, 1985a).

Moreover, ethnicity in American society is not static but dynamic, incorporating generational changes. A "minority model" has been developed to further differentiate the experiences of specific ethnic groups, namely, those which correspond to the experiences of some non-European, racially marked groups (usually called "racial minority groups"). The assimilation-acculturation model, in contrast, tends to reflect the experiences of most European groups. It is known as the "ethnic model," and is delineated by Gans's concept of "symbolic ethnicity" (Alba 1985b; Padgett 1980).

In the field of geography, scholars have also paid attention to ethnic issues along with their anthropologist and sociologist colleagues. C. Clark et al. (1984) compiled a book of studies of ethnic groups from a geographic perspective. This volume points out that ethnic groups have a clear sense of identity based upon a shared tradition, including a language, a sense of racial or biological descent, and shared territory. Ethnicity unites elements of race and culture, but not all culture is ethnicity, nor is all race ethnicity. Thus immigrant experiences involve race, ethnicity, and culture, and the immigrants' becoming integrated into the American social structure "creates social pluralism through the projection of institutional differentiation from the private into the public domain" (Clarke, Ley, and Peach 1984, 54; also see Colin et al. 1984)

Overall, these two contrasting theoretical approaches to interethnic relations—acculturation-assimilation and ethnicity-pluralism—have traditionally characterized the ethnic studies literature in the United States and have, accordingly, influenced ethnic geography.

In the 1980s and 1990s, however, social scientists began to recognize the inadequacy of the more traditional approaches to ethnic studies. Scholars have raised new questions about the meaning of and underlying reasons for ethnicity and race in American society and have characterized traditional approaches as having an establishment bias. Both acculturation-assimilation and ethnicity-pluralism are considered to belong to "order theories," which "tend to accent patterns of inclusion, of orderly integration and assimilation of particular racial and ethnic groups to a core culture and society" (Feason and Feason 1994, 29).

Similarly, Omi and Winant (1994, 48) categorize these two schools as part of ethnicity theory, which focuses on "the dynamics of incorporation of minority groups into the dominant society."

In the case of assimilation, traditional theorists developed a theoretical progression that every ethnic group was supposed to follow and then failed to recognize the many divergences from this "norm." Discrimination by mainstream society made assimilation a longed-for dream for many non-European immigrants. For example, the heyday of the assimilation concept (1870–1925) was the same era when Asian immigrants were attacked physically and barred from becoming naturalized citizens by the mainstream society, which was dominated by white Americans. The belief was that only "good groups" (defined as immigrant groups from certain European countries) assimilated well into the American mainstream (Feason and Feason 1994; Hing 1994). While ethnicity-pluralism recognizes the differences between various groups and emphasizes the benefit of a diversified American society, the theory does not explain why racial and ethnic differences and inequality exist, nor does it specify the social, political, and economic circumstances that would promote a harmonic mosaic of different groups and cultures in America. In fact, the question of whether it is possible to build such a mosaic has not even been raised, which leads to the presumption that a harmonic mosaic is possible so long as immigrants assimilate to American society. In addition, neither the assimilation nor the pluralism theory attach their ideas about ethnicity to national and global socioeconomic and political contexts, but rather they associate the assimilation and integration process solely with individual attitude and behavior.

Retheorizing Ethnicity and Race

Contemporary researchers are seeking to transition from immigration scholarship that is exclusively concerned with patterns of immigration, segregation, and assimilation to one that more consciously attempts to deal with the political/economic contexts as well as the racial/ethnic dimensions of immigration.[1] Some of these new approaches belong to the power-conflict school, which seeks to explain the persistent inequality of power and resource distribution that is associated with racial, ethnic, and gender relations. Scholars in this school emphasize "the links of the inequality to the economic institution of capitalism...; the role of the government in legalizing exploitation and segregation and in defining racial and ethnic relations; [as well as the] resistance to domination and oppression by those oppressed" (Feason and Feason 1994, 44). Such approaches often consider race/ethnicity, class, and gender as being interrelated.

With regard to race, recent critiques treat it not only as a category used by the mainstream society to differentiate among various groups of people, but also as a formation process imposed by the social structure, which closely relates to the politics and power relations in American society. Omi and Winant (1994) review three existing paradigms on American race relations: the ethnicity paradigm (acculturation-assimilation), the class paradigm (class and labor market conflicts), and the national paradigm (internal colonialism) and propose an alternative model of racial formation. They define racial formation as "the socio-historical process by which racial categories are created, inhabited, transformed, and destroyed." Indicating that both "human bodies and social structures are represented and organized," they see racial formation as being linked to "the evolution of hegemony, the way in which society is organized and ruled" (Omi and Winant 1994, 55 and 56). They emphasize that both race and racism are products of social organization and cultural representation and demonstrate racial formation as a macro-level social process, as well as a micro-level everyday experience. They identify the United States as a "racial state." Its racial formation process dates at least to the 1790 Naturalization Law, which made it clear that only "free white" persons were eligible for citizenship. The 1790 law initiated a continuous process of defining and redefining who belongs in the "free white" category, which has persisted throughout U.S. history. For example, after the United States took over California, Mexicans were considered to be "semi-civilized" and qualified for citizenship, but they were never treated on an equal basis with whites. On the other hand, Native Americans, African Americans, and Asians were thought to be "heathen" and excluded from citizenship, although all three groups were indispensable as labor in building California and were recruited specifically as such (Almaguer 1994; Barrera 1979; Saxton 1995).

In an earlier edition of their book, Omi and Winant also introduced the concept of "*racialization* to specify the extension of racial meaning to a previously racially unclassified relationship, social practice or group" (emphasis added); they underscored the notion that "racialization is an ideological process, a historically specific one" (1986, 64). Hence, race is not just a way to differentiate people, but is also an idea that shapes power relationships as well as social practices through racial formation processes. Espiritu (1992) maintains that the concept of "panethnicity" that has emerged in recent decades is the result either of mainstream society's unwillingness to recognize or of its ignorance about ethnic subgroup differences, or both. Such panethnicities include, but are not limited to, "Asian Americans," "Hispanic Americans," and "Native Americans." Panethnicity is a categorization both adopted on voluntary basis, but also imposed. I would argue that such categorization is also a racialization process, as different ethnic groups are lumped together in order for them to be treated as a racial group. Such a racialization process not only applies to minority groups but to some portions of the dominant non-Hispanic white group as well. In American history, some European immigrant groups were initially not considered "white" despite their light skin color. The Irish, Italians, and Jews were viewed as inferior to Anglos, but over time they became "white" (Ignatiev 1995; Roediger 1991). The phenomenon of panethnicity underlies the entire concept of whiteness, which has evolved into higher relief in reaction to population diversity and is amplified by the emergence of many Euro-American clubs in high schools and university campuses.

Geographical reflections upon these new approaches emphasize the following issues: (1) a reassessment of race as a social construction, (2) the examination of the complex mesh of social relations and spatial structures, and (3) a recognition of both the spatial expression of social processes and the spatial constitution of society (Jackson 1987). Jackson (1987) calls for study of the "geography of racism" to inject a more adequate theoretical conception of space and place into studies of race and racism. The added territorial dimension has important potential. Only by analyzing the socioeconomic and political contexts of society can we understand the situation of ethnic groups. Researchers must not only examine the "classified"—the various racial/ethnic groups—as they did before, but also focus more on the "classifier"—the white-dominated social structure.[2]

Anderson (1987, 1988, 1991) examines the roles of the "classifiers," especially the federal, provincial, and local governments, during the process of racialization. She demonstrates how European immigrants and native Canadians formalize "Chineseness" and the image of Chinatown. She indicates that "Chineseness" is a creation born out of the beliefs and institutional practices of white European society and that Chinatowns are the physical manifestation. Although her case study examines only Vancouver, she argues that the situation represents "more 'global' themes concerning power and racial discourse, the social construction of identity and place, the relation between ideology and institutional practice, and the formation of conceptual structures into material forms" (Anderson 1991, 250).

Ethnicity, too, has been reevaluated under the same framework. For example, Cater and Jones (1987) conclude that although ethnicity flourishes as a real, dynamic force, it must be analyzed in terms of the interests of the dominant class. I have also recently argued that there is a phenomenon called "racialized assimilation." This complement to "segmented assimilation" theory indicates that the immigrant integration process occurs not only along class lines but also has a racial dimension, precisely because of the racial dynamics in contemporary American society.[3]

Clearly, these new approaches to analyzing ethnicity and race locate ethnicity in the broader socioeconomic and political contexts in American society. Hence they explore the relationships between ethnicity/race and society more appropriately than the traditional theoretical interpretations have done. Moreover, both race and ethnicity are spatially constituted and expressed. Both arise from large-scale political-economic processes (for example, colonialism and class formation), yet they are also expressed in local economies and cultures. Studies of race and ethnicity should incorporate the spatial expressions and the economic characteristics of ethnicity/race and be multilevel in nature, and, indeed, recent geographical scholarship emphasizes how racial/ethnic identities are not only socially constructed but spatially constituted.[4] The spatial dimensions of ethnicity are what geographers can best address, not only from the perspective of spatial variations of ethnicity, but also the relationship between the spatial form of ethnic communities and ethnicity and racial formation as social constructions.

The Spatial Forms of Ethnicity and Race

The formation of ethnic communities has been explained by a number of theoretical approaches. Different spatial locations, degrees of concentration, and the forms taken by ethnic communities are good indicators of changing American racial relations and socioeconomic environments. Historically, ethnic minority groups were forced to live in contained communities due to discrimination. American urban housing dynamics are underpinned by racial discrimination that causes spatial segregation. Changing political and socioeconomic situations have resulted in dispersion but also in new forms of ethnic concentration.[5] Both processes can transform ethnic communities as well as the larger society.

Ghettoes and Ethnic Enclaves

Ethnic concentrations have traditionally taken two major forms: the ghetto and the enclave. Both result from a combination of external push factors by the mainstream society (prejudice and discrimination) and internal pull factors (ethnic solidarity and mutual interests). A ghetto is "an urban residential district which is almost exclusively the preserve of one ethnic or cultural group…where ethnic concentration results from discrimination" (Johnson 1994, 231). Philpott (1991) further differentiates slums and ghettos along race lines: poverty alone defines the slum, whereas poverty combined with racism creates the ghetto. Racism imposes severe spatial limitations on the distribution of urban African Americans and other people of color. Enclaves are more complex, being "neighborhoods or sections of a community whose key institutions and business enterprises owned and operated by members of an ethnic group cluster together" (Jaret 1991, 327). Therefore, a ghetto is mainly an ethnic residential area without an internally functioning economic system controlled by the ethnic group. An ethnic enclave, on the other hand, operates as a social and economic complex within its boundaries.

Racial segregation is by far the most thoroughly explored topic in geographical studies of race and ethnicity. In fact, the "geography of minority groups" started from research on the inner city ghetto as a territorial entity. Studies of a single minority group—African Americans—and their patterns of residential segregation composed the major focus of American ethnic geography in the 1960s and 1970s. These examinations of segregation, however, were limited to an analysis of residential choices and constraints.[6]

An extensive literature on ethnic enclaves as ethnic communities in contemporary America exists. These studies come from variety of perspectives, and collectively they offer a complex portrait of enclaves. For instance, New York's Chinatown is probably one of the most studied ethnic communities in the nation. As one of the earliest and largest American Chinatowns, it has experienced rapid changes in demographic composition, economic structure, political representation, and social reconfiguration in recent decades. Several books on this community approach its rich stories from different angles. Peter Kwong's *New Chinatown* (1987, 1996) characterizes it as a closely knit community by examining the internal structures, labor disputes, and class struggles, especially the exploitation of undocumented immigrants. Min Zhou's *Chinatown: The Socioeconomic Potential of an Urban Enclave* (1992), on the other hand, describes how Chinatown, as an enclave, provides job opportunities and eventually upward mobility for new immigrants, especially those who have little formal education and English ability. Jan Lin's *Reconstructuring Chinatown: Ethnic Enclave, Global Change* (1998) situates contemporary Chinatown in the trend of globalization by explaining how international, national, and regional structural factors, together with institutional and individual players, have shaped the changes in Chinatown. Lin's study captures the shifting nature of the enclave by documenting its economic activities in both the financial and labor-intensive sectors. These works demonstrate that the changes in Chinatowns are caused both by external forces, including global economic restructuring, the duality of ethnic economy, the situations in immigrants' origin countries, and federal and local policies, and internal factors like factionalism and solidarity within the community, community mobilization, and social change.

Invasion and Succession

The most influential explanation for the replacement of one neighborhood population by another was labeled *ecological succession* by the Chicago School of Sociology, especially in the work of Park, Burgess, and Mckenzie in the 1920s and 1930s, which dealt with the residential succession process. The "invasion and succession" model suggests that suburbanization of the middle class leaves the inner city to new minority groups, who create ghettos.[7] It theorizes that newly arrived and often poor immigrant/ethnic groups will occupy inner-city neighborhoods first; later, some economically well-off people from this group will enter the American mainstream and move to the suburbs to find better living conditions. When immigrants stay in the inner city, most live in segregated neighborhoods. When they move out to the suburbs, their experiences vary from being totally dispersed, to being relatively concentrated, to being highly segregated, depending upon the ethnic group and the time and place in question. With its concern for residential neighborhood change and succession, this model fits the experiences of many white ethnic groups.[8]

The invasion and succession model is clearly linked to the acculturation-assimilation theory of ethnic relations. Relationships between residential patterns and degrees of assimilation are articulated as residential dispersal accelerates the process of acculturation-assimilation. Empirical works demonstrate that the reasons for residential segregation are economic and racial, while residential segregation (whether in the inner city or suburb) has a strong negative correlation with assimilation, for example, with citizenship, intermarriage, ability to speak English, and occupational structure. Recent social trends may decrease residential segregation levels in some cities, but it is still not clear that interracial contact and social assimilation have increased accordingly.[9]

Downtown versus Uptown

The notion of downtown versus uptown arose in New York. Differences among people of the same ethnic group who lived downtown as opposed to those who lived in the suburbs have been documented among the Jews in New York City at the turn of the century (Sowell 1981). The downtown versus uptown model posits that within one ethnic group, those who live in downtown enclaves are usually poor, less educated, and spatially concentrated, whereas residents of uptown, that is, the suburbs, are well off, professionally trained, and live in racially or ethnically mixed residential areas. Kwong describes it as follows:

> The Chinese today basically consist of two distinct groups. More than 30 percent are in the professional category [and] ... have more education and higher

incomes than the national average. They do not live in concentrated Chinese ethnic communities. They are "Uptown Chinese."...Manual and service workers...constitute another 30 percent of the Chinese population. A significant proportion tend to be new immigrants, who are likely to live in Chinatowns, speak little English, and work at low wages in dead-end jobs. They are "Downtown Chinese." (Kwong 1996, 5)

This model, although offered by a scholar who is not a geographer, is highly spatial. There are distinctions between these two subgroups in many aspects, including geographical distribution, economic condition, and social status. Most downtown Chinese are somewhat isolated from the core society; they are in the ethnic labor market and are more likely to be owners or laborers in the Chinese restaurants, grocery stores, garment shops, and gift shops that are typical of inner-city ethnic businesses. The downtown Chinese and their ethnic businesses make Chinatown an active commercial and cultural center as well as an inner-city ethnic enclave. The well-educated uptown Chinese live dispersed in racially integrated suburban neighborhoods. They have professional occupations with a high level of upward mobility, and they interact on a higher level with the mainstream society. Such socioeconomic variations between ethnic people downtown and in the suburbs still prevail in many metropolitan areas with traditional Chinatowns, such as the Washington, DC, area and San Francisco Bay area (W. Li 1990; B. P. Wong 1998).

Similar patterns can be found among Japanese Americans. The early Japanese immigrants set up "Little Tokyos" and "Japan Towns" in Los Angeles and San Francisco and similar places in other cities. Some older Japanese Americans still live in such inner-city ethnic enclaves today, whereas subsequent generations who are economically better-off live in the suburbs (Lyman 1988). This kind of dualism may exist among other ethnic minority groups as well.

The application of the acculturation-assimilation theory can be found in both spatial models. According to assimilation theory, assimilation cannot happen "until the immigrant is able to function in the host community without encountering prejudiced attitudes or discriminatory behavior" (Gordon 1964, 63). Residential segregation, whether in the inner city or in the suburbs, is one of the main barriers to assimilation. With regard to the relationship among economic status, social status, and assimilation, both the invasion-succession and the downtown-uptown models imply that those who live in the suburbs are middle class, which makes it relatively easy for them to merge with the mainstream society. Ethnic minorities who cluster in inner-city ghettos and enclaves are poor and unassimilated, while those who live in suburbs have assimilated to the non-Hispanic white American mainstream both in terms of spatial dispersion and behavior.

Economic Structure of Ethnicity and Race

The study of ethnicity and race not only considers relationships between ethnic groups and American society, but also addresses the internal economic structure of racial/ethnic groups and their relationships to the broader socioeconomic structures in society. Recent literature focuses on the economic nature of ethnicity, especially the links between race/ethnicity and economic structure. Many studies fit what Omi and Winant (1994) refer to as the "class paradigm of race." They agree that "social divisions which assume a distinctively racial or ethnic character can be attributed or explained principally by reference to economic structures and processes" (Stuart Hall, as quoted in Omi and Winant 1994, 24). Such economic structures and processes include market relations (exchange), systems of stratification (distribution), and processes of class conflict (production). One of the principal points Omi and Winant make is that the status of subaltern groups is a result of the economic, racial and cultural domination in the mainstream society. A good example is the depressed status of Latino migrant farm workers and nonunionized immigrant workers. Almaguer (1994) and Barrera (1979) argue that throughout the history of California, American Indians, Mexicans, and Asian Americans, especially Chinese and Japanese, were concentrated in specific occupational categories due to the racialization processes. We need, therefore, to view the occupational selections and economic structures of ethnic groups within their own communities in the light of such societal forces.

When immigrants arrive in a destination country, they inevitably become integrated into the economic system either as laborers, middle-class wage-earners, or as business owner/entrepreneurs, in addition to becoming consumers. The relationship between immigrants and the native-born population changes with economic cycles. During periods of economic hardship, job competition between different groups sometimes results in conflict. Historically many conflicts between racial/ethnic groups have been caused by competition for the jobs needed for survival. Recent conflicts, however, have involved more complicated issues, such as equal opportunity as well as economic justice (Pulido 1996; Saxton 1995).

To survive in the receiving society, many immigrant groups either concentrate on certain occupations or establish their own independent firms and economic linkages. Such ethnic-owned and -operated firms are known as the "ethnic economy." Some immigrants and their descendants participate in the mainstream economy as individual players in the system, although they sometimes concentrate in specific occupational niches. In contrast, the ethnic economy includes a variety of ethnic-owned firms that often employ members of the same ethnic group although their customers may cross ethnic boundaries. Ethnic economies evolve over time and vary in spatial form. Their relationships with the broader socioeconomic system can also change dramatically.

The focus here is on the ethnic economy, for it has played an important role in the historical and contemporary development of Chinese communities in Los Angeles. Ethnic economies divide roughly into three types: ethnic economic niches, ethnic enclave economies, and contemporary integrated ethnic economies.

The Traditional Ethnic Economy of Niches and Enclaves

The ethnic economic niche is the earliest form of ethnic economy that developed in America. Niches are certain occupations or self-employment business types pursued by first-generation immigrants as pathways to economic survival. Sometimes the majority of a particular immigrant group owns or engages in one or several ethnic economic niches, and a very high proportion of such local job types may be held by immigrants. Such niches include, for example, the Greek ice-cream parlor, the Italian fruit stand, the Jewish clothing store, the Chinese laundry and restaurant, and the Armenian garbage collection service. Siu asserted that the occupational selections of immigrants are "new social inventions by these different ethnic groups in America as ways and means to struggle for existence in the symbiotic level of the community life. The occupation chosen is a form of accommodation, since its founding, it has become institutionalized with a characteristic pattern of its own" (Siu 1987, 1–2).

In American history, however, the formation of economic niches is not always driven by the free choices of immigrants, but instead is often imposed by the mainstream society. As described by the "dual labor-market" theory, these job types most likely belong to the secondary segment of the labor market, where jobs are primarily unskilled and unprotected by unions. They are niches for the immigrants not because they are particularly suitable, but because these immigrants may be restricted from other forms of employment. Lack of financial capital, English language skills, and/or job experience forces many immigrants to become manual laborers or small business operators. The businesses they set up are often ones that do not compete directly with those operated by the white majority and that require little initial capital. Siu's idea of the "immigrant economy" is similar to this concept of ethnic economic niches. He points out that the immigrants' occupations are usually not the ones that they held in their home countries. There are some exceptions, though, such as the engagement of many Japanese immigrants in garden/floral farming and in fishing, as they had been in Japan.

One characteristic of these niches is that although they are part of an entire economic structure with business linkages to the mainstream, they are relatively independent. They often operate at the periphery of the dominant economy, making them relatively less important to the system. The spatial distribution of such ethnic economic niches also varies, depending on their activities. If the clients are primarily co-ethnics, the businesses are often spatially concentrated, because early ethnic communities often cluster in small-scale downtown areas. However, if they serve a broad base of clients, or if their main purpose is to serve people other than their own group, niche businesses tend to be scattered. For example, the early Chinese restaurants tended to be spatially concentrated because they served their own community, whereas the early Chinese laundries were dispersed because they served a more general public. In such niches, since many ethnic people belong to the same class (as laborers or business partners), or have no major differences in income and social status, their economic participation and ethnic affinity reinforce each other, and serious intragroup conflicts are absent or rare.

The "enclave economy," in contrast, is an integrated set of ethnic niche activities, which forms a more or less self-contained economic system with relatively weak ties to the dominant economy. Enclave economies are a well-recognized form of the ethnic economy and have been the most widely studied by social scientists.[10] Wilson and Portes (1980) define the enclave economy as a set of firms that are established by immigrant entrepreneurs and that "hire co-ethnic workers, thus propelling and/or perpetuating the labor-market segmentation of their group" (Hiebert 1993, 247). Good examples include the Koreans in Los Angeles and the Cubans in Miami.[11]

Integrated Ethnic Economy

The contemporary integrated ethnic economy is a set of ethnic businesses integrated with the mainstream economy, but with a distinct ethnic imprint. Similar to the ethnic enclave economy, the businesses of the integrated ethnic economy are usually owned and operated by one ethnic group, and their labor force and support networks are, to some extent, provided by their own ethnic group. However, because of economic restructuring in the larger society in recent decades, many ethnic economies have become more integrated with the national and international economic systems than ever before; they have become part of the mainstream economy. The prevalence of Indian- and Chinese-owned firms in Silicon Valley has resulted in the dubbing of the

IC (integrated circuits) industry as Indian and Chinese industry (Saxenian 1999, 2002).

The contemporary ethnic economy is closely associated with and a result of the economic restructuring process. Economic restructuring involves plant closures, urban decline, shifts in migration patterns, and altered social relations. The aim of economic restructuring is to reduce costs (particularly labor costs), capture market share, and increase profits. Cost reductions are achieved both by moving labor-intensive plants overseas and by establishing plants in the United States that use cheap domestic labor. Worsening capital-labor relationships make employers seek nonunionized, low-wage laborers, and as a consequence, immigrants and the ethnic economy become more actively involved in the U.S. economic system. The establishment and prosperity of some ethnic economic sectors, like the garment industry in the Chinatowns of New York and San Francisco, are the result of a combination of U.S. economic restructuring, labor protection and immigration laws, and increasing polarization between rich and poor people worldwide. With reindustrialization creating the need to fill labor-intensive jobs inside the United States, the ethnic economy can provide the necessary workers often by circumventing U.S. labor protection laws, because in many cases the immigrant laborers are employed by their co-ethnics, not by large U.S. firms. These workers often have limited English language skills, and some are undocumented and without the means to protect themselves. In addition, since U.S. immigration laws emphasize family reunification, this has created a large reserve pool of cheap labor. International polarization further accelerates the division between rich capitalists and poor laborers. While the former come to the United States as investors and entrepreneurs, the latter can survive only by taking low-wage jobs. This causes internal differences within immigrant communities. The contemporary integrated ethnic economy comes closer to observing the typical capitalist norms of minimizing costs and maximizing profits, and as a consequence there are overlapping racial and class tensions and conflicts within, as well as between, ethnic groups. The new transnational capital and ethnic millionaires, some of whom belong to the new cadres of circular migrants—such as the trans-Pacific "space men" or transnational entrepreneurs—not only increase the size of the ethnic economy, but also the gap between ethnic employers and employees.[12]

Through widespread franchising and subcontracting, the ethnic economy itself is more directly integrated into the mainstream economy. Like vertical disintegration, franchising makes use of spacing and pricing agreements; depends on risk-taking, hard work, and thrift; and benefits from cheap labor. Subcontracting, on the other hand, in many sectors may involve below-minimum-wage payment schedules, nonpayment of mandatory overtime and social security tax, industrial homework, child labor, and substandard working conditions. Such conditions are prevalent in a new generation of sweatshops. Meanwhile some ethnic firms are also directly involved in global business cycles because they engage in international trade between the United States and their home countries, and this in turn creates a new form of the "trader-minority" (see Hiebert 1993). In Los Angeles, for instance, a large number of Chinese-owned business firms are engaged in international import and export trades.

Ethnic Economy, Ethnic Community, and Ethnicity

The spatial relationship between the ethnic economy and the ethnic community is a topic of heated debate. The question is whether an enclave can be related to a particular spatial residential form or whether it should be considered only as an economic form. Portes and Jensen strongly oppose any possible "confusion" between enclaves and immigrant neighborhoods and define an ethnic enclave strictly by place of work. Hiebert, Sanders and Nee, and Thompson, on the other hand, make some connections between the two (Hiebert 1993; Portes and Jensen 1987; Sanders and Nee 1987; and Thompson 1979). Waldinger, McEvoy, and Aldrich consider that the relationship between the ethnic economy and community "is complex, differing by type of business, and varying over time." They point out that ethnic neighborhoods are often the starting points of ethnic businesses and provide a two-by-two matrix in terms of ethnic population concentration and ethnic business specialization (Waldinger, McEvoy, and Aldrich 1990, 106 and 125).

While the separation of workplace and residence is the norm of modern capitalist society, to disconnect research on ethnic work places from research on residences is unnecessary and may have negative consequences. Only by integrating analyses of the geographies of home and work can we get a broader picture of the internal dynamics of ethnic communities and the position of the ethnic economy within larger socioeconomic systems. Many types of businesses within the ethnic enclave economy may be separated from the owners' residences. Examples include Jewish storeowners and their Korean successors in South Central Los Angeles. Alternatively, parts of the ethnic economy and community may be quite close to each other or in the same place, such as the garment sector within the growing Jewish residential clusters in Toronto during the first half of this century. In many traditional and contemporary ethnic enclaves, the close-knit ethnic neighborhoods and the ethnic economy enhance each other and support the growth of such enclaves. The situation varies depending on the economic activity, the ethnic group, the geographical area, and the time period. One hypothesis holds that the proximity of the ethnic economy and owner/worker residences reinforces ethnic consciousness and affinity. Ethnicity may also be used to consolidate scattered ethnic business owners in their economic and political pursuits.[13] Waldinger, Aldrich, and Ward propose an interactive model of ethnic business development and seek to demonstrate the relationships between spatial concentration and ethnicity. They state:

> Ethnic concentrations may also give rise to common ethnic interests, reinforcing a sense of identity. In addition, industrial or business concentrations foster competitive cross-ethnic contact, which in turn promotes ethnic consciousness and solidarity. (1990, 34)

In addition, there appears to be an increased relinking of place of work and place of residence in both the mainstream and ethnic economies. For example, both high-tech, high-wage workers and low-skill, low-wage immigrant workers are now clustering in what are called "edge cities" in the suburbs. In California, many immigrants live close to the high-tech agglomerations in Orange County and work in high-tech assembly plants.[14] It appears, therefore, that the ethnic economy and ethnic community are increasingly connected to each other not only functionally but also spatially.

Transnational Connections of Ethnicity and Race

One contemporary theoretical thread connecting international migration, ethnic and racial identity, the changing global economy, and nation-states is transnationalism. Transnationalist scholars explore the expanded and unprecedented extent and scope of cross-national movements of people, goods, information, and financial resources in recent decades. Within this field of study immigrants are no longer considered to be uprooted and transplanted migrants who will be assimilated into the receiving societies, but "transmigrants," who will keep close ties and be identified with both their origin and receiving countries and beyond (Basch, Glick Schiller, and Blanc-Szanton 1994; Glick Schiller, Basch, and Blanc–Szanton 1992, 1995). Their transnational connections are defined as "multiple ties and interactions linking people or institutions across the borders of nation-states" (Vertovec 1999, 447).

Several aspects of transnationalism warrant special recognition in the study of contemporary international migration and urban ethnicity:

1. Transnationalism is a multidimensional phenomenon. It is considered to have at least three forms: economic, political, and sociocultural. Economic transnationalism has been widely studied—its foci include migrants' remittances, cross-border economic transactions conducted by immigrant and

minority businesses, as well as the economic activities of mega-scale multinational firms. Political transnationalism encompasses issues of citizenship, nongovernmental organizations (NGOs), and other organizational forms. Among the sociocultural dimensions of transnationalism are the "relational" and the "experiential," the former describing individual movements and the latter referring to an individual's sense of identity and belonging. In fact, many empirical studies on transnational connections today address the frequency, modes, and reasoning for cross-national trips and connections for both personal and professional reasons.[15]

2. Transnationalism crosses class lines and involves multiple levels of actors, from individuals, to households, to institutions. As a result of advances in transportation and communication, cross-ocean travel is no longer a luxury of the privileged elites but is increasingly affordable for many. Transnational linkages have changed the dynamics of international migration and connections tremendously.

3. Last but not least, one specific theme identified for transnational research is the investigation of transnational social fields/spaces, including new nodes and localities within such fields (Dunn 2005; Satzewich and Wong 2006; Vertovec 1999). Thus the study of transnationalism is place-specific and spatially connected and offers geographers an expanded arena for exploration.

The study of immigrant and minority research can benefit from an examination of the transnational dimension, which can analyze how the global roots and connections of immigrants have increased ethnic, economic, and social diversities in the urban and suburban areas that the majority of immigrants call home.

⤶

Although studies of race and ethnicity in geography in particular, and in social sciences in general, have advanced tremendously in the United States since the 1960s, four issues in particular warrant further investigation:

1. The relationships between theories of race/ethnicity and ethnic spatial distribution. The prevailing acculturation-assimilation theory was accompanied by spatial models of invasion-succession and downtown versus uptown. Pluralist theory and the new theoretical approaches to race/ethnicity (which emphasize the process of racialization) also need an analysis of how they connect to contemporary spatial expressions of race/ethnicity.

2. The relationships between race/ethnicity and class. Because of historical traditions, economic restructuring, immigration waves, and international competition, there are increasing conflicts between ethnic groups as well as class conflicts within and between ethnic groups. Such processes may have

certain spatial patterns or may be place specific. These should be better addressed in ethnic geography.

3. The relationships between race/ethnicity and broader socioeconomic contexts. Although there are many studies of ethnicity dealing with ethnic communities, ethnic economic structure, and the broader socioeconomic context, few consider them as a complex and deal with them in an integrated fashion. There is a need to examine them together and search for what changing socioeconomic contexts mean for ethnic identity and solidarity, and vice versa.

4. Empirical comparative studies of changing ethnic experiences over time and across space. Comparisons are needed of different ethnic groups within one place or country, as well as among those groups in different places, and in the national and global scene. Direct comparisons are still not abundant.[16]

Chapter 2 presents the ethnoburb model, which is my attempt to address some of these outstanding questions in ethnic geography. The chapters in Part II operationalize the model and explain the processes and dynamics of spatial transformation in the Chinese community in metropolitan Los Angeles from downtown Chinatown to the San Gabriel Valley ethnoburb.

2 Ethnoburb

An Alternative Ethnic Settlement

The stereotypical traditional American suburb is populated by white middle-class American families, composed of a working dad, a stay-at-home mom, and their children. A corollary of this is that racial and ethnic minorities are mostly concentrated in inner-city ghettos or ethnic enclaves. If minorities manage to achieve the American dream of suburbanizing, they were expected to be, and likely are, spatially dispersed and socioeconomically assimilated into the mainstream society.

These conceptions belie reality because a new type of suburb, the ethnoburb, has emerged in recent decades, a product of international geopolitical and global economic restructuring; changing national immigration and trade policies; and local demographic, economic, and political contexts. Ethnoburbs express a set of contemporary ethnic relations involving interethnic group and intraethnic class tension or cooperation in a unique spatial form and internal socioeconomic structure. Ethnoburbs are suburban ethnic clusters of residential and business districts within large metropolitan areas. They are multiracial/multiethnic, multicultural, multilingual, and often multinational communities, in which one ethnic minority group has a significant concentration, but does not necessarily comprise the majority. Ethnoburbs are likely to be created through some form of deliberate efforts of that group. Ethnoburbs replicate some features of the ethnic enclave and some features of a suburb without a specific minority identity. Thus ethnoburbs offer an alternative type of ethnic settlement in contemporary urban America and coexist along with traditional ethnic ghettos and inner-city enclaves.

Using contextual analysis, this chapter delineates the conceptual model of the ethnoburb and ties it to the framework of ethnicity and space presented in Chapter 1.

Formation of an Ethnoburb

Changing dynamics at the international, national, and local levels clearly shape and propel formation of an ethnoburb. Global economic and geopolitical restructuring alters economic relations and the world order, making the flows of capital, information, and labor increasingly internationalized and creating the conditions necessary for the establishment of an ethnoburb. Changing national policies have created new needs for entrepreneurs and investors, as well as for cheap labor, and have opened the door to immigrants of different backgrounds to enter the United States and potentially populate an ethnoburb. These global and national conditions manifest themselves at the local level and are intertwined with place-specific situations. The interplay of changing geopolitical, economic, and social dynamics at the different levels express themselves spatially in the emergence of ethnoburbs in certain localities. While all these changes underlie the formation of an ethnoburb, each may play different roles and to different degrees.

Global/National Economic Restructuring

Figure 1 provides a framework of connections between global and national economic restructuring trends and possible sites of ethnoburbs. In recent decades, both the U.S. economy and the world economic system have experienced rapid restructuring with associated spatial transformations. As the U.S. economy has globalized, it has experienced two simultaneous trends: deindustrialization and reindustrialization.

Deindustrialization is caused by long-term structural trends (global competition and technical development) and short-term temporal trends (reces-

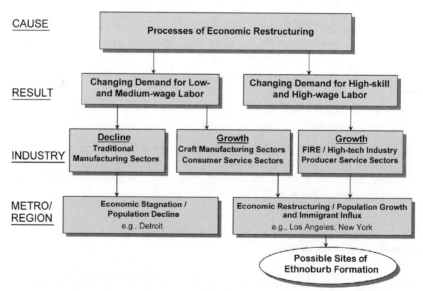

FIGURE 1. Economic Restructuring and the Ethnoburb

sions). In the contemporary world, the economy of a nation has to be more competitive in order to keep, or increase, its global market share. The United States has been facing intense competition from Japan and Germany since World War II, the four Asian "Little Dragons"—Hong Kong, Singapore, South Korea, and Taiwan—since the 1960s, and more recently China, India, and other Asian and Latin American countries in certain economic sectors. To reduce costs and increase profits, many American multinational corporations have closed their production plants in the United States and moved their capital overseas to set up factories in, or outsourced certain service functions to, third world countries, causing the loss of high-wage unionized jobs in the United States. Since small firms do not have the resources to compete with multinational corporations, deindustrialization has also made it particularly hard for small independent firms to survive and destroyed many conventional forms of entrepreneurship. At the same time, the dominant sector in the U.S. economy has shifted from manufacturing to service and high-tech industries, leading to high unemployment in manufacturing sectors and an increase of low-wage service jobs and high-wage professional jobs. Economic recession has caused industry downsizing with plant closures and layoffs.

However, many U.S. industries are not dying, but are reorganizing into new forms, that is, restructuring along post-Fordist lines in a new trend of reindustrialization. Within the manufacturing sector, several changes have been observed. One is vertical disintegration. Vertical integration, historically the dominant form of large industrial organizations, entailed the collection of a wide range of production and distribution functions (from raw materials to marketing) under the auspices of a single firm. Now, to reduce costs and risks, many large firms have been breaking off some of their former production processes and subcontracting a variety of functions. Such a process calls for new types of entrepreneurship and opens opportunities for small contractors. A second hallmark of post-Fordist industrial organization is geographical relocation and renewed concentration within the United States. Plants have been moved to areas offering lower labor costs and with other comparative advantages. A third post-Fordist characteristic is polarized reindustrialization, that is, the development of both high-tech, high-wage sectors and low-tech, low-wage sectors. On the one hand, high-tech computer, biotech, and advanced communication equipment firms have gained greater importance in the overall economy and have become increasingly dependent upon highly skilled and well-educated immigrant professionals. On the other hand, increasing numbers of technologically unsophisticated industries have re-emerged, such as the highly concentrated, vertically disintegrated garment industry. These low-wage industries are especially prevalent in large metropolitan areas with high proportions of immigrants. The trend toward polarized reindustrialization not only offers jobs for high-skill professionals (both domestic and immigrants), but also provides opportunities for ethnic entrepreneurs/subcontractors and semi-skilled and low-skilled job seekers. Economic restructuring has also taken place in other economic sectors as well. The financial sector, for instance, has undergone a transformation during the last several decades. Large U.S. banks have consolidated domestic branch operations and have looked to international lending instead, increasingly globalizing the flow of capital. Large capital investment in the United States by foreign countries has further contributed to the globalization of financial capital (Davis 1992; Dymski and Veitch 1996a, 1996b). Changing trade policies in the United States and worldwide have contributed to the globalization of the U.S. economy. In order to increase their market shares in the United States and to circumvent trade barriers and quotas, foreign multinational corporations have set up production plants inside U.S. territory. With the passage of the North America Free Trade Agreement (NAFTA), a free-trade area embracing over 360 million people and more than $6.5 trillion in annual economic activity, was established in January 1994. NAFTA removes all economic barriers between Canada, the United States, and Mexico over a fifteen-year period. The treaty not only covers manufactured goods, but also agriculture, intellectual property, investments, and services. This pact was seen by many as "creat[ing] a vision for the future of our country and of our work force that is based on expansion, growth and change."[1] Though it is a trade agreement among three North American countries, NAFTA has implications for other nations as well. It offers tremendous opportunities for foreign multinational corporations to take advantage of free trade among the three by establishing branch firms in low-wage Mexico and then exporting the finished goods to the United States and Canada. NAFTA has also facilitated conclusion of the Uruguay Round of General Agreement of Tariffs & Trade (GATT) and stimulated formation of the World Trade Organization (WTO), which aims to reduce trade barriers around the world. With the emergent economic power on the Pacific Rim, U.S. trade with the Asian Pacific Economic Cooperation Forum (APEC), which includes all three North American countries, Australia, New Zealand, and thirteen Asian Pacific and Latin American nations, has been thriving. In the early 1990s, U.S. exports to APEC members already amounted to $128 billion annually, accounting for 5.3 million American jobs; in comparison, U.S. sales to Europe totaled $102 billion annually, accounting for 4.2 million jobs (Grayson 1995). These international trade agreements at regional and world levels not only lower trade barriers between countries, but inevitably promote globalization of capital, information, technology, managerial personnel, and labor, and in so doing accelerate U.S. economic restructuring. The impact of economic restructuring has been profound throughout the United States. It has created a more polarized urban labor market by eliminating unionized manufacturing jobs; increasing low-wage, low-skill service and manufacturing jobs; and creating high-wage, high-skill financial, technical and managerial jobs. This process has increased the numbers of both upper- and lower-income households and has decreased the middle class. This has caused a U-turn in the U.S. income distribution and enlarged income gaps between different groups (Bluestone and Harrison 1982; Peterson and Vroman 1992).

The consequences of economic restructuring have dramatically different imprints on various localities. Those metropolitan areas and regions that have been centers of traditional manufacturing, like Detroit and some other cities in American's traditional manufacturing belt, have experienced absolute decline, with few new industries arriving to replace lost or diminished sectors. On the other hand, metropolitan areas with a more diversified economic structure, especially those "world cities" that are at the center of global and regional financial capital and trade transactions and activities (such as New York and Los Angeles) are in a better position (Allen and Turner 1996; Sassen 1994). Like other cities, these world cities have also experienced economic restructuring and downsizing, but they have a greater potential to recover and reorganize themselves to cope with the changes. In these favored areas, changing structural conditions at the international scale offer economic opportunities, especially for new entrepreneurs (such as subcontractors and entrepreneurs specializing in international trade, finance, as well as manufacturing) and specific segments of the labor force (including both high-wage high-skill workforce and low-wage low-skill laborers). Such metropolitan areas become potential sites of ethnoburbs, since they provide ideal geographic locations and stages for ethnic entrepreneurs and laborers to create new types of ethnic economy. These areas often have large preexisting ethnic minority communities and ethnic economic structures, which lure ethnic newcomers (both entrepreneurs and laborers) and their investments. These preexisting ethnic concentrations provide the consumer goods and cultural institutions that meet the needs of newcomers.

Changing Geopolitics and U.S. Immigration Policy

U.S. history has always involved immigrants, and U.S. immigration policies have historically been influenced by domestic and international economic conditions, geopolitical changes, and U.S. strategic interests. Immigration policies have had an enormous impact on the demographic and socioeconomic structure of the United States.

U.S. immigration legislation has historically discriminated against groups that are not of Anglo-Saxon origin. Individuals from ethnic minority groups were not given the same opportunities as their white European counterparts. The Naturalization Law of 1790 specified that only free "white" immigrants would be eligible for naturalized citizenship. The 1882 Chinese Exclusion Act aimed at barring Chinese labor from entering the United States. The 1907 Gentlemen's Agreement restricted Japanese and Korean immigration. The 1917 Immigration Act denied entry to Asian Indians and created an Asiatic Barred Zone, which essentially curbed all immigration from Asia. None of the above groups had the right to be naturalized as U.S. citizens during the nineteenth and early twentieth century. The 1924 National Origins Act gave no quotas for any group that was ineligible for citizenship, a category that included all the above-mentioned groups, and also restricted entry of immigrants from southern and southeastern Europe. The 1934 Tydings-McDuffie Act added Filipinos to the list of excluded groups. Congress also tried repeatedly to impose a quota limit on immigration from Mexico. During the Depression, Mexico workers were deported from the United States.[2] These immigration restrictions prevented certain groups from entering this country and legitimized discriminatory actions against these groups by denying them the right to become citizens. Exclusionary legislation contributed to the racialization of certain groups, and the transformation of these groups into racialized minorities with limited legal rights, which made them easy targets for exclusion. Therefore, racism in U.S. society was not only de facto (expressed by the general public in actions and sentiments against immigration), but also de jure (legal discrimination against certain racial groups).

The passage of the 1965 Immigration and Nationality Act, which marked symbolic as well as real changes in U.S. immigration history, was highly influenced by the changing international and national contexts of the 1960s. Globally, decolonization and independence of third world countries had become a worldwide movement, making the voices of developing countries heard in the international arena. Moreover, the moral victory of World War II and the economic prosperity enjoyed by the United States made it the leader of the free world, while the rise of Eastern Bloc socialist countries changed the global strategic geopolitical map giving rise to the Cold War. To win the Cold War and to improve its image as a democratic country and a world leader that did not discriminate against nonwhite groups in its own country and in the international community, the United States found it necessary to revise its traditional discriminatory immigration legislation. Nationally, the 1960s was the decade of the Civil Rights Movement, which resulted in the passing of the 1964 Civil Rights Act, the 1965 Voting Rights Act, and the 1968 Fair Housing Act. Minority groups, led by African Americans, fought for political rights and economic power. In the wake of nationalist movements overseas and the Civil Rights movements at home, Congress also passed the historic 1965 Immigration and Nationality Act, a landmark change in U.S. immigration policy. For the first time in U.S. history, every national group in the Eastern Hemisphere—all continents except the Americas—was granted an equal annual maximum immigration quota of 20,000 people.

Figure 2 summarizes the major contents of immigration legislation in the past forty years and their consequences. The results of the 1965 Immigration and Nationality Act were profound. This Act not only brought in more immigrants from third world countries, especially from Asia and Latin America, but it also changed the demographic and socioeconomic structure of immigrant populations in the United States. The 1965 legislation divided all potential immigrants into two major types, one of which was family reunification-based and the other profession-based, with a total of six different preference categories. Regarding family reunification, it gave preference to families and relatives of U.S. citizens and permanent residents, which accounted for 80 percent of all quotas, even though the immediate families of U.S. citizens—spouses, minor children, and parents—were exempted from the quota system altogether. It also provided opportunities for skilled labor and professionals needed by the U.S. economy by redesigning the preference system, which was capped at 20 percent of all allocated visas, with the possibility of exceeding 20 percent if the family quotas were not used up. The third preference targeted well-trained

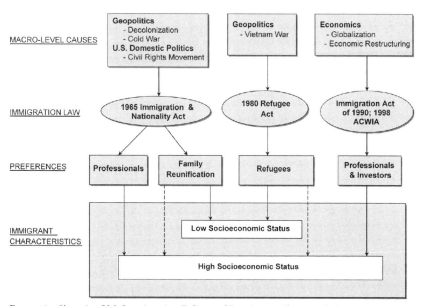

FIGURE 2. Changing U.S. Immigration Policy and Immigrant Characteristics

professionals (including engineers, technicians, and university professors), and the sixth preference was for laborers in those sectors where there existed a short-fall of domestic labor. Thus, the 1965 legislation opened the door for a more economically and socially stratified immigrant profile.

An influx of lower-skilled, poorly educated immigrants provided a labor pool for low-skill jobs and revived some diminishing traditional inner-city ethnic ghettos and enclaves. Since the majority of these immigrants did not speak English, one of the important avenues for economic survival was to live and work inside such ghettos and enclaves, with the hope of eventually achiev-ing "the American Dream." Some immigrants who were well-educated profes-sionals in their home countries but who did not have adequate English skills faced similar problems. At the other end of the spectrum, higher-skilled labor and professionally trained people with prior job experience and English ability, many of whom had been educated in the United States or other Western coun-tries, tended to find jobs in the mainstream economy, and these immigrants moved upward socioeconomically and outward spatially to the suburbs. These were the people who normally were considered as "assimilated" into main-stream society, because they gradually adopted the American way of life.

During the Cold War era, U.S. economic and military involvement in for-eign countries dramatically changed the situation both in the United States and the immigration source-countries. While U.S. foreign investment resulted in a stratified pool of potential immigrants, U.S. military involvement cre-ated refugees and other migrants displaced by the effects of war. After World War II, in order to maintain U.S. supremacy in the international arena and to prevent the USSR from expanding its influence into Asia, the United States carried out economic and military aid plans in many Asian countries. These plans were similar to the Marshall Plan in Europe but were smaller in scale. The United States encouraged these countries to develop export-oriented econo-mies. Export-led growth strategies linked local economies to the United States and helped to generate U.S. economic restructuring, as labor-intensive sectors of the U.S. economy were shifted to low-wage countries. Economic growth in these countries caused rapid urbanization and surplus labor that could not be absorbed by their own economies. The United States also invested in educa-tion systems in many developing countries, by providing faculty and exchange programs. Such programs not only exported American democratic values and ideology, but also generated a "brain drain" from sending countries (Liu and Cheng 1994). All these actions increased the wave of immigrants—unskilled, semiskilled, and highly skilled professionals—coming to the United States after the passage of the 1965 Immigration Act.

U.S military involvement in foreign countries also had important consequences in changing specific immigration policies and situations. The Korean War resulted in immigration from Korea. Over a decade of U.S. military involvement in Indochina[3] not only caused casualties for both the United States and the Indochinese countries but also created huge refugee waves, especially after the fall of Saigon in 1975. In order to accommodate this refugee population, the largest in the U.S. history, the Congress passed the 1980 Refugee Act, which separated refugees from the regular quota system. Under this act, the President, in consultation with Congress, decided how many refugees were to be admitted to the United States annually. Unlike typical immigrants, refugees from Vietnam, Laos, and Cambodia had not planned to move to the United States before the war and were not well prepared to "assimilate" into U.S. society; their arrival was the direct result of U.S. military activities in their home countries. Therefore, their resettlement into the United States resulted from forced evacuation. Many Southeast Asian refugees had lost everything during the war and their long journey to the United States—their family and friends, property, and belongings. They had to reestablish themselves in a country completely different from their own. Although many acknowledged the opportunities offered by the United States, their adjustment was often more difficult than the process was for other "ordinary" immigrants.

The Immigration Act of 1990, effective October 1, 1991, makes some further changes to accommodate economic restructuring and globalization of capital and personnel flows. It divides all immigrants into three categories: family-sponsored, employment-based, and diversity. This act treats Hong Kong as "a separate foreign state, and not as a colony or other component of dependent area of another foreign state" (U.S. Congress 1991, 4985) and gives an annual immigrant quota of 10,000 for fiscal years 1991, 1992, and 1993 to Hong Kong. This legislative change is a direct response to the geopolitical changes in the international arena, namely, the agreement between the People's Republic of China and the United Kingdom to return Hong Kong to China in July 1997. The Immigration Act of 1990 offers a total of 140,000 visas for employment-based immigrants that breaks down as follows: 40,000 are for "priority workers" ("aliens with extraordinary ability; outstanding professors and researchers; and certain multinational executives and managers"); 40,000 are for "members of the professions holding advanced degrees or aliens of exceptional ability"; 40,000 are for "skilled workers, professionals, and other workers"; 10,000 are for "certain special immigrants"; and 10,000 were for "employment creation." The last provision resulted directly from the competition posed by Canada and Australia, among others, for immigrants with financial investment resources.

The establishment of a new commercial enterprise with $1 million or more investment the United States and the creation of at least ten jobs now make it possible for an immigrant to apply for the "employment creation" category, that is, obtain an EB-5 visa. The law encourages such employment-creation immigrants to set up their enterprises in "targeted employment areas," rural or metro areas with high unemployment rates. In such targeted employment areas, qualifying immigrant employers need a smaller capital investment (only $500,000). The L-1 visa ("intracompany transferees") also encourages multinational corporations to invest and set up branches in the United States and to bring in transnational managerial personnel as potential immigrants. These L-1 visa holders are eligible to apply for permanent residency after successfully operating their businesses in the United States for a year. In this legislation, Congress also sets quotas for H-1B nonimmigrant visa, designated for "specialty occupations" that require the equivalent of a bachelor's degree whose holders are eligible to bring their immediate family and work in the United States for up to six years, during which they are eligible to apply for permanent residency. Under pressure from American high-tech companies to recruit highly educated and skilled foreign professionals, Congress has repeatedly and significantly increased the limit of H-1B visas since 1990, but especially since passage of the American Competitiveness and Workforce Improvement Act of 1998 (ACWIA). The annual quotas for H-1B visas were raised from 65,000 to 115,000, then to 195,000, until it was reverted back to 65,000 in fiscal year 2004. An additional 20,000 have been added to the quota since 2005 (which are reserved for foreign students who obtain graduate degrees in the United States) as a result of intense lobbying by knowledge-based American corporations. Higher education institutions and nongovernment organizations (NGOs) are exempted from such quotas in their hiring of H-1B visa workers.

It is obvious that in addition to stressing the traditional value of family reunion, the Immigration Act of 1990 and other recent policies promote employment-based immigration and capital investment to accommodate the increasingly globalized process of economic restructuring. These new immigration regulations have greatly altered the socioeconomic structure of the immigrant populations, especially those flowing from rapidly growing third world countries and areas such as the Newly Industrialized Countries (NICs), the Association of Southeastern Asian Nations (ASEAN), India, and Mainland China. Particularly, they offer opportunities for well-educated professional people and skilled managerial personnel. Unlike traditional immigrants, these new immigrants are usually not only well educated and professionally trained, but they are often wealthy as well, with portable assets. They may not, however, have high English proficiency, and they may not be willing to completely assimilate into the American mainstream. While some English proficiency is sufficient to handle their business, English skills are not necessarily a prerequisite for business success. These new immigrants often choose big cities with large populations of their co-ethnics in order to maintain and develop their businesses and personal networks. Since many of these immigrants deal with international trade and finance involving their home countries, the United States, or other countries, blending into U.S. society does not have to be their first priority. The development of transnational or global ties is the key. The result of the latest U.S. immigration policies is a new type of sojourner, who is as comfortable crossing oceans and countries as he or she is crossing Main Street, U.S.A.

The impact of post-1965 immigration legislation on various localities within the United States has been uneven. Only some states have become the main recipients of the new immigrants, and the immigrants are more concentrated in large metropolitan areas than they are in rural areas. Large cities with traditional immigrant concentrations, such as Chicago, Los Angeles, New York, San Francisco, and Washington, DC, have received disproportionately higher concentrations of the new, more diversified immigration. These metropolitan areas are thus more likely to be the sites of ethnoburb formation, especially if they are world cities at the center of global capital, commodity, information, and personnel flows.

Locality Conditions

Economic restructuring and policy changes at the international and national level provide the basis for possible ethnoburb development, but they do not, by themselves, guarantee the establishment of an ethnoburb. Whether a particular metropolitan area develops an ethnoburb partly depends on locally specific conditions. Locality conditions do not simply mirror global and national contexts, but have their own place-specific variations. Such conditions are based on geographic location and physical environment; on demographic, political, and socioeconomic conditions; and on the ways in which such conditions have historically been manifested. As mentioned above, world cities that play important roles in the globalization of capital, commodities, information, and personnel flows have greater potential as sites of ethnoburb formation. Those world cities with preexisting ethnic residential clusters and ethnic business districts and networks are particularly ideal for ethnoburb development. However, not every world city can be expected to witness ethnoburb development; nor will each ethnoburb be created under the same conditions.

In this section, I will focus on the Los Angeles area to explain the relationship between locality conditions and ethnoburb formation. Just as Chicago is commonly seen as the prototypical industrial city, LA is often cited as a post-modern archetype and as a world city of the twenty-first century. "The Los Angeles prototype—with its emphasis on multicentered, dispersed patterns of low-density growth—may become the new paradigm of metropolitan development" (Dear 1996, 1–2; see also D. W. Miller 2000). Los Angeles is the second largest metropolitan area in the United States. By the late 1980s a circular area with a sixty-mile diameter, centered in downtown Los Angeles, commanded 56 percent of the international trade of the State of California, its gross annual output worth nearly $250 billion. Its gross product per person ranked it as the fourth largest economy in the world, and the city itself became an international capital city with huge amounts of foreign investment (Dear 1991; Soja 1989).

Metropolitan Los Angeles has grown in a spatially fragmented manner since its earliest beginning. It has more than 14 million people, 5 counties, and at least 132 incorporated cities by the 1990s. Contemporary Los Angeles "is claimed [to be] the greatest concentration of technocratic expertise and militaristic imagination in the USA" (Soja 1989, 224). It contains striking contrasts, including many high-tech companies, especially in Orange County, as well as sweatshop garment districts. Many of the best scientists and technicians are located there, along with numerous blue-collar workers and low-skilled immigrant laborers. Beautiful beach cities and wealthy hillside communities exist side by side with poor, economically depressed slums. Los Angeles is home to some of the wealthiest people in the United States, as well as a rapidly increasing number of homeless people concentrated in the skid row area (Rowe and Wolch 1990). Non-Hispanic whites, most of whom live in the fringe areas, are no longer the majority group, while many minority immigrant groups live within the inner-city or inner suburbs. As a result, Los Angeles is the one of most ethnically diverse places in the United States. The underlying structure of LA's urban system drives the polarization of economic and social status in the region. Many groups are excluded from mainstream urban America: the unemployed poor dependent on social welfare programs and new immigrants (both legal and undocumented) with little understanding of American society, who nevertheless add to the mix with their own culture and values. LA is so complicated, so diversified in almost every aspect in its economic base and social relations, that the city presents a novel, postmodern style and a highly problematic locale, forming a new time-space fabric that characterizes the new global metropolis.

As a world city, Los Angeles provides the opportunity for immigrants to engage in international business and to restructure an integrated ethnic economy. Los Angeles/Southern California, a Pacific Coast region with large ports, has locational advantages on the increasingly important Pacific Rim. By 1994, the Los Angeles Customs District, which encompasses the ports of LA, Long

Beach, and Hueneme, as well as Los Angeles International Airport and McCarran Field, surpassed New York to become the nation's largest customs district for imports and exports (Lowenthal et al. 1996, 28). Los Angeles offers a variety of preexisting immigrant neighborhoods, like Chinatown, Little Tokyo, and the Latino barrios of East LA, and expandable business networks that attract even more new immigrants. The spatial fragmentation of Los Angeles facilitates the creation of ethnic communities in the suburbs. All of these local conditions make LA, perhaps more than any other city, an ideal site for the formation of ethnoburbs.

Process of Formation

Minorities, like most Americans, moved to the suburbs in the 1950s and 1960s to secure better housing and neighborhood environments. Some of these early minority suburbanites, including American-born generations and better-off immigrants, formed small-scale residential clusters. During this stage these suburban clusters were probably the result of a natural growth process. Soon after, however, some pioneers moved to a particular neighborhood, and their relatives and friends followed, buying properties in the same neighborhood, attracted by the same reasons that drew the pioneers in the first place. These reasons included affordability, newer housing tracts, good schools, a nice environment, and last, but not least, the acceptance by the original residents of an increase of minority residents in their neighborhood. These early small concentrations may well have served as the predecessors of more recent ethnoburb development.

But then the combination of changing geopolitical and global economic contexts, and shifting U.S. immigration policies made it possible for ethnoburbs to take root and grow. The influx of immigrants and the new economic networks created by their arrival stimulated the formation and determined the particular location of an ethnoburb within a metropolitan area. Following the passage of the 1965 Immigration and Nationality Act, unprecedented numbers of Asians and Latinos immigrated to the United States. The traditional small-scale and congested inner-city ethnic enclaves could no longer house all the new immigrants. As a result, many settled directly in the suburbs without ever having experienced life in an inner-city ethnic enclave. Such was the case in the San Gabriel Valley, where waves of new Asian immigrants settled as soon as they arrived in America, partially because the valley already housed large numbers of Asian Americans. In many high-tech areas of the nation, such as Silicon Valley, and many New Jersey towns, immigrants, especially high-tech professionals, including H-1B visa holders, settled in the suburbs to be close to their jobs and to guarantee their offspring the best education America could offer. These locations are often the ones with superior school districts. Later, chain migration played an important role in the further agglomeration of immigrants in such areas.

Regardless of the reason for the increased ethnic presence in the suburbs, this minority population created a demand for ethnic-specific businesses and professional services such as grocery stores; realty companies; immigration, financial, and legal services; language schools; and travel agencies. As the ethnic population became more visible, ethnic businesses prospered, and the two reinforced each other by attracting a wide spectrum of new immigrants as residents and workers. Development sometimes led to tensions between long-time residents and immigrant newcomers, and this in turn prompted political activism among the minority residents. As more immigrants became American citizens, many sought to participate actively in grassroots and electoral politics and to engage in local social, cultural, and economic affairs. It was under these conditions that some of these suburbs emerged as or were transformed to ethnoburbs. During this stage of ethnoburb formation, a particular minority group might expend deliberate efforts to further the process of agglomeration. For example, ethnic realtors would help direct new immigrants where to live, and ethnic financial institutions similarly channeled residential and business loans to certain areas.

Ethnoburb: Position and Relationship

A new type of suburban ethnic concentration area, ethnoburbs occupy a unique position in the contemporary socioeconomic and political fabric, and they engage in different kinds of social and economic relationships. Ethnoburbs are fully functional communities, with their own internal socioeconomic structures that are integrated into both national and international networks of information exchange, business connection, and social activity.

Compared with the old ethnic enclaves, ethnoburbs offer ethnic populations more space and more diversified economic activities. Economic activities in ethnoburbs not only incorporate the traditional ethnic economy, but also involve functions that result from the globalization of capital and the international flow of commodities and labor, whether skilled, semi-skilled, or unskilled. The establishment of ethnic-owned and -operated businesses attracts more immigrants to the suburban clusters, while increasing numbers of immigrants, who are entrepreneurs, laborers, and customers of ethnic businesses, strengthen the ethnic socioeconomic structure in the ethnoburbs. This also, however, increases the potential for tension and conflicts among different classes within the ethnic group itself. Nonetheless, ethnoburbs have replaced

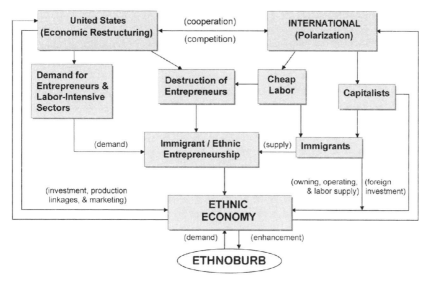

FIGURE 3. The Ethnic Economy and the Ethnoburb in Socioeconomic Contexts
Source: Modified from Light and Bonacich 1988, 427, fig. 5

or are replacing traditional inner-city enclaves as the important ports of entry, or gateways, for new immigrants in some large American metropolitan areas. Once established, ethnoburbs continue to grow and diffuse spatially and to develop socioeconomically.

Ethnoburbs in a Socioeconomic Context

Figure 3 delineates the relationships among an ethnoburb, its ethnic economy, and globalized capital and personnel flows.

Competition and cooperation in the world economy have stimulated increased polarization between the wealthy and the poor worldwide and have brought about economic restructuring in the United States. For example, reindustrialization and cheap domestic labor have provided opportunities for new entrepreneurship and labor-intensive sectors that can compete with such sectors overseas. The trend toward worldwide polarization of economic well-being further bifurcates populations, producing ever greater distinctions between cheap labor and capitalists. Changing immigration policies and geo-politics stimulate both laborers and millionaires to join new immigrant waves. Thus, the ethnic economy receives investment resources from ethnic capitalists (both immigrants and those who stay in the native country but invest in the United States) but also relies on a labor force dominated by poor immigrants. Ethnoburbs attract investment by ethnic millionaires and encourage poorer people to immigrate for work. The formation of an ethnoburb calls for a strong ethnic economy, and the ethnic economy enhances the ethnoburb. The integrated ethnic economy in an ethnoburb is formed by the linkages of investment, production, and markets to the mainstream economy. The formation of the ethnic economy itself further accelerates economic restructuring and the international polarization of wealth, as it becomes increasingly integrated into national and global economic systems.

Socioeconomic Relationships in Ethnoburbs

Figure 4 illustrates socioeconomic relationships within the ethnoburb. It depicts ethnic community formation and racial/class conflicts within and between ethnic groups (intra- and intergroup relations).

An emerging ethnoburb generates the need for an ethnic economy to serve its consumer market. This economy benefits the ethnoburb by creating business opportunities and providing jobs to ethnic people, and the establishment of ethnic-owned businesses attracts more people to live and work in the ethnoburb. The increasing numbers of new immigrants, who bring their skills and labor to open and operate ethnic businesses and patronize other businesses, in turn strengthen the ethnic socioeconomic structure and enhance the ethnic identity of the ethnoburb.

At the same time, a large influx of ethnic newcomers to traditionally white American "turf"—the suburbs—rapidly changes the residential landscape and business environment at the local level. What may result are misunderstandings,

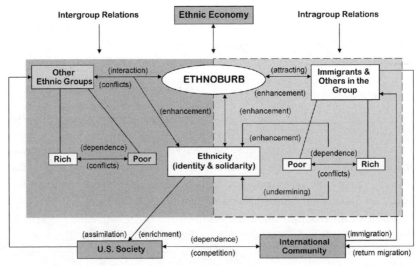

FIGURE 4. The Ethnoburb in Socioeconomic Contexts

distrust, and tensions between the new ethnic minorities and longtime residents of various ethnic groups. Sometimes these tensions are racialized and evolve into conflicts between groups regarding economic development, social adjustment, cultural settings, and political participation. But such conflicts also serve as opportunities for both the minority group and the dominant group to reassert their own ethnic consciousness and identity and, in some cases, solidarity. In other words, the emergence of an ethnoburb is likely to reinforce the ethnicity for all groups and to reinforce existing divisions.

An ethnoburb can also divide people from the same ethnic background by raising class consciousness, and this can increase the potential for conflict between different classes within the ethnic group. Interdependency between rich and poor within a group enhances ethnicity whereas conflict between them undermines ethnic solidarity. Ethnic people in an ethnoburb also have interactions with other groups, but these conflicts between groups tend to enhance ethnicity. Sometimes class interests transcend ethnic boundaries to become the main reason for conflict. Therefore, tensions and conflicts within and between ethnic communities are not only race related, but also class based.

Ethnoburbs Distinguished from Ghettos and Enclaves

Ethnoburbs differ from the traditional ethnic settlement types of ghetto and enclave in the following ways (see Table 1).

TABLE 1. Comparison among Ghetto, Enclave, and Ethnoburb

Characteristic	Ghetto	Enclave	Ethnoburb
Dynamics	forced segregation	forced & voluntary	voluntary
Spatial form	small scale	small scale	small to medium scale
Population	high density	high density	medium density
Location	inner city	inner city and suburbs	suburbs
Economy	few ethnically owned businesses	bias towards services and labor-intensive sectors	ethnically owned business of all kinds
Internal stratification	minimum	not much	very stratified
Interaction	mainly within group	mainly within group	both within and among different groups
Tension	intergroup	mainly intergroup	inter- & intragroup
Community	mainly inward	mainly inward	both inward & outward
Example	traditional Chinatown (nineteenth century)	contemporary Chinatown	Chinese ethnoburb in the San Gabriel Valley

1. Dynamics. Ethnoburbs may result from a deliberate effort by the ethnic groups involved to set up their own job and consumer markets in order to fit into broader national and international socioeconomic and geopolitical contexts. Unlike ghetto residents, who lack economic power, the creators of ethnoburbs are able to choose potential locations because of their economic strength. Unlike ghettos where ethnic residents do not own many of the businesses in their own neighborhoods, in ethnoburbs the ethnic residents own a good portion, or key components, of the businesses. Economic activities in ethnoburbs not only incorporate the ethnic economy in the traditional sense, but participate in the globalization of capital and international flows of commodities and skilled, high-tech, and managerial personnel. The situation may vary among ethnic groups, depending on their population size, willingness to relocate, and economic capacity, and it is also affected by local response, perhaps resistance, from the majority community and by promotion or restriction because of government policies. Ethnoburbs are not the result of forced segregation, as are ghettos, but are voluntary concentrations of ethnic people to maximize their own personal network and business connections and to create a community with a familiar language and culture.

2. Geographical locations and density. Ethnoburbs are located in suburbs where they have larger geographical areas, a larger ethnic population, and lower density than exist in ghettos and enclaves. They may include many municipalities and unincorporated areas, rather than just blocks or sections in the inner city, as is true of most ghettos and ethnic enclaves. Although there may be more ethnic people in ethnoburbs than in traditional ethnic neighborhoods, the proportion of one particular ethnic group is not as high as in the traditional neighborhoods. The percentage of ethnic people in ethnoburbs may be as low as 10 to 15 percent in some places, and they seldom become the majority of the community, although their presence can transform the local residential composition and business structure and can stamp an undeniable ethnic signature on the local landscape. Both ethnic residences and businesses tend to be relatively concentrated within identifiable clusters in ethnoburbs, but they are not highly concentrated in one single location. Unlike the sharp boundaries of ghettos and enclaves, boundaries for ethnoburbs are fuzzy and largely arbitrary.

3. Internal stratification. Socioeconomic status and the occupational structure of ethnic residents in ethnoburbs are far more polarized than is the case in ghettos and enclaves. As a consequence, ethnoburbs may generate not only racial tensions between different ethnic groups, but also class conflicts within a single ethnic group. Both wealthy and poor people live in ethnoburbs, although often in different sections of the community or in different but nearby communities. The establishment of ethnic-owned and -operated businesses, both

"ethnic" in traditional terms and "professional" in modern terms, attracts more new immigrants to live and work in these suburban clusters. Increasing numbers of immigrants strengthen the ethnic socioeconomic structure, even as that structure also increases the potential for class conflict within the ethnic group.

4. Functionality. The nineteenth-century ethnic enclaves of European Americans in the suburbs primarily were the result of "invasion and succession," in which concentrations of better-off longtime immigrants and/or later generations moved in from downtown districts. In contrast, ethnoburbs are "ports of entry" for new immigrants of all different socioeconomic backgrounds. Unlike the traditional ethnic enclaves and ghettos, where the ethnic group primarily looked inward and formed self-contained communities, ethnoburbs are more open to the mainstream society as multiracial and multicultural suburbs. Many Americans go to inner-city enclaves like Chinatown to get a sort of "exotic" experience as tourists and then go home after a day's excursion. But in ethnoburbs, your next door neighbors are minority people and your neighborhood stores may look like the shops you see in Chinatown. Given this mixed environment and daily contacts with people of different backgrounds, ethnic minority people in ethnoburbs are both inward and outward looking in their socioeconomic and political pursuits. They have more contact and interactions with other ethnic groups in terms of economic activities, social affairs, and political involvement. They are more actively involved in mainstream politics and community affairs than the residents of ghettos and enclaves. But they also maintain and exhibit their ethnic affinity through the very establishment of ethnoburbs. Once an ethnoburb is established, it becomes a new hub for the ethnic group. Ethnicity is reinforced through a network of economic, social, and political relations. Although there are class differences and conflicts within the ethnic group, the group often unites in solidarity to fight for their rights whenever those rights are threatened. Cultivating an ethnic consciousness leads to growth and prosperity.

Ethnoburbs and Theoretical Considerations

The ethnic population that still lives in inner-city enclaves is usually poor and less educated and more likely to consist of low-skilled workers in an ethnic job market. However, the traditional image of an assimilated, well-off, and dispersed minority population in the suburbs has changed because of the emergence of ethnoburbs. In the ethnoburbs, ethnic minority people are not only spatially concentrated within their residential and business clusters, but they are also stratified in economic and social structures. Because of this clustering, the assimilation process within the ethnic group slows in ethnoburbs and takes different forms.

Assimilation continues to occur within ethnic groups. However, an ethnic group with a certain population size, continuing immigration, relatively large concentrations, and that maintains close transnational ties may maintain high levels of ethnic consciousness, identity, and affinity, symbolically as well as substantively. Therefore, assimilation and ethnic identity coexist as complementary processes. Further, the ethnoburb model can elaborate pluralism and newer perspectives that have focused on the social construction of and links between race, class, and gender, by revealing the spatial dimensions of these dynamics and their social-theoretical rationale.

The rise of an ethnoburb ultimately challenges the conventional assimilation theory fundamentally. Assimilation theory assumes ethnicity is a temporary and static feature that will gradually cease to exist; all ethnic groups will eventually merge with Protestant white American society. But with the establishment of ethnoburbs and the influx of new types of immigrants, assimilation may not necessarily be an inevitable process for immigrants. While these new immigrants may be law-abiding residents or citizens of the United States, they may not be ready (in the case of some refugees) nor willing (in the case of some transnational personnel or investment-linked immigrants) to assimilate fully. With recurrent immigrant-bashing nationwide and the rise of a new cultural racism, especially in the debate about who should be "Americans," it remains to be seen just how well the general public and state apparatus will tolerate the ethnoburb phenomenon and how these reactions will shape or limit the future of ethnoburbs.

Assimilation itself requires certain societal conditions. Only when the society provides a level playing field for every ethnic group, free of prejudice and discrimination, can assimilation of minorities be possible. Many non-European groups in the United States suffered severe discrimination, even violent attacks, so assimilation was only a distant promise to them. Since racialization dynamics still exist and function in society, it is hard to believe that assimilation can be the answer to all societal problems related to immigration and minority groups. Moreover, is cultural and behavioral assimilation of all different groups to a single white Protestant society in the best interest of the United States? This remains an open question, but globalization and transnationalism suggest otherwise.

Perhaps the assimilation process should be redefined as a two-way separation-integration continuum along which groups can move in either direction, instead of assuming a one-way process that transforms immigrants, at least figuratively, into white Americans. The ethnoburban Chinese in LA's San Gabriel Valley represent a new type of ethnic community, one that has partially merged with American society socioeconomically and politically, yet retains its own identity and cultural heritage. They may ultimately transform mainstream American society, while being transformed themselves during the process, illustrating how the assimilation process may increasingly have become a two-way street.

By linking ethnoburban settlement patterns with political, social, and economic contexts at several spatial scales, the ethnoburb concept provides a stronger social-theoretical basis for understanding changing ethnic relations than is possible if we rely on either assimilation or pluralism alone. And clearly it best elucidates the sociospatial manifestation of contemporary ethnic settlement dynamics today.

PART 2

The Los Angeles Chinese Ethnoburb

3 Changing Chinese Settlement

One of the earliest immigrant groups to settle on the west coast of the United States, the Chinese, like other racial minority groups, were victims of racial discrimination and scapegoating during periods of economic hardship. They faced prejudice and violence, exclusion and deportation, and were forced to retreat to their own social and spatial world—inner-city Chinatowns. Their fate in this country can be seen to mirror changing global, national, and local circumstances. When the United States and China are allies, the Chinese in this country become a symbol of friendship between the two countries; when the two countries become enemies in the international arena, the Chinese face hostility, even though many are American citizens.

The circumstances for Chinese immigrants in the United States changed considerably with the passage of the 1965 Immigration and Nationality Act. Many new immigrants came in what can be called a chain migration because the coming of one person stimulated not only the coming of family members but also relatives and friends. This includes those with more education and specialized training as well as those simply willing to work; all have made important contributions to the U.S. economy, politics, and society. As a result of changes in the composition of Chinese population, their settlement forms have altered a great deal over time. In many U.S. urban areas, Chinatowns have been transformed from traditional ethnic ghettos or enclaves to sites for international investment and urban renewal efforts. In addition, a new form of ethnic settlement—the ethnoburb—has arisen and matured.

Chinese Settlement in the United States before 1965

The Chinese were among the earliest Asian immigrants to migrate to North America.[1] They started to come to the United States in large numbers after 1850. While reportedly only 46 China-born Chinese came to the United States between 1820 and 1850, the number increased to 41,397 in the next decade

(U.S. Bureau of the Census 1864, xxii). Heavy taxation, corruption, and oppression by the Qing Dynasty government in China during the second half of the nineteenth century, in addition to population pressures and natural disasters, caused food shortages, social unrest, and rebellion. Many people, especially peasants from southern Guangdong Province, boarded boats in a search of survival abroad. The Burlingame Treaty of 1868 between the United States and China further insured free Chinese immigration and encouraged a steady labor supply for the United States. Pulled by the gold rush and better opportunities in the United States, many of these early Chinese immigrants came as "sojourners," hoping to find their fortune, support their families, and eventually return to China. Most were young males who settled on the west coast, particularly in California. These Chinese were recruited to meet the demand for labor for the economic development of the western frontier. They worked as manual laborers in mines, railway construction sites, manufacturing, or in farming and fishing. In 1880, the Chinese population of the United States reached 105,000 (Table 2).[2] In California alone, the Chinese accounted for 10 percent of the total population, and one-quarter of the labor force (Chinese Historical Society of America 1994; Mangiafico 1988).

While the Chinese brought with them a culture that differed considerably from the white European American norm, it was the combination of social tensions and economic competition that provoked the hatred toward the Chinese. Initially, employers welcomed the Chinese and often hired them as strikebreakers since they were cheap and industrious labor. This caused intense job competition between Chinese and white workers. Not surprisingly, white mobs who engaged in anti-Chinese violence during the late nineteenth century were mostly working class. The economic situation worsened after the stock market collapse in 1872 and a severe drought in 1876, which caused massive business failures and job losses. Led by the Workingmen's Party, militants demanded "the Chinese Must Go." It became the leading slogan, and anti-Chinese violence broke out in several western states. Cultural difference was deployed only later to unite whites against the Chinese, who now accused the Chinese of remaining unassimilated. Thus, the Chinese became scapegoats during periods of economic recession, and a racialized group under continuous socioeconomic pressure in American society.

Although early anti-Chinese sentiment was clearly linked to economic competition, it also reflected a deep-rooted racist attitude towards nonwhites that stressed white superiority over "yellow inferiority." The Page Act (An Act Supplemental to Acts in Relation to Immigration, March 3, 1875) was the first federal legislation to restrict female immigration. In particular, this act attempted to prevent the importation of Chinese women on the explicit assumption that

TABLE 2. Numbers of Chinese in the United States (1850–2000)

Year	Total	Male	Female	Male: Female Ratio	Foreign Born: Native Ratio
2000	2,865,232	1,387,290	1,477,942	0.94:1	1.63:1
1990	1,648,696	821,542	827,154	0.99:1	2.26:1
1980	812,178	410,936	401,242	1.02:1	1.73:1
1970	433,469	227,163	206,306	1.10:1	0.89:1
1960	236,084	135,430	100,654	1.35:1	1.53:1
1950	117,140	76,725	40,415	1.90:1	0.63:1
1940	106,334	73,561	32,773	2.24:1	0.92:1
1930	74,954	59,802	15,152	3.94:1	1.43:1
1920	61,639	53,891	7,748	6.96:1	2.41:1
1910	71,531	66,856	4,675	14.30:1	3.84:1
1900	89,863	85,341	4,522	18.87:1	8.97:1
1890	107,488	103,618	3,869	26.78:1	35.69:1
1880	105,000	n.a.	n.a.	n.a.	88.15:1
1870	63,199	58,649	4,550	12.89:1	121.25:1
1860	34,933	n.a.	n.a.	n.a.	n.a.
1850	758	n.a.	n.a.	n.a.	n.a.

Sources: T. Almaguer 1994, 156; S. Chan 1991, 94; M. Zhou 1992, 44, Table 3–1; and U.S. Bureau of Census, under the following census years:
1860: p. xxviii;
1890: table 12, p. 474;
1910: table 4, pp.79, 82;
1920: table 20, p. 94; Table 22, p. 104; Table 71, p. 302;
1930: vol. III, pt. 1, table 17, p. 123; vol. II, table 1, p. 25;
1940: vol. II, pt.1, Table 22, p. 52;
1950: P-E No.3B, table 5, p. 19; table 29, p. 87;
1960: table 4, p. 4; table 26, p. 91;
1980: PC–80–2–1E, table 1, pp. 2–3;
1990: CP–3–5, table 1, p. 6;
2000: http://factfinder.census.gov/servlet/DTTable (accessed: 1/7/04).

many of them were prostitutes. Then, in a report issued on February 25, 1878, the House Committee on Education and Labor singled out the Chinese male as "an undesirable citizen" for three reasons: his effect on the labor market, his debilitating effect on society, and his inability to assimilate (Chinese Historical Society of America 1994; Leong 1994). In 1879, California adopted its second constitution, in which the Chinese were declared "undesirable." These legislations reflected the interrelations between race and gender ideologies, which were used to exclude the Chinese in general and Chinese women in particular.

In addition, it is clear that for the Chinese at least, assimilation was not a voluntary goal among immigrants wanting to merge into American society, but a condition of cultural acceptance imposed upon them. When they were perceived as not satisfying these cultural demands, the Chinese were labeled "unassimilable." Assimilation thus became an important criterion as to whether a group should be allowed to immigrate.

Anti-Chinese sentiment in the west prompted Congress to pass the Chinese Exclusion Act (An Act to Execute Certain Treaty Stipulations Relating to the Chinese), signed by President Chester Arthur on May 6, 1882. It was the first, and the only, federal law to exclude a group of people based solely on their race and class. The Chinese Exclusion Act barred both skilled and unskilled Chinese labor from coming to the United States for a period of ten years. It began by stating that "in the opinion of the Government of the United States the coming of Chinese laborers to this country endangers the good order of certain localities" (U.S. Congress 1882, 211). The Chinese Exclusion Act was revised or renewed in 1884, 1888, 1892, 1893, 1898, 1901, 1902, and finally 1904, when it was extended indefinitely. Chinese exclusion became known as "the Chinese Question" in American domestic politics during this period, and Congress enacted a total of fifteen anti-Chinese laws between 1882 and 1913. For example, the 1892 Geary Law required all Chinese to prove legal residency to any law enforcement officer on demand, and failure to do so could result in a jail sentence and deportation. It is not too difficult to see that one of the provisions of Proposition 187, passed by California voters 102 years later, and later ruled in violation of current state law, resembles this historical law with its provision that immigrants should carry IDs at all times.

The Chinese Exclusion Act also served as the precedent for later exclusionary policies used against other racial minority groups in the United States and became a model for similar laws in other countries, such as Canada and Mexico. Canada imposed a head tax on all Chinese immigrants between 1885 and 1923, when it enacted its own version of the Chinese Exclusion Act in 1923. During the first forty years that the Chinese Exclusion Act was in operation, the total Chinese population in the United States (including the American-born generation) fell to less than 62,000 in 1920, a little more than half of the number in 1880. In west coast states such as California and Oregon, the decrease was even more severe (Table 2 and Map 1).[3]

Desperate to find prosperity in the United States and to circumvent the exclusion laws, many Chinese came in the early twentieth century as "paper sons." Following the 1906 San Francisco earthquake and fire that destroyed official documents, including birth certificates, the opportunity to claim to be children of American-born Chinese was immediately seized. In response, the

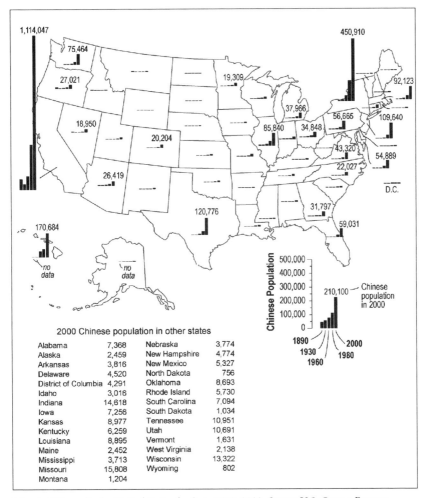

Map 1. Chinese in the United States, by State 1890–2000. *Source:* U.S. Census Bureau.

United States set up a detention and interrogation center on Angel Island, just offshore in the San Francisco Bay, which was meant to ferret out those who tried to enter the country under false pretenses. It was reported that between 1910–1940, about 50,000 Chinese were confined for weeks, months, or even years and repeatedly interrogated to determine their fates.

Under the shadow of exclusion and violence, the Chinese changed their economic strategies, residential patterns, and geographical locations in order to cope with the harsh conditions imposed by the host society. They ceased to work in occupations that directly competed with white labor and turned to businesses that required less capital to start. Thus Chinese laundries and restaurants became the two major Chinese-owned businesses in this country until after World War II. What is ironic is that these were two types of activity that they had rarely performed in China. The Chinese left small towns and rural areas and established Chinatowns that stimulated social cohesion and ethnic solidarity, which dominated Chinese settlement in large cities until the 1960s. Chinatowns were usually in depressed downtown areas, where immigrants lived, worked, and sought to protect themselves from discrimination in the host society. Chinatowns became "a sanctuary, a residential neighborhood, [an] economic zone, and a place to practice traditional culture" (B. P. Wong 1982, 77). Loo and Mar note that "Chinatown provide[d] many of its residents with convenient access to shopping, transportation, restaurants, foods, and place of work; and it provide[d] the opportunity to live among Chinese-speaking persons" (1982, 95). Most Chinese lived and worked in restaurants and related service industries inside Chinatown. The exceptions were those who opened other ethnic businesses (mainly hand laundries) and located their businesses and residences in other parts of cities. Many Chinese opted out entirely of the hostile west, moving to other parts of the country, including large east coast cities, where the Chinese population increased and many Chinatowns were formed during this time.

The impact of the Chinese Exclusion Act on the Chinese community was severe. It caused a situation unique to the Chinese among all major ethnic groups in the United States. The rights of Chinese men were keenly circumscribed; they were prevented from bringing their wives to the United States, but anti-miscegenation laws forbade their forming lasting legal relationships with white women, which added to a sense that their only avenue was to earn enough money to return to China. Generations of Chinese men traveled back and forth between the Americas and China, where they could visit their families and father children, and sojourning became their way of life. According to a 1934 law (H.R. 3673), for a child born of an American citizen to be a citizen of the United States, that child had to reside in the United States for at least five continuous years before age eighteen. Therefore, Chinese boys of American-born Chinese fathers had to leave their mothers in China and come to the United States no later than age thirteen; only a few Chinese girls made this journey. The restrictions against Chinese women immigrants and the establishment of family ties for the majority of Chinese men in the United States resulted in an extremely unbalanced sex ratio (see Table 2). Chinatowns were communities of fathers and sons, uncles and nephews, male relatives and friends. This demographic situation in turn contributed to the social problems and vice in

Chinatowns, such as gambling and prostitution. Because of discrimination and the immigrants' language difficulties, the Chinese were forced to stay in their own social world.[4]

The era of Chinese exclusion lasted for a period of sixty-one years, and the Chinese Exclusion Act was not repealed until 1943, when China became a war ally of the United States. During World War II, there were strong voices for repealing the Chinese Exclusion Act at both local and national levels. Many local institutions, particularly those in the west, passed resolutions supporting the repeal by early September 1943. A Chinese newspaper in San Francisco listed the following repeal supporters: the American Legion, California Department; the Veterans of Foreign Wars, California Department; the California Council; the City of San Francisco, San Francisco Chamber of Commerce; the Oregon Council; the Chambers of Commerce in Portland, Seattle, and Houston.

Several repeal bills were introduced in Congress, listing three main reasons for repeal: "(1) as a measure of *war expediency*, to strengthen Chinese morale; (2) as an act of overdue justice to a *friendly people* against whom humiliating discriminations have been made; (3) as a means of cementing the good will of a great nation *with whom post-war trade will be highly profitable*" (*Chinese Press 1943*, "Repeal of the Chinese Exclusion Act," rpt. in Chinese Historical Society of America, 1994, 8 [emphasis added]). In his letter to the Congress on October 11, 1943, President Franklin Roosevelt indicated that

> by the repeal of the Chinese Exclusion Laws, we can correct a historic mistake and silence the distorted Japanese propaganda.... The Chinese quota would therefore, be only about one hundred immigrants a year. There can be no reasonable apprehension that... will cause unemployment or provide competition in the search for jobs (quoted in L. L. Wang 1994, 69).

Taken together, both Congress' reasons and Roosevelt's letter undoubtedly suggest that the repeal was not primarily motivated by justice for the Chinese, but was more a measure of bolstering the image of United States and its strategic interests in the war.[5] The repeal act was signed on December 17, 1943 (An Act to repeal the Chinese Exclusion Acts, to establish quota, and for other purposes, Public Law 199). This one-page act repealed all exclusion acts against the Chinese passed in previous years, allowed Chinese immigrants to become naturalized citizens, and established an annual immigration quota of 105 for China computed on the basis of the 1924 Immigration Act. That Act stated that "up to 75 per centrum of the quota shall be given to Chinese born and resident in China" (U.S. Congress 1943, 217). This actually limited the annual Chinese immigrants coming directly from China or born in China to 71. A total of 383 Chinese were admitted into the United States under this immigration category during 1944–1949.

The number of Chinese immigrants to the United States rose as a result of the passage of the War Brides Act (Public Law 713) on December 28, 1946, and the Fiancées Act of June 29, 1946. These laws allowed Chinese wives and minor children of American citizens (especially GIs) to enter the United States on a nonquota basis. They resulted in the entry of 5,687 Chinese and reduced the male-to-female ratio of the Chinese in the continental United States from 2.85 in 1940 to 1.89 by 1950 (W. H. C. Chen 1952; H. M. Lai 1994.) The establishment of People's Republic of China in 1949, and the outbreak of the Korean War in the early 1950s, reversed the geopolitical relations between the United States and China and the favorable attitude toward the Chinese in America. Between 1956 and 1966 the Confession Program was instituted; this allowed those Chinese who confessed to immigration authorities that they entered the United States under a fraudulent identity (as paper sons) to adjust their immigration status and to bring their families to the United States. A total of 13,897 Chinese confessed in the ten-year period under this program (Lai 1994). This same program, a product of the McCarthy era, however, was used to tightly control the Chinese community through suspicion, stress, and anxiety in an effort to expose so-called "red agents" and "Red China" sympathizers (Zhao 2002).

Fueled by anti-Communist fervor, Congress enacted programs to assist Chinese students and scholars who were enrolled in the U.S. colleges and universities[6] to establish residency after their graduation and to help other Chinese immigrants—political refugees, merchants, professionals, and former diplomats—to find "refuge" in the United States. The influx of these highly educated, elite immigrants, the twentieth-century Chinese "forty-niners," altered the composition of the Chinese population in the United States. Unlike the nineteenth-century Chinese "forty-niners," who were mainly laborers and sojourners, these new immigrants were the elite of Chinese society and came to the United States to stay. They were the first generation of Chinese immigrants who brought fortunes with them, instead of seeking to earn money here to send back to China. Many of them did not live in Chinatowns, but became the predecessors of the present-day suburban-bound immigrants.

Chinese Immigration since 1965

As S. H. Tsai has noted: "The presence of sharp ethnic and class distinctions and a politically fragmented population were characteristics of the post-1965 Chinese-American community" (1986, 157). Unlike the traditional, "old immigrants" *(lao qiao)* who came mostly from Guangdong Province and spoke Cantonese, the new immigrants *(xin qiao)* come from different geographic areas, including Taiwan, Mainland China, Hong Kong, and other parts of the world, and possess a higher level of education and job skills overall. The new immigrants include both millionaires and poor people who are largely confined to the ethnic economy.

From 1960 to 1990, the Chinese population in the United States almost doubled in every decade, while maintaining a relatively balanced sex ratio. By 1990, the Chinese population had reached 1,645,472 and become the fourth largest ethnic group in the United States according to origin. (The three larger groups were Mexicans, Puerto Ricans, and American Indians.) The 1990s witnessed another 42.5 percent increase. Spurred by an increase in quotas—that offer Mainland China and Taiwan each 20,000 immigration visas per year—the number of Chinese immigrants surpassed the number of native-born Chinese Americans. Although the native-born population exceeded the immigrant population by a ratio of 0.89 immigrant per native-born Chinese American in 1970, the trend has reversed in recent decades (see Table 2). Legal immigrants who came in under quotas plus those who came in on a nonquota basis totaled about 50,000 or more Chinese immigrants entering the United States every year during 1982–1992 (U.S. Immigration and Naturalization Service, 1993 *Statistical Yearbook of the Immigration and Naturalization Service*). Of the 1,825,285 foreign-born Chinese in 2000, 42 percent immigrated to the United States during the1990s alone. China (including Hong Kong and Taiwan) became the second largest immigrant source country, second only to Mexico in 2000. The 2006 American Community Survey reveals that the total Chinese population reached 3,090,453.[7]

The Chinese population continued to concentrate in several states like California, New York, Hawai'i, Texas, and New Jersey, which together accounted for 69 percent of all the Chinese population in 2000. But states such as Florida, Georgia, Virginia, and Washington also experienced rapid growth between 1980 and 2000 (see Map 1). The Chinese have tended to live in urban areas; 98 percent of all the Chinese population lived in urban areas in 2000, much higher than the national average of 79 percent. Three metropolitan areas—New York, San Francisco, and Los Angeles—still dominate, accounting for 48 percent of the nation's Chinese population in 2000.

The dramatic increase in immigration after 1965 meant that congested small downtown Chinatowns were no longer able to house all the new immigrants. A smaller proportion of Chinese continued to live in Chinatowns, mainly the elderly and the poorer of the new immigrants. Most Chinatowns had, and continue to have, poor housing, overcrowding, and crime. "Residents want to stay not because it is an ideal place of residence, but because of social, economic, and language disadvantages relative to white American society" (Loo and Mar 1982, 95). Chinatowns today in many cities function mainly as tourist attractions, showcase small-scale ethnic businesses, and offer modest housing (W. T. Chow 1977). However, in recent decades Chinatowns in big cities have gone through gentrification, which makes housing affordability an increasing concern. Manhattan's Chinatown, for instance, is becoming a place for hip young urban professionals.

In more recent decades, many better-off Chinese have moved to suburbs for better housing and neighborhoods. As predicted by the assimilation theory, many of them became spatially dispersed and socioeconomically assimilated into the mainstream society. Some of these residents were economically better off second- or later-generation Chinese Americans. Others were immigrants with high educational attainment and professional jobs.

But in the shifting socioeconomic and political contexts, the Chinese communities in the suburbs of some large metropolitan areas, such as those of Los Angeles, Chicago, Houston, New York, San Francisco, and Washington, DC, have become relatively concentrated. Living in the suburbs no longer necessarily means spatial dispersion for ethnic people, but, in some cases, residence in new ethnic concentrations. Unlike the immigrants of the previous periods and the better-off immigrants and native-born Chinese Americans who made their move from inner city to suburbs, these new immigrants have never experienced living in an American downtown; they have bypassed inner cities to settle directly in the suburbs. This diverse mix of suburban-bound immigrants includes not only wealthy people bringing cash, but also poor, unskilled workers.

Racialization and Spatialization of the Chinese Community in Los Angeles

Early History
It has been reported that one of the twelve householders who founded the village of El Pueblo de Nuestra Senora la Reina de Los Angeles de Porciuncula in 1781, Antonio Rodriguez, was a man of Chinese origin, who had adopted a Christianized Hispanic name. This is the earliest record of a Chinese settler in Los Angeles. In 1850 there were two Chinese male house servants, Alluce and Ahfou, in Los Angeles, according to the Census. The first Chinese woman reportedly arrived in Los Angeles in 1859. Ten years later, the total number of Chinese had increased to sixteen (Table 3). They worked in laundries or were employed in Caucasian households as domestics or laborers. The earliest

TABLE 3. Number of Chinese in Los Angeles County, 1850–2000

Year	Total	% of Population	Male	Female	Male:Female Ratio
2000	323,093	3.39%	156,931	166,162	0.94:1
1990	248,033	2.80	120,850	124,183	0.97:1
1980	93,747	1.25	47,090	46,657	1.0:1
1970	40,798	0.58	21,073	19,725	1.1:1
1960	19,286	0.32	10,836	8,450	1.3:1
1950	9,187	0.22	5,574	3,613	1.5:1
1940	5,330	0.19	3,751	1,579	2.4:1
1930	3,572	0.16	2,701	871	3.1:1
1920	2,591	0.28	n.a.	n.a.	n.a.
1910	2,602	0.52	n.a.	n.a.	n.a.
1900	3,209	1.88	n.a.	n.a.	n.a.
1890	4,424	4.36	n.a.	n.a.	n.a.
1880	1,169	3.50	1,302	69	21.0:1
1870	234	1.53	195	39	5.0:1
1860	16	0.14	n.a.	n.a.	n.a.
1850	2	0.06	2	0	2.0:1

Sources: U.S. Bureau of Census, under the following census years:
1890: table 2, p. 9; table 13, p. 477; table 14, p. 516;
1910: table 13; p.33;
1930: vol. III, pt.1, table 17, p. 226;
1940: vol. I, pt.1, p. 122;
1950: vol. I, table 5, pp.5-12; vol. II, pt. 5, table 47, p. 179;
1960: vol. I, pt. 6, pp.6–22; vol. I, table 28, p. 196;
1970: PC(1)–136, table 34, pp. 6–310;
1980: vol. 1, pt. 6, table 50, pp.6–679;
1990: CP–1–6, table 55, p. 270;
2000: http://factfinder.census.gov/servlet/DTTable?_ts=41623892875.

reported Chinese business was a merchandise store on Spring Street, opposite the Court House. It was established by Chun Chick on July 13, 1861, and was mostly patronized by white customers. Several Chinese-owned businesses followed, including an herb shop, a restaurant, a curio store, and several laundries. Most of them catered primarily to the Anglo community.[8]

The number of Chinese increased to 234 in 1870; 39 of them were women, for a sex ratio of 5:1. They lived in 108 households, about half of them (52) family households. This demonstrates that even at the very early stage of Chinese settlement, the Chinese immigrant population in Los Angeles was not composed just of male "birds of passage." About one-third of all Chinese in town lived in the first Chinatown of Los Angeles, a block adjacent to the south side of the original Plaza. Its main street was known as Calle de los Negros, or Negro Alley. In the early 1870s, there were at least two Chinese fraternal organizations, Hong Chow and Nin Yung (Lou 1982; Mason 1967).

Railroad construction in Southern California in the mid-1870s caused a boom in the local Chinese community. Chinese workers were brought in to build the South Pacific railway links between Santa Monica and Los Angeles and between San Francisco and Los Angeles, which included digging the San Fernando Tunnel. These workers patronized local Chinese businesses, and some eventually became settlers themselves after the railroad work was completed. As a result Chinatown expanded eastward to the Los Angeles River and southward. Since most people considered the land adjacent to the Los Angeles River to be undesirable, it was cheaper than the area west of the Plaza. But since foreign-born Chinese were barred from owning land at this time, they rented instead, paying the landlords high rents. Three types of businesses dominated the Chinatown economy of the mid-1870s. One type provided goods and services mostly to white people, such as employment agencies, labor contractors, laundries, and vegetable peddlers. The second primarily served the Chinese and included money lenders, barbers, priests, and Chinese grocers. These types of business were stimulated by the increase in the Chinese population and their denial of access to businesses that served mainly whites. The third type catered to both Chinese and white customers and included retail merchants, restaurants, grocers, butchers, jewelers, tailors, and physicians. Grocers and physicians in this third group were often set up initially to serve the Chinese, but their price and quality attracted white customers. According to a Chinese Directory compiled by Wells Fargo & Co., there were forty-one Chinese businesses in Los Angeles by 1882, including eighteen laundries and eleven merchants.[9]

By 1880, there were 1,169 Chinese in Los Angeles County, comprising 3.5 percent of the total population (Table 3). With the influx of male laborers, the sex ratio among the Chinese increased to 21:1. The number of Chinese households increased to about 240. By 1890 the Chinese population reached a peak of 4,424, constituting an all-time high of 4.4 percent of the total population in the county. More than two-thirds of all Chinese in Los Angeles City lived in what was then Chinatown, and the Chinese population was the largest minority group in the city.

The Chinese Exclusion Act began to have a major impact on Los Angeles at the turn of the twentieth century. While the overall population of the county increased rapidly, the number of Chinese residents decreased to 3,209, comprising only 1.9 percent of total (Table 3). The number of Chinese family households increased marginally, to 290. Because of their exclusion from Anglo economic activities, the Chinese were forced to be economically self-sufficient, and this affected the local occupational distribution. From 1880 to 1900, the number of Chinese engaging in business (including all retail services) increased from 50 to 285, and Chinese laundries increased from 152 to 575. The Chinese dominated the laundry business during this period in Los Angeles County. Restaurants, dry goods merchants, groceries, and shops offering services for Chinese clients were thriving, and the earliest Chinese advertisement in the *Los Angeles Times* was placed in 1882. The Chinese garment sector was emerging, and by 1894 there were six Chinese restaurants in Los Angeles. During the same period, however, the number of laborers dropped from 195 to 132, a decrease from 28 percent to 2.1 percent of the total labor force. For instance, Chinese truck gardeners decreased from the 1880s number of 208 (89 percent of all gardeners in the county) to the 1900s total of 95 (21 percent). The four predominant occupations among local Chinese in 1900 were agriculture (44 percent), laundry (19 percent), cook (11 percent), and business (9.5 percent).[10] The number of Chinese in Los Angeles County continued to decline even though the total population steadily increased. By 1920, only 2,591 Chinese were counted, 0.3 percent of the total population in the county; the Chinese population had dropped rapidly from the peak year of 1890. Growth began again soon after this low, mainly due to natural growth, but it did not surpass the 1890 peak until 1940, when it reached 5,330 (Table 3).

At this early period of Chinese settlement, the Chinese were constant targets of white mobs. During 1870–1900, there were a total of thirty-four robberies and eight murder cases in which the victims were Chinese. Eleven to twenty-seven incidents of anti-Chinese violence (abuse, assault, robbery, and murder) were reported for every five-year period. In the most infamous Negro Alley massacre of October 24, 1871, violence broke out in Chinatown, triggered by the death of one white man caught in gunfire between the two rival Chinese associations. A mob of several hundred whites shot, hanged, and stabbed nineteen Chinese to death in retaliation, while the robbing and looting that followed caused $20,000 to $40,000 in losses to the Chinese. Another well-publicized case was the expulsion of the Chinese from Pasadena in 1885, which involved a downtown fire, allegedly caused by a Chinese arsonist. All Chinese people were forced to leave downtown Pasadena within twenty-four hours. Most did leave immediately and moved to Los Angeles' Chinatown, while others were chased to the southernmost boundary of Pasadena, away from the central business district. Chinese were also forcibly driven out of Norwalk, Burbank, Vernon, and what is today's Hollywood.[11] These incidents were part of broader general violence against the Chinese in the western United States during that period.

The Los Angeles Chinese also suffered from another type of organized harassment, in the form of economic exclusion, which especially targeted Chinese small businesses—laundries, merchants, peddlers. Since Chinese laborers were mainly employed in domestic service and agriculture, two occupations not popular among whites, agricultural workers and domestics were not the primary targets in the anti-Chinese movement in Southern California. Instead, the first effort to restrict Chinese participation in the local economy focused on the laundry business, when in 1872 the City Council passed a $5 license tax ordinance aimed at hand laundry establishments. Virtually all fifteen Chinese laundries refused to pay. Their proprietors were arrested and taken to court. Some of these then paid the tax, but the others served the five-day jail sentence instead. In 1874, the *Evening Express* published an editorial demanding that the City Council take action against the spread of Chinese laundries by restricting their locations within residential neighborhoods. These local efforts against Chinese laundries intensified in concert with national anti-Chinese movements. In spite of these actions, however, Chinese-owned and -operated laundries reached a peak of fifty-two in the city in 1890, and were estimated to employ more than 500 people.

Another example was the attempt to exclude Chinese vegetable peddlers from the city. Chinese immigrants had a near-monopoly on the fresh vegetable business in Southern California, where they grew, distributed, marketed, and sold practically all produce consumed in the region. By 1880, fifty out of the sixty registered vegetable peddlers in the city were Chinese, but they were the target of continuous harassment. In 1876, the City Council passed an ordinance requiring peddlers to acquire a permit before selling within city boundaries. This ordinance directly targeted the Chinese, since white farmers were exempt from such requirement. The Council increased license tax rates to $10 per month after the landslide victory by the Workingmen's Party in 1878. It was not until a successful strike by the Chinese peddlers, during which no vegetables were made available to customers for several weeks, that the Council finally reduced the permit fee to $5.25.

The Migrations of Los Angeles Chinatown

Exclusion served to contain and confine the Chinese within their own social world. Chinatown became a sanctuary to the Chinese, but not by choice. A local scholar recognized "the isolation of Chinatown [is] a semi-product of our civilization" (Sterry 1923, 326). But the very existence of this sanctuary was repeatedly threatened. Besides violence and organized restrictions against the Chinese, there were continuing efforts to remove Chinatown altogether. The socially marginalized Chinatown had to move twice during a fifty-year period before it was finally able to establish itself in today's location.

The earliest attempt to remove Chinatown surfaced during the 1870s, with a proposal to extend Los Angeles Street through the center of the Negro Alley Chinatown. In a report entitled "Chinatown: The Crying Evil of Our City," the City Council's "Subcommittee on Chinese" condemned Chinatown as a "great social evil in every respect." During the same period, the Cubic Air Ordinance, ostensibly to prevent overcrowding but specifically targeting Chinese-occupied buildings, was enforced more harshly. There were several attempts to burn down Chinatown as well. Fires set by arsonists in June 1887 destroyed almost a whole block in Negro Alley, but the arsonists went unpunished. Then acting Chinese consul, Colonel Bee, came to Los Angeles to conduct an independent investigation, but reached no conclusions. White residents convinced him that although they needed the services provided by Chinese businesses, they did not want the Chinese as neighbors. Bee believed these wishes were "reasonable," promised to satisfy them, and actually found a new location away from the heart of town for the Chinese.

In January 1888, the extension of Los Angeles Street was started, and most buildings in Los Angeles' first Chinatown were demolished. Only by fighting for their existence, did the Chinese retain the east side of Negro Alley. The rest of Chinese residents and businesses had to evacuate to a new area, the "Second Chinatown," at the present site of Union Station. The new enclave included the Plaza, North Main, Spring, and Los Angeles Streets, Ferguson Alley, and was bordered by Macy Street to the north, and Commercial Street to the south. This location was an undesirable area in every respect, for it was close to a main railroad line and bordered on two sides by railroad yards. Two blocks to the east was a gas plant. The two main commercial strips in Chinatown were Marchessault and Apablaza, which were intersected by thirteen thoroughfares without paving. Despite being such an undesirable location, by 1923 there were 184 shops, two small factories, and four large warehouses in this new Chinatown.[12] Chinatown at this time contained the worst housing problems in the city. In a survey carried out by the State Commission of Immigration in 1916, 878 out of the 1,572 rooms visited in Chinatown were found to be totally dark and windowless. These conditions were mainly due to the desire of building owners (none of whom were Chinese) to acquire the highest rental income by utilizing the maximum space in the buildings. They were unwilling to have their income reduced by housing and health regulations. There was no official count on numbers of Chinese during this period, but in the Macy Street School district (one-half of a precinct), there were about 100 Chinese voters, approximately

FIGURE 5. Chinatown Gate (author photo, 1995)

half of all registered voters. Since foreign-born Chinese were not eligible to become naturalized citizens, all these Chinese voters were adult American-born Chinese or China-born sons of Chinese-Americans. There were five Chinese schools, two Buddhist temples, a Chinese Chamber of Commerce, and two Chinese *tongs* (fraternal and political organizations—the Hop Sing and the Bing Gong) that had been established in order to maintain Chinese cultural heritage and keep social order (Sterry 1922, 1923).

The second Chinatown faced demolition and the displacement of residents in the early 1930s, when Union Station was constructed. Peter Soo Hoo, a University of Southern California-trained Chinese electrical engineer, along with Herbert Lapham, a Caucasian developer, coordinated the acquisition of a piece of land and the establishment a "New Chinatown" in the former Little Italy. Bordered by North Broadway, Castelar (today's Hill Street), Bernard and College Streets, this section became the center of contemporary Chinatown. For the first time in history, the Chinese themselves would own the land of the new Chinatown. The land was offered at 20 cents per square foot. The Chinese established the Los Angeles Chinatown Corporation with a sum $54,650 (546.5 shares, $100 each share) to purchase the land. The New Chinatown (Central Plaza)—the nation's first planned Chinatown—opened on June 25, 1938, with three sets of building and eighteen Chinese businesses. It catered primarily to tourists and secondarily to Chinese residents. The Chinatown gate and the other buildings constructed then still exist today (Figure 5). At the same time, close to New Chinatown on North Spring Street, just across from the famous Olvera Street, an exotic Chinese village-like "China City" was built to attract tourists.[13]

The Beginnings of Chinese Population Dispersal

Although most of the early Chinese settlers in Los Angeles clustered in Chinatown, there is evidence that Chinese residential patterns began to decentralize early in the twentieth century. Map 2 illustrates that the spatial center of the Chinese population in Los Angeles shifted southward slightly during the first

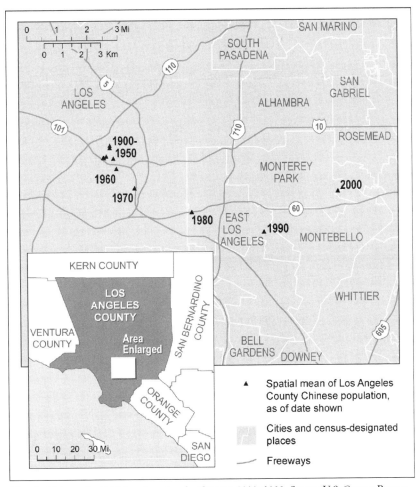

MAP 2. Chinese Spatial Mean Los Angeles County, 1900–2000. *Source:* U.S. Census Bureau.

half of the twentieth century.[14] The anchor of the first major concentration outside of Chinatown, the City Market, was built near Ninth and San Pedro Street in 1909. It was established through the cooperative efforts of Caucasians, Chinese, and Japanese. Led by Louis Quan, a Chinese-owned stock company was formed with 373 stockholders; this company raised $82,000 or 41 percent of the capital needed to build stores for produce businesses. The Chinese slowly began to move to the West Adams area in the 1920s, and that area is considered as the first Chinese "suburb" in LA.

By the 1930s, there were three main areas of Chinese concentration. They included the Second Chinatown in North Alameda Street and an expansion area around the City Market. Both were inner-city mixed residential and business districts with congested neighborhoods and crowded housing. The third area was west of Main Street, not far from the University of Southern California. This was mainly a residential area, with properties actually owned by Chinese. In Chinatown itself, the main business included bazaars, grocery and herb stores, import and export firms, restaurants, produce markets, and laundry shops.

The Chinese population continued to disperse south of downtown; there were three Chinese areas by the early 1940s. The first and the heaviest concentration of Chinese was around New Chinatown (the third Chinatown), the center of Chinese activities and community in Los Angeles. The second and third zones were both around the University of Southern California. The second was east of USC and west of Main Street, bordered by Broadway, Figueroa, Adams, and Exposition Boulevard. The third zone was located west of USC from Vermont and westward to Normandie and Arlington. The second and third zones, known as "zones of workmen's homes," were mainly middle class residential sections.[15]

However, Chinese movement into areas formerly restricted to Caucasians did not proceed without resistance, especially in wealthier Westside. A survey of ten residential districts in the City of Los Angeles conducted in 1940 found only two districts that permitted Asians (known as "Orientals" at the time) to live in them (Ferguson 1942, 38). Lawsuits were filed against Chinese households that dared to move to a "white area." After the U.S. Supreme Court barred restrictive covenants in 1948, thereby eliminating de jure residential segregation by race, some Chinese families moved into West Los Angeles, Hollywood, and Beverly Hills, which had been previously exclusively Caucasian. There were several reports of Chinese residents being misidentified as live-in housemaids in these affluent neighborhoods, although some of these rich Chinese families were probably the twentieth-century "forty-niners," who possessed ample financial resources. For example, a Chinese housewife who had just moved to a wealthy community became friendly with an African American housemaid working at her neighborhood. The latter was surprised to discover that this Chinese lady was not a fellow housemaid but a homeowner. In another incident, a USC sociology Ph.D. student who lived in Westside at the time was repeatedly asked by salesmen if they could see her "house lady." She felt annoyed and decided that she would respond to such questions according to her mood. If she was busy, she would simply answer, "My house lady is not at home." Otherwise she would say, "I AM the house lady!" Another example involved a male Chinese professor who went to an appliance store to buy a refrigerator for his family. As soon as he said he was looking for a refrigerator, he was led to see the industrial-use types. The salesman simply assumed that his Chinese client must either work at a restaurant or a laundry and was later astounded to learn the professor's true identity and purpose (W. H. C. Chen 1952; M. S. Lee 1939). A Chinese family moved to a Westside neighborhood and was the only Chinese family on a street full with large homes. The family hosted a housewarming party for more than 200 guests, including their Caucasian neighbors. Afterwards, some of their white neighbors exchanged remarks such as, "Gee, I didn't know Chinese people would be so nice" (author interview, Wilbur Woo, August, 1999). The experiences of the Chinese who chose to live in these affluent areas, as illustrated by the above examples, were shaped by the historical stereotype of Chinese as working-class poor, domestic servants, and the cultural "other." These illustrations also reflect the imposed racialized image of Chinese people as a low-status nonwhite group, attitudes that also permeated the notions of self-identity within the Chinese community. Those who worked, lived, and had social contact with white Americans were considered to have higher social status than the "Chinatown people." Although there were not many employment opportunities for Chinese youth in Chinatown except inheriting their parents' business, most of these youngsters considered jobs in Chinatown to be a last resort. They wanted to move out.

By the early 1950s, there were about 350 Chinese laundries, 60 Chinese produce businesses, 30 Chinese grocery stores, 40 gift shops, and 35 Chinese herb doctors in Los Angeles (W. H. C. Chen 1952, 59; M. S. Lee 1939). By 1960, there were almost 20,000 Chinese living in LA County (Table 3). Chinatown remained the main business district, residential area, and the social and cultural center of Chinese community. While some Chinese lived in the area outside Chinatown, scattered in communities in metropolitan Los Angeles, no single jurisdiction except LA City had a Chinese concentration of more than 350 Chinese. The City of Monterey Park, the largest Chinese concentration outside LA

City, had only 346 Chinese residents at the time. Nonetheless, as Map 2 reveals, the center of the Chinese population in 1960 was shifting southeast, because of the suburbanization trend and the rise of Monterey Park as a secondary Chinese population center.

Chinese Residential Patterns in Los Angeles: 1960–2000

The immigration law of 1965 brought a large flow of new Chinese immigrants to Los Angeles. The limited resources in Chinatown could not cope with their needs for housing and employment. Jobs were few, and wages were low. Rents were high, and living conditions were bad. The 1960 census showed that one-third of all housing in Chinatown was substandard. A 1968 survey of 193 Chinatown families indicated that the majority of them spoke only Chinese at home. One-third of the families survived on less than $4,000 a year. Despite these undesirable conditions, the population of Chinatown continued to grow at a rate of almost 50 percent between 1970 and 1980, from 5,839 to 8,652. In 1974 there were at least fourteen garment factories owned and operated by Chinese in the Chinatown area, reportedly employing fewer than 1,500 Chinese workers, mainly female immigrants who lacked English and job skills and who needed money to support their families.[16]

The end of the Vietnam War in the mid-1970s brought a huge influx of Southeast Asian refugees to the United States. Many of them were ethnic Chinese from Vietnam, Laos, and Cambodia who resettled in the Chinatown area. These new immigrants changed the demographic composition, language patterns, and streetscapes in Chinatown from a primarily Cantonese-speaking community made up of immigrants from Guangdong Province, to a multilingual one speaking Cantonese, Mandarin, Vietnamese, and Cambodian. The 1970s became a boom time in Chinatown. Some of the newcomers became business owners. By 1984 the Vietnamese Chinese owned half of all Chinatown businesses (Lew 1988). Shop signs became trilingual, in Chinese, Vietnamese, and English. On the window of the Chinatown Plaza, the three large painted characters in Chinese actually mean Vietnam, Cambodia, and Laos, suggesting that many Chinatown businesses were catering to customers from Southeast Asia. Chinatown continues to be a traditionally congested neighborhood, as well as a tourist attraction (Figure 6). Ethnic Chinese accounted for 62 percent of all the residents in the small Chinatown area in the early 1990s (Seo 1992), including an older generation of Cantonese-speaking Chinese and new immigrants from Southeast Asia. Most of them were poor, with limited education. In recent years however, LA Chinatown has undergone gentrification due to its revival as a location for artists' studios and galleries and as a popular nightclub scene (the Firecracker Lounge, for example) for young twenty-somethings.

FIGURE 6. Broadway Street (author photo, 2001)

In recent decades the majority of the Chinese in Los Angeles County no longer live in Chinatown. While in 1970 Chinatown still accounted for 14.3 percent of all Chinese in the county, by 1980 the percentage had decreased to 9.2 percent (Calculation based on CRA 1985 and Table 3). The declining importance of Chinatown as a population center coincides with the emergence of a new form of Chinese concentration, the ethnoburb, in the eastern suburbs of Los Angeles. The San Gabriel Valley Chinese ethnoburb is a new urban geographic phenomenon emerging on a larger spatial scale and in different locations than the older Chinatown form.

The 1970 census data show that outside Los Angeles' Chinatown, the largest Chinese concentration was located in the City of Monterey Park. Monterey Park led the way in increasing Chinese population density in LA County between 1960 and 1970, followed by some other western San Gabriel Valley communities (see Map 3).[17] The trend continued in the next decade. Both the western and eastern parts of the San Gabriel Valley increased in Chinese population density between 1970 and 1980, as did the southeast part of the county in the Artesia and Cerritos area. By 1980 the number of Chinese in Los Angeles County had grown, but it was still highly concentrated. About three-fourths of all census tracts had less than 50 Chinese. Only seven tracts had more than 1,000 Chinese each. The tract with the largest Chinese population, 2,929, was in Chinatown. But extending from the Chinatown cluster was a path of Chinese settlement leading to the eastern suburbs and centered around the City of Monterey Park. This pattern indicates that by 1980 the Chinese ethnoburb in San Gabriel Valley had already formed but had not yet become detached from Chinatown, the traditional center of Chinese people in LA.

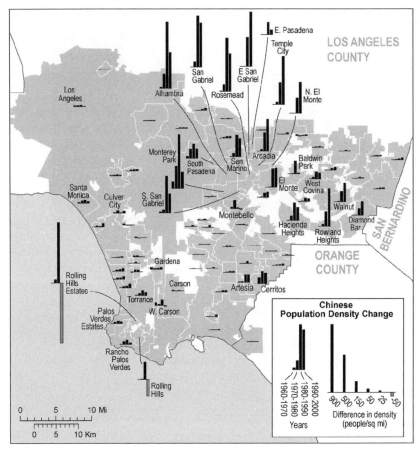

MAP 3. Changing Chinese Population Density, 1960–2000. *Source:* U.S. Census 1960–2000.

In the ten years that followed, the Chinese population in LA continued to increase rapidly and remain highly concentrated. In 1990 the number of tracts with fewer than 50 Chinese fell to less than half of all tracts. On the other hand, the tracts with more than 1,000 Chinese increased to forty-nine. The Chinese distribution in Los Angeles by then had multiple clusters: one in the downtown Chinatown area and the other in the eastern suburban zone. There were more than 158,000 Chinese in the San Gabriel Valley in 1990 (calculation based on the U.S. 1990 Census, STF1). The ethnoburb was not only growing, adding a large number of Chinese, but it was maturing in the sense that it had formed its own center and distinctive spatial form. The largest Chinese population in one single tract rose to 3,834 and was located in the ethnoburb. Similarly, most tracts with 1,000 Chinese and over were in the ethnoburb. It is obvious that in terms of its spatial scale and the number of Chinese, the San Gabriel Valley ethnoburb had become, by 1990, a more important Chinese residential area than Chinatown. Moreover the ethnoburb had not only grown at its original site during this ten-year period but had expanded to the eastern part of San Gabriel Valley. Map 3 shows that in the whole San Gabriel Valley, particularly in the west part, the Chinese population density increased dramatically compared with other parts of the county. In the southwest and southeast parts of the county, especially in the wealthy neighborhoods of Rolling Hills and Palos Verdes, as well as the Cerritos area, the Chinese population density also increased rapidly. The 1990s, however, saw slow growth of Chinese population in the western San Gabriel Valley but a much faster pace in the eastern part. Map 2, of the spatial center of Chinese population, shows that the second half of the twentieth century witnessed increasingly rapid eastward movement, especially in the later decades. The map offers visual proof of the spatial transformation of LA's Chinese community from the downtown Chinatown to the San Gabriel Valley ethnoburb.

The emergence of the Chinese ethnoburb not only changed the population composition of the area, but it also altered architectural forms and styles, street scenes and signs, which makes today's San Gabriel Valley a multiracial, multicultural, multilingual area with a strong ethnic Chinese signature. Many multifamily dwellings, including apartment buildings and condos, have replaced the formerly dominant single-family homes. New building styles mix with old houses, and wealthy people built their mansion-like dream-houses in rich neighborhoods such as Arcadia and San Marino (see Figure 7). Hsi Lai Temple,

FIGURE 7. Old versus new single-family houses in Arcadia (author photo, 2001)

Figure 8. Hsi Lai Temple in Hacienda Heights (photo courtesy Min Zhou, 2004)

the largest Buddhist temple in the western hemisphere, not only aims to set up a worldwide Buddhist organization, but attracts many tourists, residents, and businesses to the Hacienda Heights area (see Figure 8).

The business landscape has also altered with these rapid demographic changes. The first Chinese street mall in the San Gabriel Valley was set up at the corner of Atlantic and Garvey and was named "Deer Field" (Lu Yuan). More than two decades ago, the mainstream Alpha Beta supermarket chain remodeled its Monterey Park store on Atlantic Boulevard, installing a pagoda-style roof in order to attract the growing local Asian (especially Chinese) customer base. It was soon taken over by a Chinese supermarket company—Ai Hoa. In 1992 the store changed hands again when it was sold to a Vietnam-raised ethnic Chinese, who renamed it Shun Fat Supermarket. San Gabriel Square at Valley Boulevard and Del Mar Avenue boasts the largest Chinese commercial mall in the Southland and attracts many visitors from mainland China and Taiwan; its business signs feature Chinese more prominently (see Figure 9). However, the ethnoburb is still a multiethnic community, which is evident in the multilingual business signs and Chinese supermarkets that employ, and are patronized by, people of different ethnic backgrounds (see Figure 10).

Figure 9. San Gabriel Square (photo courtesy Min Zhou, 2004)

Figure 10. Street sign, Rowland Heights (author photo, 2001)

The explanations of the San Gabriel Valley transformation lie in the process of the formation and development of the San Gabriel Valley Chinese ethnoburb, in the relationships between the Chinese ethnic economy and the Chinese community in the ethnoburb, and in the socioeconomic characteristics of the Chinese residents inside the ethnoburb. These matters form the focus of the next four chapters.

4 Building Ethnoburbia

The establishment of the Chinese ethnoburb as a new type of ethnic settlement in the San Gabriel Valley has occurred within a framework of global, national, and place-specific conditions. Without changing global geopolitical and economic contexts, and shifting national immigration policies, the ethnoburb phenomenon might never have emerged. It is also likely, however, that without certain locality-specific circumstances, such as demographic changes, local politics, and business dynamics, the ethnoburb would not have been established either, or at least not in its present manifestation. Place-specific conditions have led to subtle, variegated social constructions of race and expressions of racialization. Since its formation, the ethnoburb has generated self-perpetuating processes of expansion by diffusing to adjacent communities spatially and increasing the Chinese population numerically, maturing with new functions, and playing different roles in local socioeconomic and political structures.

Stages in Ethnoburb Formation

Surpassing Chinatown as the center of Chinese residential, business, and community life in the Los Angeles area, the ethnoburb was built through the deliberate efforts of individual Chinese people and key business leaders operating in the context of various international, national, and local arenas in a new era, in a new locality.

Depending on the size of the local Chinese population and the spatial scale of the relevant Chinese communities, formation of the San Gabriel Valley ethnoburb divided roughly into three main stages:

1. Emergence of a suburban Chinese residential concentration area (1960–1975). The ethnoburb started to emerge in one of Los Angeles' eastern inner suburban towns, the City of Monterey Park. This settlement began because Chinese people started moving out of the inner-city area as part of the overall

American suburbanization process. Later, this population was reinforced by a new wave of immigrants settling in the San Gabriel Valley during the early 1970s.

2. Expansion of the ethnoburb's Chinese population and ethnic economy (1975–1990). This period witnessed the arrival of large numbers of immigrants from a variety of origin countries and areas, although most were from Taiwan, Mainland China, Hong Kong, and Southeast Asia. They displayed a wide range of socioeconomic characteristics and their immigration status varied considerably. During this period of time, the ethnoburb surpassed Chinatown as the primary set of Chinese residential neighborhoods and consumer-serving business districts.

3. Establishment of the ethnoburb as a global outpost and racialized place (1990–present). The ethnoburb has grown rapidly, causing overcrowding in its original sites in the western part of San Gabriel Valley, especially in the City of Monterey Park. The settlement has leapfrogged to such outlying eastern San Gabriel Valley communities as Hacienda Heights, Rowland Heights, and Walnut (which the Chinese call "the eastern district"), giving the ethnoburb a barbell shape. The ethnoburb continues to expand and develop international economic ties.

Budding Stage

The Chinese ethnoburb began in the City of Monterey Park. This city is 7.5 miles east of downtown Los Angeles and has an area of 7.72 square miles. It is bordered by seven cities and Census Designated Places (CDP), including Alhambra, Rosemead, San Gabriel, South San Gabriel, Montebello, East Los Angeles, and the City of Los Angeles (see Map 3).

When it was first incorporated in 1916, Monterey Park was a small town with a collection of chicken and truck farms. It was planned as the Beverly Hills or Bel Air of the San Gabriel Valley but ended up a typical suburban bedroom community and remained so for over a half century. At the end of World War II, Monterey Park was still an ordinary white suburban town. In 1950 99.9 percent of its total population were white Americans, including some Hispanics. There were fewer than ten Chinese and a total of twenty-three Asian-born residents in the city at that time. There was no significant difference between Monterey Park and any other suburban town of the Los Angeles area in terms of the number of Chinese residents (see Tables 4 and 5).

By 1960 a budding Chinese cluster had emerged in Monterey Park; the community already had the second highest share of the Chinese population in Los Angeles County, next only to the City of LA itself. Monterey Park surpassed Pasadena in terms of the number of Chinese in Los Angeles' suburban zone.

TABLE 4. Population Composition in Monterey Park, 1950–2000

	1950	1960	1970	1980	1990	2000
Total Population	20,395	37,821	49,166	54,338	60,738	60,051
Asian	<0.04%	2.8%	15.3%	34.1%	57.5%	61.8%
Chinese	*<0.04%*	*0.9%*	*4.5%*	*14.9%*	*36.2%*	*41.3%*
African American	0.06%	0.04%	0.2%	1.3%	0.6%	0.4%
Hispanic	n.a.	11.6%	34.0%	38.8%	31.3%	28.9%
Non-Hispanic White	99.9%	85.6%	50.5%	25.8%	11.6%	21.2%

Sources: Barron, 1991; Fong 1994, p. 22, Table 1; U.S. Bureau of Census, Census of Population 1950, 1960, 1990 STF1; 2000 http://factfinder.census.gov/servlet/DTTable?_ts=41626581531.

The trend continued for the next ten years. The number of Chinese reached 2,200 in 1970, a 536 percent increase during the ten-year period. Monterey Park not only outnumbered other suburban towns in terms of Chinese population by 10 to 40 times, but also had the highest percentage of Chinese among its total population. The number of Chinese in Monterey Park was much higher than any of the surrounding communities: Alhambra, East Los Angeles, Montebello, Rosemead, or South San Gabriel. The rate of Chinese population increase in Monterey Park during the 1950–1970 period was also the highest in the whole Los Angeles area. As early as 1970 a Chinese residential cluster had clearly been established in Monterey Park.

What had happened in Monterey Park to make it emerge as the largest suburban Chinese concentration area at this stage?

The growth of the minority population in Monterey Park during this period appears to have been a "natural" process that lacked triggering events or prominent figures (author interview, Wilbur Woo, August, 1999). The initial increase of Chinese in Monterey Park was part of the general postwar trend of suburbanization. Statistics indicate that the share of the county's Chinese population living in the City of Los Angeles decreased, whereas in suburbia, especially in Monterey Park, it increased dramatically between 1950 and 1970. In 1950 the Chinese in Los Angeles City accounted for 87.8 percent of all Chinese in the county, while Monterey Park only had about one-tenth of one percent. In 1970, however, the proportions had changed to 67.0 percent and 5.4 percent, respectively (see Table 5).

During this period different kinds of Chinese people migrated to Monterey Park from different areas. A majority of them were of working age, had families, and held jobs in downtown Los Angeles. Many worked in the public sector, especially as engineers, because there was less job discrimination in the public sector than in private businesses. Some of the suburbanized Chinese had come

TABLE 5. Chinese in Selected San Gabriel Valley Cities as Percentage of Total Chinese Population in Los Angeles County, 1950–2000

City	1950	1960	1970	1980	1990	2000
Alhambra	0.29%	0.29%	0.80%	4.31%	8.69%	14.55%
Arcadia	0.01	0.10	0.06	0.68	2.93	9.28
Covina	n.a.	0.16	0.16	0.19	0.41	0.70
Diamond Bar	n.a.	n.a.	0.04	0.43	1.78	5.21
El Monte	n.a.	0.08	0.19	0.35	2.77	6.04
Hacienda Heights	n.a.	n.a.	0.28	1.70	3.20	6.18
La Puente	n.a.	0.13	0.06	0.09	0.23	0.43
Montebello	0.00	0.05	1.30	3.11	1.43	1.43
Monterey Park	0.11	1.79	5.39	8.62	8.97	12.81
Pasadena	1.55	1.45	1.95	1.81	1.27	2.16
Rosemead	n.a.	0.09	0.23	1.41	4.42	7.94
Rowland Heights	n.a.	n.a.	0.07	0.34	1.90	7.24
San Gabriel	0.12	0.09	0.12	0.90	3.12	6.85
San Marino	0.01	0.02	0.04	0.52	1.37	2.73
South El Monte	n.a.	n.a.	0.06	0.08	0.22	0.48
South Pasadena	0.15	0.06	0.65	1.44	1.27	2.00
South San Gabriel	n.a.	0.09	0.15	0.16	0.47	0.83
Temple City	n.a.	0.03	0.12	0.36	1.48	4.76
Walnut	n.a.	n.a.	0.06	0.27	1.49	4.45
West Covina	n.a.	0.15	0.29	1.25	1.79	3.92
Ethnoburb	*2.24*	*4.59*	*12.02*	*28.03*	*49.21*	*59.89*
Los Angeles City	*87.81*	*80.07*	*67.03*	*47.31*	*27.42*	*18.42*
Number of Chinese, LA County	9,187	19,286	40,798	93,747	245,033	323,093

Sources: Bureau of the Census, for the following census years:
1950: pt. 5, California Table 47, p.179;
1960: pt. 6, California Table 26, pp.189–195;
1970: pt. 6, California Table 23, pp.100–101;
1980: pt. 6, California Table 15, pp.20–29;
1990: *Census of Population and Housing,* Summary Tape File 1A;
2000: http://factfinder.census.gov/servlet/DTTable?_ts=41624594765.

as foreign students to Los Angeles or other areas in the United States, gotten jobs after graduation, and then settled down. Some followed a step-wise migration pattern, living first in the downtown Chinatown area or another adjacent inner-city neighborhood, and then moving to Monterey Park when their economic circumstance improved and their families grew. Despite the stereotype of professionals with their advanced academic degrees being the only immigrant Chinese to "make it," that is, to move to the suburbs, some blue-collar workers were also able to move to Monterey Park (Monterey Park Oral History Project, 1990; author interview, Mr. and Mrs. C, and Ms. M 1992).

The suburbanization of the Chinese was also prompted by an unexpected incident: the 1965 Watts civil disturbance in South Central LA. Many oldtimers (*lao qiao*) had already moved into different parts of Los Angeles City by that time, and many were longtime residents who owned grocery stores or other small businesses in South Central. Many Chinese storeowners in the area suffered financial loses in the riot, and as a result, more and more Chinese moved either to Chinatown or the eastern suburb of San Gabriel Valley. For those who moved to the valley, Monterey Park was the first stop (author interview, Wilbur Woo, August 1999; Li et al. 2002; C. C. Wong 1980). While the suburbanization trend provides a general backdrop for the Chinese move to the suburbs, it does not explain why Chinese people went to Monterey Park instead of any of the other suburban communities in Los Angeles. Responses to a migration history survey and in-depth interviews provide some answers. When asked why, at that particular time, respondents moved to Monterey Park, these Chinese provided the following main reasons.

First, they cited unfavorable conditions in and around downtown Chinatown. Chinatown had become too congested, and the price of property was very high, usually $40–50 per square foot. In adjacent neighborhoods, like Echo Park and Silver Lake, where many other Chinese lived, it had become hard for a family with children (sometimes pets as well) to find an affordable apartment or house to rent or purchase. Those who were upwardly mobile chose to migrate to a suburban bedroom community with bigger houses, better living conditions, nicer neighborhoods, and better school districts (Monterey Park Oral History Project 1990; author interviews, Ms. M 1992 and Lucia Su 1995).

Second, they cited the accessibility of Monterey Park. Monterey Park is bordered by three major freeways: Interstate 10 (the San Bernadino Freeway) to the north, Interstate 710 (the Long Beach Freeway) to the west, and State Highway 60 (the Pomona Freeway) to the south (see Map 2). Such a high level of freeway access is not very common even in the freeway-oriented Los Angeles area. Monterey Park was a short hop on the freeways from any direction, making it easier to get downtown, where most jobs were located, and to Chinatown, where the new Chinese suburbanites could shop at Chinese groceries, eat Chinese food, and socialize. At that time, neither Chinese restaurants nor grocery stores had opened in Monterey Park (the first Chinese grocery store did not open until the early 1970s) (C. C. Wong 1980; Monterey Park Oral History Project 1990; author interview, Lucia Su 1995). By making the relatively short move to Monterey Park and retaining their jobs locally, these Chinese extended their activity space, remaining "partial displacement" migrants.[1]

Third, respondents spoke of prior ties to Monterey Park. Some migrants to Monterey Park had contacts with local residents, many of whom were their friends or relatives, prior to their move. From these people they gained an image of Monterey Park as a quiet suburban community and decent place to live. They also learned that housing prices were reasonable, with an ordinary single-family two- or three-bedroom house priced at about $40,000. Many purchased properties in Monterey Park and settled down. Some migrants had some very early personal impressions of Monterey Park. One eighty-year-old Chinese gentleman, a former Chinese Air Force officer who had received his training in Southern California during World War II, remembered clearly that back then "Monterey Park was all but a sleepy small town on the outskirts of Los Angeles. On both sides of Atlantic Boulevard, there were mostly barren patches of land with overgrown bushes and weeds. There were very few retail stores."[2] When his three sons came to California to study in the 1960s and 1970s, and when he and his wife immigrated to the United States in the mid-1970s, all of them selected Monterey Park as their new home. His three-generation extended family of sixteen members all lived in Monterey Park, although in different residences, in the early 1990s.

A fourth reason given for choosing Monterey Park was its relative diversity. Compared with many of the surrounding communities, where Anglos dominated the population, Monterey Park had a more diverse population. Even at the city's beginning there were already a few Japanese families, who lived in an area called Yokohama Village, just south of what is now Monterey Park. Japanese farmers had built a smooth roadway, the Coyote Pass (now Monterey Pass Road), across the hills to ship their produce to the Los Angeles markets.[3] Among the white population there was also a large proportion of Jews, who themselves had suffered tremendous discrimination throughout history and therefore tended to be more tolerant of other minority groups. In the mid-1950s Monterey Park was called the Mexican Beverly Hills by Latinos in adjacent East Los Angeles. The city drew Latinos from East Los Angeles, who totaled over one-tenth of the population in 1960 (see Table 4). Japanese Americans came from the west side of Los Angeles after returning from the World War II internment camps. Along with the Chinese from the downtown Chinatown area, these groups formed into part of the postwar wave of suburb-bound minority American middle- or working-class families. The population base in Monterey Park was more diverse than most suburbs, and Monterey Park became known for its warm welcome of racial and ethnic minority groups, particularly in the relatively wealthy areas in the city. At the same time, many of the surrounding communities still had restrictive covenants.[4]

Respondents also mentioned the practices of developers and realtors in Monterey Park. In the beginning, Monterey Park did not open its arm to all racial and ethnic minorities. In a well-known case, an African American professional couple successfully sued a developer for discrimination after they were excluded from Monterey Park. But when new tracts of houses were built in the Monterey Highlands section in the late 1950s, developers encouraged Japanese American households to purchase properties there. Clearly, therefore, realtors also helped channel and facilitate the movement of Asian Americans from the inner city to Monterey Park area during this time period.

Some respondents cited the superior *feng shui* of Monterey Park: The word "Monterey," meaning "King's Hills" in Spanish, describes the hilly parts of Monterey Park. According to Chinese folklore, hilly areas with better views are considered to have better *feng shui*, which brings good luck.[5] These hilly areas also reminded immigrants of the places they came from, such as Hong Kong and Taiwan. Following the Japanese settlement pattern, the Chinese soon moved into houses in the hilly Highlands area of the city (Census Tracts 4820.01 and 4820.02). At that time Monterey Park came to be known as the Chinese Beverly Hills among the Chinese, and later on the community continued to be very popular among Chinese in Los Angeles and abroad (author interview, Lucia Su 1995).

Although it seems that there were no major differences between the Chinese and other ethnic groups in their reasons for moving to the suburbs in the late 1950s and 1960s, the focus on Monterey Park as their destination differentiates the residential choices made by Chinese households. For instance, white people moved to the San Fernando Valley, Westside, and other areas on the periphery of Los Angeles County, and African Americans concentrated in Inglewood, Compton, and other adjacent communities in the southern part of the county. For the Chinese, push factors led to moves out of the inner city. Poor living conditions in Chinatown and the downtown area in general pushed Chinese households to move out and seek nicer neighborhoods. The pull factors associated with Monterey Park made it an ideal destination. A combination of major freeway access, affordable housing, good schools, a relatively diverse population base, and auspicious *feng shui*, all worked to attract people to the budding ethnoburb.

The move to Monterey Park for some of the earliest Chinese families, however, did not proceed without resistance. Wilbur Woo, father of the first Chinese American LA City councilman Michael Woo, bought a house and moved his family of three generations to the highland area of Monterey Park in the 1960s. At the time the hilly area was just being developed, with only a few houses in the lower $40,000 range, and a monthly mortgage payment of $40–50. Many empty lots were selling for $10,000–12,000 each. Soon after, Woo's friends visited his house and decided that they, too, would move their families to Monterey Park. Word of mouth about the reasonably priced houses, good neighborhoods, and good schools gradually attracted more Chinese American families. However, their arrival also sparked controversy. When Woo's family first moved in, they received anonymous phone calls with death threats and demands that they move out of the neighborhood. Woo's friends rallied behind him; some even offered firearms for the family's defense. The threats did not stop until Woo called the Monterey Park police, who strengthened their patrols in the neighborhood and even stationed officers at Woo's house for a few days. As a result of the harassment of the Woo family, Monterey Park's first Community Relations Commission was formed. Wilbur Woo and Betty Chu, a Chinese American lawyer and banker, were among the first of its commissioners (author interview, Wilbur Woo, August 1999).

Blooming Stage

During the 1970s and 1980s rapid shifts in population composition took place in Los Angeles County in general, and in Monterey Park City and San Gabriel Valley in particular. The Chinese population grew from 15 percent (8,082) to 36 percent (21,971) of Monterey Park's total population between 1980 and 1990 (see Table 4). Monterey Park thus had the highest percentage of Chinese population of any community in the Los Angeles area. While the proportion of the county's Chinese population living in Los Angeles City continued to decline, the percentages in Monterey Park increased from 8.6 percent to 9.0 percent in the same period (see Table 5).

Monterey Park, along with eight neighboring west San Gabriel cities (Alhambra, Arcadia, El Monte, Pasadena, Rosemead, San Gabriel, San Marino and South Pasadena), had formed a clear area of Chinese concentration by 1990. The lowest share of Chinese in these eight cities of the total Chinese population in Los Angeles County in 1970 was 0.03 percent (San Marino) and the highest was 2.0 percent (Pasadena). By 1990 the shares of all eight cities had increased in a range of 1.3 percent (Pasadena and South Pasadena) to 8.7 percent (Alhambra). The area gained some 66,000 Chinese residents in the 1980s, 45 percent of total increase of Chinese population experienced by Los Angeles County during this time period. Not only did the western part of the San Gabriel Valley become an area of large Chinese concentration, but the eastern part of the valley also witnessed large increases in Chinese population. Cities and areas like Diamond Bar, Hacienda Heights, Rowland Heights, and Walnut in the eastern part of the valley formed what the Chinese people and media termed the Eastern District (Deng 1995). The ethnoburb now comprised two major portions, with concentrations at either end of San Gabriel Valley. In between these two areas, the Latino population comprised a majority. Map 2 shows how the spatial center of Chinese population in Los Angeles County moved eastward at a faster pace in the 1990s.

The sweeping changes to the U.S. immigration law in 1965 set the stage for large numbers of Chinese to immigrate to the United States. The Chinese American community, however, was not just a passive beneficiary of this legislation. In fact, local Chinese Americans had contributed to its passage. A delegation of Chinese Americans, including longtime community leaders and lawyers from LA and San Francisco, headed to Washington, DC, in 1965, when Congress was debating the proposed changes of immigration laws. They met with Senator Edward Kennedy who was the chairman of the Immigration Sub-Committee at the time. They also testified in a congressional hearing, urging Congress to increase the immigration quotas (author interview, Wilbur Woo, August 1999). The Chinese immigrants, who came to the United States for family reunification as well as for professional development, rapidly populated the budding ethnoburb in the San Gabriel Valley.

In addition to immigration law change, other factors at the international and local level also made important contributions to the development of the ethnoburb during this period. In 1971 the members of the United Nations voted to let the People's Republic of China hold the seat for China instead of the Republic of China (Taiwan). President Richard Nixon visited Mainland China in 1972 and established a quasi-official relationship with the Chinese government. By the end of 1978 President Jimmy Carter announced that the United States and China would establish formal diplomatic relations, effective on New Year's Day of 1979. The United States would send its ambassador to Beijing and terminate its official diplomatic relationship with Taipei. The bipartisan U.S. policy of normalizing the relationship between the United States and the People's Republic of China made the people in Taiwan feel abandoned by the United States, which had guaranteed their safety and security for three decades after World War II. Political instability and uncertainty fueled massive emigration out of Taiwan. Given their urban background, many Taiwanese emigrants preferred to stay in Pacific Rim cities, which are geographically and psychologically close to home. Among the different options on the west coast of the United States, the northwest and even San Francisco were considered too cold by the Taiwanese, who were accustomed to much warmer weather. Many thought Southern California was an ideal place to settle. Large numbers of Chinese immigrants had parents who did not speak English and did not drive. They thus sought places that were within walking distance of relatives and friends, Chinese shops, Chinese restaurants, and Chinese newsstands and bookstores (Monterey Park Oral History Project 1990; author interview, Mr. and Mrs. M 1992). Migration to such cities was therefore possible without a substantial change in lifestyle.

The number of Chinese households moving to the ethnoburb continued to increase in the mid-1970s. At that time, "whenever a white moved out, a yellow moved in, including Chinese, Japanese, and Korean" (author interview, Lucia Su 1995). Many of the original white residents were elderly; they sold their properties and moved out to retirement homes or other communities. Some people took advantage of the profit they could make by selling their homes in a price-inflated housing market. Even the older houses in Monterey Park, such as those along Alhambra and Orange Avenues, on small lots of 50 or 55 ft x 300 ft., sold well. One Chinese resident moving into Monterey Park in the 1960s joked that at that time, "Even if you bought a toilet in Monterey Park, you can sell it for good money" (author interview, Lucia Su 1995). Housing prices skyrocketed again in the 1980s. Newcomers to Monterey Park area who purchased these properties were a mixed group of old and young. Many of those who arrived from Hong Kong, Taiwan, and Malaysia were rich and purchased properties with cash. Local banks responded by discouraging cash sales, because they were losing the interest revenue they would otherwise make from mortgage loans. But the financial resources of these new immigrants made it possible for them to buy directly into a middle- or upper-class neighborhood during a time when some original residents were ready to sell and move out, which dramatically changed the population mix of these communities.

During this period of ethnoburb development, unconventional types of immigrants also emerged. For example, some Taiwan and Hong Kong entrepreneurs came to start businesses; they became a new type of sojourner by choice, sending their wives and children to live in Monterey Park or other adjacent communities while they themselves shuttled between Taipei, Hong Kong, and Los Angeles. These trans-Pacific nomads were nicknamed "spacemen" or "astronauts" (Kotkin 1991; Tanzer 1985). In their home countries, such words as *tai kong ren* (astronauts) or *nei zai mei* (inner beauty) took on new meanings. Since both *tai tai* and *nei ren* mean "wife" in Chinese, these two words, *tai kong ren* and *nei zai mei*, actually mean "men with wife absent (from home)" and "wife in America," respectively. Some Taiwanese parents sent their children to study in the Monterey Park area to avoid the highly competitive college entrance examinations in Taiwan and the compulsory military service required of every young Taiwanese man. Some of these "little overseas students" were as young as eight to fourteen years old, yet they lived alone in properties bought by their parents or with relatives or friends. This situation generated some social problems in the Chinese community, for some poorly adjusted youngsters joined gangs, and some wealthy children became targets of crime such as kidnapping for ransom. These young immigrants have been called "parachute kids," referring to the fact that they have been precipitously dropped into a dramatically different environment and expected to function normally with little or no parental supervision (Chou 1996).

Because of the large Chinese population influx into Monterey Park, many real estate firms chose to do business there. Monterey Park contained half of all the ethnoburban real estate firms, with a total of forty firms in 1982 (*Chinese Yellow Pages* 1983). This was a clear sign of a booming real estate sector and newly arriving residents with purchasing power. The number of Chinese involved in real estate also increased during this time. Many Chinese professionals working in the public sector saw good opportunities in real estate, so they got training and began to handle real estate transactions. For some, real estate became their primary career. A common practice was to purchase residential properties and convert them to business premises or multifamily dwellings for new migrants. In many cases Chinese buyers offered higher than regular market prices, sometimes twice as much, and convinced owners to sell.[6]

One of the most frequently mentioned names during this period of Monterey Park development history is Frederick Fukang Hsieh. A first-generation immigrant, Hsieh was born and raised in Mainland China. Coming to the United States as a foreign student, he got a Master of Science degree in water resources engineering in 1969 and began work as an engineer for the City of Los Angeles immediately thereafter. Hsieh started to purchase properties in the downtown area of Echo Park and Silver Lake and took a real estate course to get his broker's license in the early 1970s. He bought his first house in Monterey Park in 1972. When he had moved there, he had noticed a lot of vacant, overgrown land and thought Monterey Park could become a place that would attract many immigrant Chinese. Soon after he became the first and only Chinese realtor in town and opened Mandarin Realty at Garvey Boulevard. He bought a mobile home park at the corner of South Atlantic and Garvey, which later sold for $7.50 per square foot. This was an unheard price at the time, when most comparable property was selling for around $3–5 per square foot. Hsieh was guided by a vision of Monterey Park as an emerging Chinese concentration area, which he called the "New Chinatown." He even advertised Monterey

Park as the "Chinese Beverly Hills" in Taiwan and Hong Kong. He was actively involved in such transnational real estate transactions and investment until his death in May 1999.[7]

Longtime original residents were aware of, and became concerned about, the prospect of a large immigrant influx. There were mixed feelings about the Chinese newcomers. On one hand, the booming real estate market driven by Chinese investment dollars made many original residents' property values rise, and they earned spectacular profits from them. At the same time many residents felt they were losing control of their own community and were reluctant to see the symbols of that community fading away, such as the closing of the famous Paris Restaurant and the transformation of a former bowling alley into a Chinese "Hong Kong Supermarket."[8] Sensitive to these concerns, Hsieh spoke to local business leaders at a Chamber of Commerce lunch meeting in 1977 and told them that Monterey Park was going to become a Chinese-oriented community and a Chinese business mecca serving not only Monterey Park but surrounding communities as well. The Chinese population wanted this to be an orderly transition, smoothing the way for assimilation, and minimizing conflicts. The Chinese were not going to "take over" the city, but they wanted their elderly Chinese relatives and country people who were new immigrants to live in decent neighborhoods (Arax 1987; Monterey Park Oral History Project 1990). With the Chinese community's economic ability, persuasion, and sometimes, through personal relationships of trust with business leaders of other ethnic backgrounds,[9] Chinese businesses and real estate developers achieved a relatively peaceful transition.

The Chinese media in both the Los Angeles area and in Asian home countries strongly promoted the Monterey Park area. Many immigrants had heard about Monterey Park from secondary sources, such as newspapers, magazines, and TV, well before they actually migrated to the United States.[10] Some decided they would look for places to live in Monterey Park as soon as they arrived or before their non-English-speaking spouse or parents were scheduled to join them. Many advertisements about the commercial investment potential and residential opportunities in Monterey Park appeared in public media in both Taiwan and Hong Kong, a few dating back to the 1970s. In the Asian media, Monterey Park is referred to as the "Chinese Beverly Hills" and "Little Taipei," the latter in reference to the large influx of Taiwanese immigrants. Locally, the LA area had long been known among the Chinese as "Los Province" (Luo Sheng), and during this period Monterey Park came to be labeled "Mon City" (Meng Shi). Soon after Mon City became an important symbol of the Chinese community in Southern California and was regarded as such in Asian countries.

In the 1980s there were several Chinese-language newspapers in the San Gabriel Valley. The largest Chinese newspaper in North America, the *Chinese Daily News* ("world journal"), which is owned and funded by the largest Taiwanese news company, opened its new headquarters in Monterey Park. Two other major papers, *Singdao Daily* and *Qiaobao,* also had their offices there (Arax 1987; author interview, Mr. M 1992). Several Chinese TV and radio stations operated daily in the Los Angeles area, some of them headquartered in Monterey Park or other San Gabriel Valley communities.

Activities sponsored by the City of Monterey Park and other local institutions had a powerful impact on Chinese migrants and potential migrants. Mounted as the city's response to the large influx of Chinese immigrants (author interview, Judy Chu 1995), these city-sponsored activities played an important role in bringing Chinese people into the city to spend their leisure time. Over time, the activities reinforced the image of Monterey Park as a hub for the Chinese population. For instance, Langley Senior Center provided various activities for the elderly (Chinese and non-Chinese alike) in Monterey Park in addition to offering lunches for $1.25 in a big lunch room Monday through Friday and free barber services for senior citizens. The center's recreation room was equipped with table tennis and pool tables, and the mahjong room, with its four tables, allowed thirty-two people to play at the same time. The mahjong room catered mainly to elderly Chinese, who had been coming regularly for a long time, and this made it difficult for new people to join. The center also housed several Chinese organizations, including the Chinese senior citizen's club, a Chinese Peking Opera association, and the Evergreen Chorus, a choir group of elderly Chinese. On any given day, over forty Chinese seniors would spend their day there, some staying all day long. Often, Chinese residents from either Monterey Park or one of the surrounding cities would drop their parents off at the center before going to work and then pick them up later in the afternoon.[11]

Other examples of Chinese-oriented activities or facilities include the Golden Age Village, one of the two senior-citizen complexes that opened in 1980. Chinese elderly occupied about 100 of the village's 120 apartments. Many of these residents were not able to afford their own houses or unable or unwilling to live in their children's households (Barron 1991; author interview, Mr. C 1992). Also nine out of ten of the Chinese Peking Opera clubs in Southern California meet regularly in Monterey Park because the city offered free sites for their activities.

In summary, the development of Monterey Park as an ethnoburb during the "blooming stage" was facilitated by factors operating on several levels that promoted the concentration of Chinese in this area. Once begun, migration took on the character of a chain reaction, with the presence of a Chinese community acting to attract more and more new immigrants to live in the city and surrounding communities. As one woman who had arrived in the 1980s responded when she was asked why Chinese people chose to live in Monterey Park:

> Why? Because in living here we feel just like home. There are so many Chinese people and Chinese stores, restaurants, banks, newspapers, radios and TV, almost everything you need. Nowhere else can provide us such comfortable living environment and so many kinds of services in such a compact geographical area. Those born in the United States do not care whether to live close to Chinese or not. But we do care as new immigrants with poor English or no English skill at all. We like to live close to our kids but not totally depend on them. We like to have our own activities. (Author interview with Ms. X in Mandarin, 1992; translated by author)

Another 1980s immigrant reinforced this perspective:

> My friends who live in other states, like the Midwest, have to go back to Taiwan to stay for several months every year because they feel so isolated, lonely, and uncomfortable. They have no "ear and mouth" [can neither understand nor speak English] to communicate and no "leg" [cannot drive] to go around. But we who live here in Monterey Park feel no difference from living back in Taiwan, especially us elderly people. (Author interview with Mrs. C in Mandarin, 1992; translated by author)

But perhaps most telling was this response:

> Want to know why I moved here? Let me tell you something: I usually take a morning walk along Monterey Park's streets. You know what? All I see are Chinese, there are no *foreigners* at all! (ibid., emphasis added)

Maturation Stage

Since the late 1980s this Chinese ethnoburb has completed its transformation from an ethnic cluster to a global outpost of the internationalized economy. This most recent period has seen the number of Chinese residents and businesses increase, but the ethnoburb has also experienced problems never faced before. The large influx of Chinese immigrants in a short time period has made longtime residents worry about losing control of their communities, which has caused intergroup tension to build, and new processes of racialization to surface. They are caused by cultural differences, language barriers, and sometimes outright mistrust of "others." The City of Monterey Park was a symbol of racial harmony in the early and mid-1980s. On November 28, 1983, Lily Lee Chen was inaugurated as the nation's first female Chinese American mayor in Monterey Park, an event well publicized in both the United States and China as "a symbol of the growing numbers and political sophistication of Asian Americans" (Mathews 1983). In 1985 the city won the title of All America City from the National Municipal League and USA Today. "Citing effective citizenship and significant civic accomplishments brought through a blending of private and public efforts, Monterey Park was one of the eight national winners and the only California city honored that year" (Barron 1991, 49). A documentary film entitled *America Becoming*, produced and broadcast by PBS, showed how ethnic diversity had been addressed by six cities across America, and included Monterey Park.

The superficial appearance of racial harmony, however, was soon to evaporate, and a backlash against immigrants erupted in the city. As the Chinese ethnoburb grew spatially and the Chinese population increased dramatically, a form of racialization evolved that was different from the sort experienced in the earlier enclave or ghetto. As large numbers of nonwhite immigrants "intruded" into the traditional turf of white Americans—the suburb—and developed their own suburban residential neighborhoods and business districts, competition increased between longtime original residents of other ethnic backgrounds and the new Chinese residents and businesses. Competition erupted into conflicts, and public discourse concerning cultural and political concerns, economic development, and even religious issues became tinged with racial rhetoric and nativist sentiment. Chinese residents, business people, political candidates, and religious institutions became the racialized targets of resentment.

The most widely known, well publicized, and overtly racialized conflicts revolved around the "slow growth" and "English only" movements in the City of Monterey Park in the late 1980s.[12] In 1986 three minority council members, including Lily Lee Chen and two Mexican Americans, were swept out of office, and three Anglos were elected to the city council. Longtime white residents regained control over the city. The new council charged its predecessor with allowing excessive growth in the city and failing to control the proliferation of business signs in languages other than English. Ironically, in fact, it had been Lily Lee Chen herself, who, as a city council member, had sponsored an ordinance requiring some English on Chinese commercial signs, an ordinance that had been made into law. In the same year that the new council members were elected, the council passed two major resolutions: one imposing a building moratorium and the other supporting English as the nation's official language

(Horton 1995, 82; author interview, Lucia Su 1995). Behind these economic and cultural moves lay a strong current of nativism, since it had been the large influx of Asian (especially Chinese) population that had stimulated the city's rapid development and the appearance of non-English signs.

With the increasing numbers of Chinese residents and voters, attempts were made to elect more Chinese to office in order to represent the general community, as well as the interests of the Chinese population. During local elections in the late 1980s and first half of the 1990s, there was always at least one Chinese candidate on the ballot in Monterey Park. In 1988 a UCLA-trained East Los Angeles College psychology professor of Chinese origin, Dr. Judy Chu, campaigned on a platform of controlled growth, ethnic diversity, and racial harmony. She was elected to the city council, earning the largest share of votes. She was then depicted by *Citizens Voice*, a local newspaper representing the interests of some long-term white residents, as a "dragon lady" who served Chinese interests only (author interview, Judy Chu 1995). Despite these charges, Chu was reelected for a second term in 1992, again earning the highest number of votes.[13] In 1990 a Chinese engineer and lawyer, Samuel Kiang, was also elected to city council with the highest total votes. The city council was two-fifths Chinese American then, which approximated the proportion of the Chinese population in Monterey Park (36.2 percent).

In the 1994 election there were a total of three Chinese candidates, including incumbent Kiang. During the campaign, the possibility of electing the first Chinese-majority city council in the United States received much media attention, and nativist forces were mobilized in response. Two direct mail campaigns were mounted. One involved an official-looking bilingual document labeled "Voting Guide," which warned residents that fines of up to $10,000 and/or penalties of up to thirty-six months in prison could result from illegal voting practices and stressed the necessity of understanding and obeying election laws. A total of 13,000 such "Voting Guides" were mailed to Monterey Park households. Some voters were intimidated by these notices, which had been prepared by a consultant for a real estate development company. Coincidentally, the development company had sponsored a casino project the year earlier, which had been defeated by the city council, led by the two Chinese council members, Chu and Kiang (*Chinese Daily News* 1994, April 7; *Los Angeles Times* 1994, April 14). At the same time, the Residents Association of Monterey Park (RAMP), a group largely composed of longtime residents, also mailed letters to households throughout the community. Both RAMP and *Citizens Voice* opposed all three Chinese candidates; they charged incumbent Samuel Kiang, a strong opponent of the casino project proposal, with serving Chinese interests only, with getting campaign funds from outside the city, and with not understanding or believing in democratic politics. The three Chinese candidates were characterized as a slate that aimed to take over the city council, although in fact they disagreed with each other on many issues (*Chinese Daily News* 1994, April 6, 7, May 8; author interview, Judy Chu 1995). Animosity against the Chinese candidates spread, the campaign was transformed into a referendum on the change of the city's racial makeup, and all three Chinese candidates were defeated in the election.

The construction of Hsi Lai Temple (Figure 8), located in the eastern San Gabriel Valley community of Hacienda Heights, was a good example of how changes in the built environment became racialized. Founded in Taiwan in the 1960s, Fu Kuang Shan (Buddhist Lights, a branch of Buddhism) sought to promote the Buddhist religion overseas by establishing branch temples on foreign soil. A piece of land was donated to the order by a friend, but it turned out to be inappropriate for development. Then, in 1978, Fu Kuang Shan finally obtained land along Hacienda Boulevard. The parcel was an ideal site for a temple, up on a hill offering a panoramic view of the San Gabriel Valley. The proposed temple, which Fu Kuang Shan named Hsi Lai Temple (Coming West Temple), was designed to attract more believers and to promote cultural exchange between East and West. However, due to strong local opposition construction of the temple did not begin until eight years later, in 1986. Longtime residents feared a housing price surge, traffic jams, and tourists. The business community, especially some Jewish storeowners, worried that the temple might ruin their businesses. Many people did not want to see the establishment of a Buddhist temple in their largely Christian neighborhood. Others interpreted the temple plan as a racial issue, seeing it as a means through which the Chinese would establish a dominant position in their community. During this planning stage, Buddhist monks and nuns went door to door explaining their good intentions and the benefits they could bring to the neighborhood. They also mounted a petition drive to help secure the permission to build. There were a total of six public hearings before the plan was finally approved. Hsi Lai Temple, the largest Buddhist monastery in the entire western hemisphere—it occupies fifteen acres—was completed at the end of 1988. After its completion, the temple became an attraction in the San Gabriel Valley, drawing many tourists each year from different parts of the United States and the world.[14] It also attracted new residents, many of whom were Buddhists. In addition, the temple generated business revenue for the local community. It organized charity activities and a New Year prayer service—along with local Christian and Mormon churches—emphasizing the importance of understanding and peace in eliminating racial and religious conflict (*Buddhist Lights Century*, January 16, 1996; author interview, Juefa 1996).

Similarly, rapid changes in the residential landscape also generated objections, even heated tensions between ethnic newcomers and longtime residents. In Monterey Park and Alhambra, people did not want high population density, which had become a concern due to the construction of condominiums and apartment buildings. In upscale cities like Arcadia and San Marino, however, many large new houses were built for rich Chinese households. There was even a trend toward construction of grand mansion-like houses. Local residents had mixed feelings about this. They were delighted to see their communities retain their high property values even as new households of different ethnic backgrounds entered their neighborhoods, but many disliked the appearance of those new houses. They felt that such architecture did not fit their communities. One mansion-style house in Arcadia, owned by a Japanese-American actor and his Chinese-American wife, was vandalized several times. The wall was covered by graffiti, and rocks were thrown through the windows (author interview, Thomas Jablonsky 1994). The establishment of the Chinese ethnoburb in San Gabriel Valley rapidly changed the business landscape as well. Like other businesses, the Chinese business sector faced the challenge of how to respond to and serve the fast-changing multiethnic consumer markets in the San Gabriel Valley. Many longtime residents felt uncomfortable about these changes, and Chinese businesses, as a whole, were subjected to a variety of charges and stereotypes. Some were accused of putting up only Chinese signs to discriminate against non-Chinese customers; Chinese street-corner mini-malls (which longtime residents called "ugly development") were targeted for not generating enough sales tax revenue for local governments. And Chinese businesses were condemned for not hiring people from other ethnic groups. In reality, however, there are many sizable Chinese malls in the San Gabriel Valley, and two of the largest generators of city revenue in Monterey Park were Chinese restaurants: Harbor Village and Ocean Star. Of the smaller family-owned Chinese businesses, some do hire people from other ethnic backgrounds, though sometimes as low-wage workers (author interviews, Judy Chu and Lucia Su, 1995). In some of the most flagrant cases of racially based conflict, some Chinese businesses were accused of engaging in illicit activities. For instance, about a dozen Chinese bridal shops had sprung up along Las Tunas Boulevard in the early 1990s. During the 1994 local election, one candidate for Temple City's city council, a retired white police officer, accused all these bridal shops of conducting suspicious illegal activities (money laundering and prostitution), but he provided no concrete evidence supporting his claims. The Chinese owners of the bridal shops fought back and demanded an apology from this candidate. They also placed big "open house" signs on their premises, letting people know that they were legitimate enterprises and had done nothing wrong. That candidate did offer an apology to the bridal shop owners, and he was defeated during the election. Later an undercover investigation proved these bridal shops "were as pure as the image they portrayed" (*Los Angeles Times*, November 1996).

These incidents reveal that in its maturation, this ethnoburb was marked by processes of racialization. Intergroup relations reflect the fact that the ethnoburb is a multiracial community, which distinguishes it from either ghettos or enclaves. As three-term Monterey Park councilwoman Judy Chu has clearly stated:

> The community is a much-mixed one [in terms of ethnic composition]. This is not your traditional ethnic enclave, like you think in terms of Chinatown or Little Tokyo. This is not that at all....I see Monterey Park is a community of different ethnic groups trying to get along with one another. That is my challenge. That is the challenge that we are facing. (Author interview, Judy Chu, 1995)

Efforts to Build a Multiethnic Community

Conflicts and the need for consensus led to active efforts to promote racial harmony and ethnic diversity in the San Gabriel Valley. To achieve those goals, tremendous efforts were made by different groups inside the ethnoburb. For example, during her first term as councilwoman, Judy Chu initiated a Harmony Week in October 1990 that included a citywide essay contest focusing on what it means to live in a multicultural society and a community dinner honoring citizens, businesses, and service clubs for their efforts to promote harmony. Harmony Week has become a community tradition and is held every October. Community Roundtable discussions, in which community leaders shared their opinions on major issues facing the city, were also conducted for several years in Monterey Park. As one of the facilitators for these discussions, Lucia Su clearly remembers that although people disagreed with each other on many issues, and although tensions sometimes developed during discussions, participants all expressed their concerns and listened to one another. These discussions successfully made possible open and frank dialogue among people of different backgrounds and with different community interests.

A community-wide debate in Monterey Park in the 1990s on whether to allow billboards inside the city's boundary demonstrates how pan-ethnicity can be utilized to unite different groups of people to fight for the same cause. A large mainstream advertising company proposed setting up billboards along the south border of the city and made contributions to local organizations to win support ($10,000 to the Chamber of Commerce; $5,000 to the Boys and

Girls Club). All city council members except Judy Chu, the only Chinese American on the council, were in favor of the proposal because they believed it would help to relieve the city's budget crisis. But many local residents were strongly against the proposal. Led by three co-chairs of different ethnic backgrounds (Chinese American and longtime community activist Lucia Su, a Hispanic, and a white), residents started an initiative called "Citizens Against Billboards." Volunteers from the group collected more than 5,000 signatures from registered voters during a two-month period in 1995 to get their anti-billboard initiative on the city's ballot in the 1997 local election. Just a month before the election, the advertisement company sued the group for not following the proper procedures in putting the initiative on the ballot and asked the court to nullify the initiative. With legal help from the family of Lucia Su and another co-chair, "Citizens Against Billboards" prevailed in California Superior Court, which ruled in their favor in February 13, 1997. The anti-billboard initiative was passed overwhelmingly (by 86.3 percent) in the local election on March 7 and claimed the highest-ever margin of victory in the city's election history. Judy Chu was elected to a third term, again with the highest number of votes. Lucia Su, reviewing the two and half years of struggle over the billboard initiative and the strategies she deployed, told me in an interview:

> This [was] a community-wide, grassroots, multiethnic struggle. I wanted it to be a fight for the whole community. I was elected to lead such a citizen's initiative drive, but decided to have two other people to co-chair with me, so that we can represent residents of different ethnic backgrounds. Monterey Park is an Asian American majority city, the advertisement company probably thought that we are less likely to be interested in politics, therefore maybe easier to be pushed around and for them to push forward their agenda. I strongly believe that we should be involved in mainstream politics and have our voices heard. Together with other ethnic groups, we can build better community for all residents. (Author interview, 1997)

Local municipality governments have promoted multiculturalism and Chinese cultural heritage. In 1992 the cities of Alhambra and Monterey Park combined to host their first Chinese New Year parade with the theme of "The World Welcomes the Chinese New Year" (see Figure 11). The city of Monterey Park withdrew the next year to have its own celebration activities, so the city of San Gabriel took Monterey Park's place and became co-hosts for the event. This San Gabriel Valley parade has become the nation's fourth-largest Chinese New Year parade, after those in San Francisco, New York, and Los Angeles' own

FIGURE 11. Inaugural San Gabriel Valley Chinese New Year celebration (author photo 1992)

Chinatown. It is surely one of the largest parades that celebrates ethnic heritage to be held in any American suburb. The event draws thousands of spectators from the San Gabriel Valley and other communities each year. Many mainstream corporations, like AT&T, MCI, and Southern California Edison, recognize the business opportunities offered by such an event and the purchasing power of Chinese Americans. They have become major sponsors, and they also have distributed bilingual publications during the events. Although the ethnoburb has transcended the boundaries of municipalities, local governmental attitudes toward the ethnoburb have played an important role in its emergence and will continue to play a vital part in its future development.

5 From Ethnic Service Center to Global Economic Outpost

One of the most important forces behind the formation and evolution of an ethnoburb is the interdependence between the ethnic economy and the ethnic population. As the ethnic population and neighborhoods grow, they call for a larger ethnic economy to provide not only business opportunities and consumer necessities, but also job markets for immigrants. As the globally linked ethnic economy develops, it creates the need for both professional and managerial personnel as well as a low-skill, low-wage labor force. The combination in one location—the ethnoburb—of both an ethnic residential area and a business district is not only vital during its formation, but it also becomes a prerequisite for continuous growth.

In the 1950s and 1960s an initial group of suburban-bound Chinese people moved to Monterey Park. Many of them commuted downtown for work and drove to Chinatown to fulfill their ethnically specific consumer needs, such as shopping at Chinese grocery stores and eating at Chinese restaurants. Chinatown was still the center of Chinese business, cultural activity, and social connection. As earlier Chinese residents recall, there was no Chinese restaurant or grocery store in Monterey Park until the early 1970s when a shopping center opened on South Atlantic Boulevard. It was built by a Taiwanese Chinese developer, the son of a Taiwanese legislator. The shopping center housed the first Chinese grocery store in town, DiHo Market, along with a couple of Chinese restaurants, including Pung Yuan, the name of a famous restaurant in Taiwan. These new businesses, however, could not fully compete with their Chinatown counterparts until larger numbers of Chinese people moved to Monterey Park and the surrounding area (author interviews, Lucia Su 1995; Wilbur Woo August 1999).

Emergence of an Ethnic Service Center

The demand for an ethnic economy to fulfill consumer needs grew alongside the increasing numbers of Chinese residents after the late 1970s. Chinese businesses were quickly set up in Monterey Park and gradually appeared in other neighboring communities in the San Gabriel Valley. Some of them were typical ethnic enterprises: Chinese restaurants, grocery stores, bookstores, and gift shops. Others were professional firms: doctors' offices, banks, law offices, and real estates firms. By the second half of the 1970s, Monterey Park was functioning as a new Chinese community with large clusters of Chinese residents and various Chinese businesses. There were even suggestions to establish an independent Chinese chamber of commerce, but after considering the possible negative impact, the Chinese merchants decided to stay within the city's Chamber of Commerce and set up a Chinese committee instead (Monterey Park Oral History Project 1990).

By 1980 the 8,082 Chinese residents in Monterey Park composed 30.8 percent of the total ethnoburban Chinese population (26,273). Monterey Park had 340 Chinese businesses in 1982, accounting for 56.5 percent of all Chinese firms in the San Gabriel Valley. Dominating Chinese economic activities in the ethnoburb, Monterey Park functioned as a concentrated residential center and a business hub for the Chinese community. In the incipient ethnoburban communities in eastern San Gabriel Valley (Hacienda Heights and Rowland Heights), the share of Chinese businesses was tiny (3 percent), even though the Chinese population there represented 7 percent of all ethnoburban Chinese.[1] The eastern San Gabriel Valley Chinese communities were largely residential at this time.

In the early 1980s the ethnoburb was mainly an ethnic community with an ethnic economic structure primarily fulfilling daily needs. Ethnoburban Chinese businesses targeted Chinese residents primarily as their customer base. In 1979 and 1980 alone, three Chinese American banks established their headquarters or branches in Monterey Park. Real estate firms accounted for the largest ethnoburban Chinese business category in terms of total number in 1982, a reflection of the demand for housing by newcomers and of their financial wealth. The other top five categories were all consumer based: medical and dental services, restaurants, travel agencies, beauty salons, and barber shops. Table 6 lists all types of Chinese business in LA County for 1950, 1982, and 1996. It reveals the shifting nature of the Chinese ethnic economy over time. In 1950, for example, the Chinese ethnic economy was dominated by three traditional categories: laundries, restaurants, and food stores. Producer or professional services were almost nonexistent. In the second half of the century, the establishment and growth of producer services and other consumer services geared toward a clientele of higher socioeconomic status across the county, but in the ethnoburb in particular, signaled a fundamental shift in LA's Chinese ethnic economy.

TABLE 6. Chinese Businesses in Los Angeles County, 1950, 1982, and 1996

Category	Total Number					Share Ethnoburb/Co		Rank				
	Ethnoburb		LA County					Ethnoburb		LA County		
	1982	1996	1950	1982	1996	1982	1996	1982	1996	1950	1982	1996
Doctor	71	706	10	127	974	55%	73%	2	1	7	3	1
Restaurant	49	503	180	240	880	20	57	3	2	3	1	2
Dentist	32	396	7	64	562	50	71	4	3	10	7	4
School	5	393		19	570	26	69	22	4		24	3
Insurance	16	273		34	369	47	74	7	5		14	6
Attorney	9	258		69	437	13	59	20	6		6	5
Beauty salon/ barber	20	244		38	298	53	82	6	7		11	9
Realtor	80	236		152	327	53	72	1	8		2	7
Auto repairing	16	233	2	26	305	62	76	8	9	18	17	8
Accountants/ CPA	10	204		36	255	28	80	17	10		12	12
Travel agency	21	193		63	257	33	75	5	11		8	11
Loans & mortgage		169			215		79		12			12
Computer & service		167			252		66		13			13
Construction	11	158		31	220	36	72	16	14		15	14
Acupuncture	10	143		21	214	48	67	18	15		21	16
Bank	14	135		36	259	39	52	12	16		13	10
Chinese medical clinic		130			182		72		17			20
Printing shop	10	128	4	24	172	42	74	19	18	13	18	21
Immigration service	112			153		73		19			23	
Advertising		109			134		82		20			26
Trading company	15	107	8	76	213	20	50	9	21		9	17
Food products	15	84	187	62	197	24	43	10	22	2	9	19
Furniture store	12	83		28	136	43	61	14	23		16	25
Auto-dealer	15	79		22	158	68	50	11	24		20	22
Boutique	8	77	4	14	138	57	56	21	25	13	25	24
Herbalist- Wholesale	2	67	35	20	102	10	66	25	26	6	23	31
Gift shop	12	64	40	43	107	28	60	15	27	5	10	30
Hotel & motel	14	60	8	80	205	18	29	13	28	8	4	18
Bakeries	4	60	4	9	114	44	53	24	29	13	27	29
Pharmacy	5	47		11	119	46	40	23	30		26	27
Laundry			350							1		
Produce (wholesale)			60							4		
Other			17									
Total	604	9,656	923	1,773	14,709	34.1%	65.6%					

Sources: H. Chen, 1952, 59; *Chinese Yellow Pages,* 1983 and 1996.
Note: Blank space means no data available.

Not all these business types had the same location patterns. Due to their different nature and their primary customer base, the distribution patterns of these Chinese businesses varied even at this early stage of ethnoburb development. For instance, Chinese attorneys, doctors, and real estate agents mainly serve Chinese clients, and so they were concentrated where Chinese residents lived. On the other hand, Chinese restaurants, which cater to a wide range of customers, opened all over metropolitan Los Angeles (see Maps 4a and 5a).

Despite the focus on local needs, however, Chinese economic activities in this period were already linked to international capital and the global economy. Many wealthy Chinese, who had emigrated because of political insecurity, brought large amounts of money to purchase properties as well as to make capital investments (author interview, Lucia Su 1995). Therefore, banks and other financial institutions became a very important industry inside the ethnoburb, with a total of eighteen establishments, 35.3 percent of all Chinese financial institutions in LA County in 1982. Also, trading companies involving various import and export activities grew rapidly during this period.

Transformation to a Global Economic Outpost

The most recent period of ethnoburb evolution has been the most active time of Chinese population growth and business development. Since the late 1980s, the ethnoburb has completed its transformation from an ethnic cluster to a global outpost, which plays an active role in the internationalized economy.

Expansion of the Ethnic Service Center

The number of ethnoburban Chinese in 1990 comprised almost half of all Chinese in LA County, but at the same time all of San Gabriel Valley's population accounted for only 11.6 percent of LA County. Hence the ethnoburban share of Chinese in the county was much higher than the San Gabriel Valley share of total population in the county. While Chinese residents in the ethnoburb accounted for 11.7 percent of the total population in the San Gabriel Valley in 1990, the county average was only 2.8 percent ethnic Chinese. The ethnoburban Chinese population had increased 359 percent from 1980 to 1990, and the number of ethnoburban Chinese business grew from 604 in 1982 to 9,656 in 1996, an increase of almost 1,500 percent. The growth rates of both the Chinese population and their businesses in the ethnoburb were more than double the county average. The ethnoburb's share of the county's Chinese population increased from 28 percent in 1980 to 49 percent in 1990, and Chinese businesses from 34 percent in 1982 to 66 percent in 1996. These are good indicators that

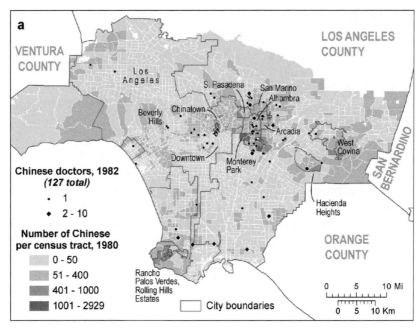

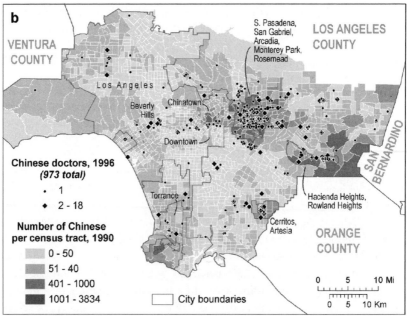

MAPS 4a and 4b. Chinese Population and Doctors in Southern LA County, 1980 and 1990. *Sources:* U.S. Census Bureau; *Chinese Yellow Pages.*

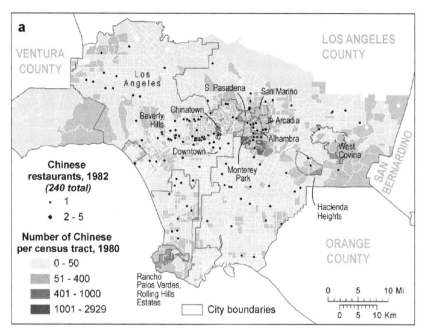

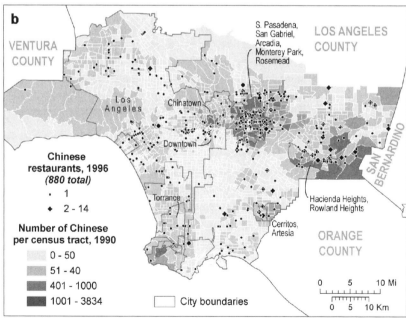

Maps 5a and 5b. Chinese Population and Restaurants in Southern LA County, 1980 and 1990. *Sources:* U.S. Census Bureau; *Chinese Yellow Pages.*

the ethnoburb was a primary magnet for Chinese people and their businesses in the 1980s and first half of the 1990s.

The most recent period of development has been marked by the continuous expansion of the ethnoburb as an ethnic service center. Back in 1982 most of the top twenty Chinese business types inside the ethnoburb provided consumer services. By 1996, due to the rapid growth of the Chinese population, some consumer service sectors had increased rapidly, becoming the top categories within the Chinese ethnic economy (doctors, dentists, and restaurants). These Chinese businesses continue to be concentrated inside the ethnoburb, whether they belonged to the traditional ethnic or professional service categories (see Table 6; Maps 4b and 5b).

One interesting phenomenon of ethnoburban development during this period was the dramatic increase in the numbers of Chinese schools between 1982 and 1996; they went from a total of 5 to almost 400. This clearly signifies that the ethnoburb had become a cultural center for Chinese communities in the Los Angeles area. Moreover, there were also more schools teaching English than Chinese, which suggests that the ethnoburban Chinese immigrants were eager to learn English in their adopted homeland, while at the same time hoping to help their children keep Chinese cultural traditions and learn their heritage.

During the early stage of ethnoburban development, Chinese residential concentrations attracted ethnic Chinese businesses, as in the case of Monterey Park. This is consistent with Waldinger, McEvoy, and Aldrich's (1990) model of the early stage of ethnic economic development and Kaplan's (1998) "Incubator" model. Later on, however, the development of Chinese residential communities and the growth of Chinese business districts created a self-reinforcing cycle, and the evolution of the two became ever more tightly linked. The development of Chinese businesses appears to have had some impact on the residential choices of Chinese newcomers and to have generated an agglomeration effect among commercial establishments. For instance, Tawa Supermarket Companies (more commonly known as 99 Ranch Market in English) was founded in 1984 by Roger Chen, a Chinese immigrant from Taiwan. Its first two supermarkets opened in Orange County in the mid-1980s. Due to the influx of Chinese residents into the ethnoburb, the next two supermarkets were set up in Montebello (1987), just across State Highway 60 from Monterey Park, and Rowland Heights (1989). Tawa also created a development division, Tawa Commercial Property Development Corp., in 1988. This division was responsible for the construction of Rowland Heights Shopping Plaza, where one of its supermarkets was located. This shopping plaza helped to bring more Chinese businesses to the "eastern district," which in turn drew many Chinese residents to live in surrounding neighborhoods. Prior to the arrival of Tawa and the other Chinese businesses in the eastern part of San Gabriel Valley and south into Orange County, Chinese in those areas commuted to Monterey Park for their ethnic shopping and socializing needs, just as two decades earlier, Monterey Park residents had gone to Chinatown.

In the 1990s Tawa Investment Inc. was established and led the construction of the largest Chinese shopping center in Southern California, the San Gabriel Shopping Plaza, commonly called San Gabriel Square (see Figure 9). Considered the crown jewel of Chinese retail success in the Southland, this mall was financed by First Commercial Bank, one of the major commercial banks in Taiwan and parent bank of FCB Taiwan California Bank based in Alhambra. The deal was brokered via a Chinese banker, the CEO of a local Chinese American bank. From a distance, this shopping center looks like any typical Southern California outdoor mall—an L-shaped two-story building in Mediterranean style. However, as one enters, one can see that every single store has a Chinese sign. This shopping center is anchored by a 99 Ranch Supermarket and an upscale Chinese department store called Focus.[2] It also houses jewelry stores, bookstores, music and VCD/DVD stores, a few professional services, and at least a dozen restaurants, which makes it probably one of the largest Chinese restaurant agglomerations in the LA area. These range in size and type of Chinese cuisine, from the anchor restaurant, of the Sam Woo chain (owned by two brothers originally from Hong Kong), to a restaurant named after a well-known shopping street in Taipei Hwasi Street,[3] to a famous franchised Beijing-based Mongolian restaurant called Dong Lai Shun. This shopping center attracts a large Chinese clientele, both local and foreign, including tour busloads of visitors from Taiwan or Mainland China. During weekends, in particular, the center is filled with shoppers, making parking difficult despite a large surface lot and an underground parking garage.[4]

Between 1990 and 1996 Tawa opened five more supermarkets inside the ethnoburb in San Gabriel, Arcadia, Rosemead, Monterey Park, and Rowland Heights, by establishing their own or by taking over other Chinese supermarkets in the area. By 1996 Tawa had thirteen supermarkets under its flag in Southern California, more than 1,200 employees, an average growth of 10 to 15 percent each year, and an annual sales volume in excess of $150 million. A TV advertisement for Tawa that runs frequently on local Chinese TV stations claims that "wherever there are Chinese, there are Tawa Supermarkets." Tawa owns or jointly owns four shopping plazas in Southern California, and a total of twenty-six supermarkets, including eight in the San Francisco Bay Area, two in Seattle, and franchised stores in Honolulu, Las Vegas, and Phoenix.[5] Tawa used to have one store in LA's Chinatown, but closed it in early 1998, citing lease expiration.

Tawa has also helped to build supermarket plazas in Las Vegas and Toronto and has become the largest Chinese supermarket chain in the United States.

The success of Tawa Supermarkets can partially be explained by the Chinese cultural tradition of gourmet food. For over thousand years the Chinese have said that "the top priority for human beings is to feed themselves" (*min yi shi wei tian*, literally, "food is the sky for human beings"). Wherever there are large numbers of ethnic Chinese, Chinese grocery stores are bound to be established to serve their needs. Tawa's success, however, may owe much to its mission and strategies. From the very beginning, Roger Chen and his associates envisioned a Chinese supermarket chain, stocked with Chinese ingredients—fresh fruits and vegetables, live fish and crabs—but as spacious and clean as any mainstream supermarket chain. This vision clearly departed from the images of cramped rooms and unpleasant odors that people associated with most traditional Chinese grocery stores, especially those in Chinatowns. Tawa stores targeted a middle- and upper-class clientele, and they wanted their supermarkets to be in a class of their own. Like other supermarkets, Tawa also stocks some specific nonethnic items that can easily be found in any supermarket, such as baby items and bathroom supplies. Thus, Tawa markets not only lured Chinese customers but also people from other Asian and non-Asian ethnic backgrounds.

Tawa markets have had an impact beyond their own clientele. Many other Chinese businesses have tried to follow Tawa Supermarkets to new locations to piggyback on the firm's vast clientele. In addition to anchoring several major Chinese malls in LA and Orange County, Tawa Supermarkets are often the anchor store in large Asian or Chinese malls in northern California and beyond. The same names and chain stores or restaurants can be found not only in the Rowland Heights shopping center and San Gabriel Square, but also in Cupertino Village and Milpitas Square in Silicon Valley and the Chinese Cultural Center in Phoenix. For instance, one Taiwan restaurant, Ban Mu Yuan, advertised in 2000 that it had a history of thirty years in Taipei, twenty years in LA, and eight years in the Bay Area (*Chinese Yellow Pages* 2000). This suggests that the development of Tawa has both been caused by, and has contributed to, the growth of Chinese residential neighborhoods in many areas, but particularly in the ethnoburb. The success of Tawa has also prompted mainstream supermarket chains to stock Asian food items. Tawa envisions expanding into Asia by setting up joint ventures in Indonesia, Taiwan, and Hong Kong (Hamilton 1997; Tawa Supermarket Companies flyer 1996). This vision of development strategies across the Pacific demonstrates the transnational nature of the ethnoburban population and their businesses.

However, the expansion of Tawa also contributed to the stiff competition among Chinese supermarkets. In the early and mid-1990s, there were more independent Chinese supermarkets in the San Gabriel Valley than there are today. These included Ai Hoa, Hoa Ping, Ta Fu, and Sieu Thi T &T (*da xin*). Ta Fu, for instance, was a spin-off operation from Tawa. Established by a former Tawa manager, it had two stores, one each in Montebello (where the original Tawa store was located) and Rowland Heights (across State Highway 60 from Tawa's own Rowland Heights store). Competition among these supermarkets in the early and mid-90s was so intense that every single one of them offered deep discounts and bonus buys, plus mail coupon campaigns and further discounts depending on money a customer spent per shopping time. The strategies and tactics these supermarkets used generated debate among the Chinese media about the motivation and consequences of such vicious competition. Because of it, Tawa reclaimed the two Ta Fu stores and made the Rowland Heights store a healthy vegetarian store called Green Market. T & T became a Tawa subsidiary, and its stores were eventually renamed.

Other surviving Chinese supermarket chains have also vigorously expanded their operations. Shun Fat supermarket[6] also became a large chain that established stores in northern California and crossed the state line to open a store in Las Vegas. Shun Fat took a vacant former Target store at the southwest corner of Valley and San Gabriel Boulevard and made it a Shun Fat Superstore. This store is more of an indoor shopping fair than simply a supermarket and offers products and services ranging from watch battery exchange, fast food, a liquor store, a bookstore, boutiques for jewelry, and an art gallery.

Rising Global Economic Outpost

During the 1980s and 1990s, not only did ethnic Chinese businesses grow rapidly, but the role of the ethnoburb changed from an ethnic cluster to a global economic outpost. The producer service sector made tremendous gains and became very important during the late 1980s and 1990s. For instance, finance, insurance, and real estate (FIRE) accounted for a total of 1,006 firms in 1996, more than 11 percent of all ethnoburban Chinese businesses (*Chinese Yellow Pages* 1996). Due to data constraints, it is impossible to pinpoint firms that serve the global economy (that is, that have active international transactions) as opposed to those that primarily serve local needs within the FIRE sector. However, data on firms with direct international ties can be used to support the global economic outpost argument. The real estate market has become increasingly internationalized. For instance, George Realty, a San Gabriel Valley-based realty company has forty offices in Taiwan. Its San Gabriel Valley operation averaged about $1 million a day in transactions for six years in a row (Klein 1997). Other business types clearly linked to the global economy, including import/export, air cargo service, custom house, and freight forwarding, grew rapidly inside the ethnoburb for a total number 330 establishments by 1996. This number accounts for over two-thirds of all such Chinese businesses in the county.

Therefore, it appears that the ethnoburb functions not only as an ethnic residential center and a hub for the traditional ethnic service economy, but increasingly it is also a focal point for globalized economic activities and international capital circulation. This has clearly been the case since the relaxation of Taiwan's rigid foreign exchange controls in 1986, which allowed the export of Taiwan's capital for the first time since 1949, and the new international trade agreements in the 1990s. The San Gabriel Valley has become an ideal site for direct Chinese investment, particularly during times of uncertainty in the investor's country of origin. For example, during the build-up of tensions across the Taiwan Strait in the spring of 1996, a large amount of money poured from Taiwan into San Gabriel Valley's Chinese-owned banks. One large Chinese American bank received wire transfers of $30 million in two weeks during that period (author interview, M. Chang 1995; and bank interview 1999, no. 19).

The prosperity of the San Gabriel Valley and the Greater Los Angeles area is supported by and relies upon a globalized economy and the rise of the Pacific Rim nations. In seeing this, many local communities have actively embraced international business activities and capital circulation. About 60 percent of all businesses in Alhambra were owned or operated by Chinese by the mid-1990s, and these businesses played vital roles in the city's economy. In order to accelerate business activities and to help understand each other's cultures, the City of Alhambra has established sister-city relationships with several cities in both Mainland China and Taiwan. The Chamber of Commerce of Alhambra has vigorously promoted direct foreign investment (especially from Asian countries) and international business transactions, hoping to act as a bridge between East and West. Some Asian companies have taken advantage of this. A Hong Kong-based bank, CITIC Ka Wah Bank Ltd., built a three-story building on Valley Boulevard in Alhambra for its overseas headquarters. Ka Wah Bank was a commercial bank in Hong Kong with a history of some eighty years, but China International Trust and Investment Corporation (CITIC), based in Mainland China, acquired a controlling interest in it in 1986 (National Association of Chinese American Bankers 2000, 20). Foreign and domestic banks have given Alhambra, a suburban city with a total population of 85,804 in 2000, one of the highest densities of banks in the Los Angeles area. At the end of 1999 the headquarters or branches of eight different banks were situated within a half-mile stretch along Valley Boulevard between Atlantic Boulevard and Garfield Avenue, including six locally based Chinese American banks. Chinese American bank executives said that "there are more banks than restaurants or gas stations along Valley Boulevard" and call Valley Boulevard "the Chinese Wall Street" (bank interviews 1999, nos. 8, 11, and 14).

The establishment of the ethnoburb added a layer of ethnic economy to the local mainstream economy, which then transformed itself into a global economic outpost with direct international capital investment. This has made the ethnoburb a vital area of economic activity and job opportunities. As a result, during the economic recession of the early 1990s, the San Gabriel Valley had lower unemployment rates and lower commercial vacancy rates than did Los Angeles County in general (author interview, Judy Chu 1995).

As a global economic outpost and a new type of ethnic settlement, different from the traditional ethnic enclave, the ethnoburb is characterized by its number of professional businesses. Although the majority of Chinese business categories grew at least tenfold between 1982 and 1996, there were fast-growing and relatively slower-growing sectors. Generally speaking, the fastest-growth categories were in producer service sectors that employ professionals, such as insurance, law firms, and accountancy firms, all three belonging to the top ten categories. In terms of geographical concentration, professional services are more likely to locate in the ethnoburb. Among the top thirty Chinese business types, average shares of professional services in the ethnoburb are higher than firms linked to the traditional ethnic economy in both years (42 percent versus 27 percent in 1982; 67 percent versus 60 percent in 1996). Moreover, two out of the three business types (accountant firms and schools), which moved from being under-represented in 1982 to over-represented in 1996, were the ones that were mainly hiring professionals. Four out of the five business types not previously listed but over-represented in 1996 can be categorized as producer services (advertising agencies, financial loans and mortgage institutions, immigration services, and computer dealerships and services). Thus producer services in the ethnoburb are far more important than in today's downtown Chinatown ethnic enclave. On the other hand, some traditional Chinese ethnic economic niches did not grow as fast. For instance, food products, wholesale, and gift shops increased only five or six times in the fourteen-year period (Table 6). This also reflects the changing economic role of the ethnoburb. These are good signs that the ethnoburb is a new type of ethnic settlement, in which professional services are more important than in a traditional Chinese ethnic enclave.

One phenomenon that warrants special notice is commercial real estate ownership as an investment strategy among ethnoburban Chinese. The Chinese have traditionally valued property ownership, which they consider as a safe investment compared with other forms. After purchasing homes for their own families, many Chinese make investment in other properties. High Chinese property ownership in the San Gabriel Valley has not only changed the valley's property ownership pattern, but also created business opportunities for financial institutions, mainstream and Chinese-owned alike. Chinese banks, for instance, make financing commercial real estate one of their main lines of business (Li and Dymski 2007). Map 6a illustrates Chinese ownership of selected categories of commercial property in eighteen San Gabriel Valley cities/CDPs in 2001.[7] Chinese (including local and out-of-state owners) own a total of 271 office buildings, 124 warehouses and distribution centers, 51 shopping centers and 31 hotels/motels in this area. Their ownership of warehouses and distribution centers reflects the fact that many ethnoburban Chinese are directly or indirectly involved with international trade, especially import trade, which demands the stocking of merchandise imported from source countries before it is distributed to various places in the United States. Map 6b depicts the complicated picture of Chinese ownership of residential property ownership in the ethnoburb. They own a total of 1,924 two-unit properties, 989 three-unit ones, 616 four-unit ones, and 1,333 five-unit or more properties in these eighteen cities. Among these, 99.6 percent in the two-unit category, 73.2 percent in the three-unit one, 82.8 percent in the four-unit one, and 94.3 percent in the five-unit or more category are not the owners' primary residences, that is, they are either a second home or income property. This reflects their investment strategy of focusing on either end of the residential market. The four west San Gabriel Valley cities—Alhambra, Rosemead, Monterey Park and San Gabriel (in that order)—topped Chinese residential property ownership in the ethnoburb. Map 6a shows the total numbers of Chinese population and Map 6b the total households by census tract in 2000. Comparing Maps 6a and 6b with Maps 4a and 4b and 5a and 5b, one can conclude that not only has the total number of Chinese increased over the decades, but that they are geographically spread out as well.[8] In fact tracts having more than 1,000 Chinese people increased from seven in 1980, to forty-nine in 1990 and sixty-five in 2000. Such rapid growth in both population and businesses mark the ethnoburb as an ethnic place that not only houses large and diverse populations but localizes the financial resources brought in and generated by immigrant and native-born Chinese alike as these resources are transformed into nonliquid assets in local communities.

Internal Differences among Ethnoburban Communities

Differences exist among ethnoburban communities as well. Not all businesses are equally distributed among these communities. As the two largest communities in terms of the number of Chinese residents, Monterey Park and Alhambra were home to one-third of all Chinese businesses in the ethnoburb in 1996

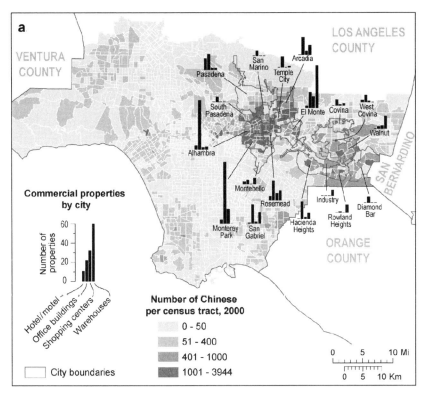

Commercial properties by city

Number of properties

60
40
20
0

Hotel/motel
Office buildings
Shopping centers
Warehouses

Number of Chinese per census tract, 2000

0 - 50
51 - 400
401 - 1000
1001 - 3944

City boundaries

0   5   10 Mi
0   5   10 Km

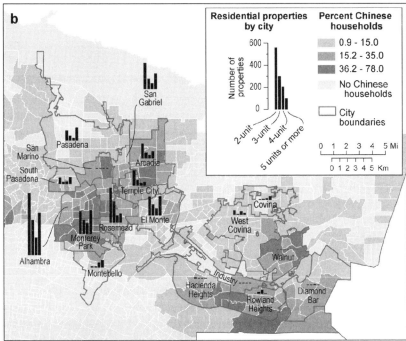

Residential properties by city

Number of properties

600
400
200
0

2-unit
3-unit
4-unit
5 units or more

Percent Chinese households

0.9 - 15.0
15.2 - 35.0
36.2 - 78.0
No Chinese households

City boundaries

0 1 2 3 4 5 Mi
0 1 2 3 4 5 Km

MAPS 6a and 6b. Chinese Population and Commercial and Residential Property Ownership, 2000. *Sources:* U.S. Census Bureau; a Chinese company.

(Table 7). The next two, San Gabriel and Rosemead, account for another 20 percent. Thus more than half of all ethnoburban Chinese businesses were located in these four cities, which suggests that western San Gabriel Valley still functions as a primary Chinese business center. Eastern San Gabriel Valley did, however, increase its importance as a Chinese business center in the 1990s. Rowland Heights, the City of Industry, and Hacienda Heights together were home to about 14 percent of all ethnoburban businesses. The ethnoburban share of

TABLE 7. Chinese Businesses in Ethnoburban Communities, 1996

City	No. of businesses	Share of business	Share of population	Doctor	Restaurant	Attorney	Insurance	Realtor
Monterey Park	1,692	17.5%	18.2%	30.3%	18.7%	24.4%	29.7%	13.1%
Alhambra	1,527	15.8	17.7	13.7	14.5	32.2	14.3	12.3
San Gabriel	1,214	12.6	2.9	13.0	16.5	6.2	9.2	12.7
Rosemead	809	8.4	9.0	5.2	9.5	2.3	9.5	7.2
Rowland Hts	541	5.6	3.9	6.1	11.1	3.1	3.7	4.7
Arcadia	514	5.3	6.0	4.5	4.8	1.9	4.8	13.2
El Monte	491	5.1	5.6	3.1	3.0	3.5	4.4	1.3
City of Industry	444	4.6	0.0	1.8	3.0	4.3	4.4	3.8
Temple City	358	3.8	3.0	0.9	1.2	0.8	2.2	3.4
Hacienda Hts	353	3.7	6.5	11.1	4.6	0.8	3.7	5.1
South El Monte	330	3.4	6.3	0.0	0.6	0.4	0.0	0.4
Pasadena	311	3.2	2.6	1.6	3.6	15.1	1.5	1.7
Walnut	260	2.7	3.7	0.1	0.8	0.8	2.2	4.2
W. Covina	150	1.6	3.0	1.8	1.8	0.4	0.4	0.9
Montebello	149	1.5	2.9	3.8	2.6	1.2	1.5	0.9
Diamond Bar	121	1.3	3.6	0.3	1.4	1.2	1.8	3.8
San Marino	110	1.1	1.0	0.4	0.2	0.8	3.3	9.8
La Puente	98	1.0	0.5	1.4	0.6	0.0	0.0	0.0
Covina	86	0.9	0.8	0.4	1.2	0.0	1.8	1.3
South Pasadena	85	0.9	2.8	0.3	0.2	0.8	1.8	0.4
South San Gabriel	2	0.02	0.5	0.0	0.2	0.0	0.0	0.0
E. Pasadena	1	0.01	0.0	0.0	0.0	0.0	0.0	0.0
Ethnoburb Total	9,656	100%	100%	706	503	258	273	236
% of LA County	65.6%			72.5%	57.2%	59.0%	74.0%	71.7%
LA County Total	4,709			974	880	437	369	329

Sources: Chinese Yellow Pages 1996; U.S. Bureau of Census, 1990 STF1a.

Chinese businesses was almost 2.5 times as high as that of Los Angeles City in 1996, making the ethnoburb a much more concentrated Chinese business hub than Los Angeles City (calculations based on *Chinese Yellow Pages* 1996).

There are clear internal differences in the economic structures among ethnoburban communities. In 1996 the City of Monterey Park continued to have the largest number of businesses among all ethnoburban communities and dominated in terms of consumer services, such as doctors, attorneys and insurance agencies, as well as restaurants, hotels, and motels. Due to the fact that Monterey Park is built out and has limited space for further real estate development, the share of Monterey Park's Chinese real estate firms has declined from 50 percent in 1982 to 13.1 percent in 1996. However, in upscale communities like Arcadia and San Marino, Chinese realtors are clearly over-represented at 13.1 percent and 9.7 percent respectively, as those cities' shares of all ethnoburban Chinese businesses are just 5.3 percent and 1.1 percent. These facts indicate that many Chinese residents and potential residents are economically well off and can afford to live in these wealthy communities. The relatively newly developed eastern district was mainly residential, with only a few businesses in 1982. Yet by 1996 Rowland Heights became the fifth largest Chinese business district among all ethnoburban communities and had an economic structure similar to that of Monterey Park. This again illustrates the close ties between ethnic residential community and business activities. Similarly, in 2001 Chinese-owned shopping centers were largely located in the western part of the valley, especially Monterey Park and Rosemead, as well as in newly developed eastern areas such as Diamond Bar (see Map 6a).

On the other hand, in the City of Industry, a primarily industrial and commercial area, computer dealerships and auto dealers were over-represented, and all other types of business were below average. This also indicates the overall agglomeration effect in these businesses, as they need to be close to each other in order to maximize profits. In a similar vein, El Monte, while having a lower percentage of Chinese population compared with the adjacent cities, had the largest number of Chinese-owned warehouses and distribution centers among the eighteen San Gabriel Valley cities in 2001, with 36.3 percent of the total. Similar situations can be found in Alhambra, Pasadena, and West Covina, where auto dealers are more concentrated than in other cities, since there exist large auto dealer complexes operated by other ethnic groups as well.

Ethnic Economy and Community Development

One of the major challenges faced by ethnoburban residents and businesses is how to develop a healthy and inclusive economy and a harmonious multiracial society. The solutions developed by Marshal Chuang, a successful Chinese auto dealer in Alhambra, are good examples of the complexities of building and maintaining the ethnoburb. Chuang, with a master's degree in food processing, began to work in the fast food business, then ran his own electric appliance shop before starting to sell motorcycles and then cars. The reason he chose to locate his business on the Alhambra Auto Row, along Main Street, in the late 1980s was the preexisting complex of auto dealers, as well as the potential market represented by the Chinese community in the San Gabriel Valley. As soon as he started his auto sale business, he faced the challenges of serving both Chinese and non-Chinese customers, developing new markets, and understanding intergroup ethnic characteristics and relations in this multiethnic setting.

In the first half of the 1990s, California's economy was hard hit by recession and so were auto sales. Based on consumer surveys and marketing analyses, Chuang decided to carry used cars to better serve the local communities, especially his Latino customers. He hired Spanish-speaking salespeople to handle such transactions. His sixty employees were divided evenly among Asians, Latinos, and Anglos, although Chinese workers were under-represented in auto parts and repair departments. Because of the increasing needs within the Chinese community, he hired more Chinese salespeople than ever before in the 1990s. About half his customers were Chinese. Chuang also investigated the consumer behavior of different groups and found that they preferred different incentives: Whites and Latinos liked lower down payments, while Asians preferred rebates. Chuang then dealt accordingly to promote car sales and became so successful that he was one of the top contributors to the city's tax revenue base; auto sales in Alhambra generated one-third of the city's overall revenue budget (author interview, Marshal Chuang 1995).

Chuang was also actively involved in community life and was a community leader. He encouraged Chinese business people and residents to learn English and to embrace American society, while at the same time maintaining their ethnic identity and heritage. He fought racialization but sought to minimize the "threat" to longtime residents. A board member of Alhambra's Chamber of Commerce for twelve years, he finished his term as its president in the mid-1990s. During his tenure, Chuang organized numerous events to help needy people and promote multiculturalism. He led the efforts of the Chamber of Commerce to bridge the gap between East and West and among different ethnic groups by promoting international businesses, cultural exchanges, and mutual understanding. He also donated money to establish a scholarship, in his father's name, to help Asian youth. Chuang's efforts have been well received in the community and stand as a model of how to develop healthy community relations and the local economy (author interview, Shea 1995). The challenges faced by Chuang and his colleagues are the same ones facing the entire multiracial San Gabriel Valley ethnoburb.

Analysis of the San Gabriel Valley ethnoburb reveals multiple paths and different trajectories of Chinese ethnoburb formation: its original site—Monterey Park—started with a large wave of in-migrants, followed by Chinese businesses. In other residential areas, like the eastern district community of Rowland Heights, certain key Chinese businesses have promoted Chinese residential concentrations by the establishment of significant business institutions, which stimulated the growth and expansion of the ethnoburb toward the east San Gabriel Valley.

Examination of the Chinese ethnoburb reveals its transformation from an ethnic service center to a global economic outpost, through its business transactions, capital circulation, and personnel flows (including both entrepreneurs and laborers). Its ethnic economy not only plays important roles in the ethnoburb's socioeconomic structure, but, depending on the sizes, types, and functions of the local ethnic economies, it helps to define the region's role in the national and global economies. The economic nature of the ethnoburb as a global outpost also gives localities a better chance to integrate the ethnic economy with mainstream economic life, to take advantage of immigrants' skills and resources, to adopt alternative strategies during periods of recession, and to strengthen its position in the global economy.

Therefore, in many respects the ethnoburb reflects the ability of highly mobile capital to set up effective outposts in global cities like Los Angeles, from which it can direct international business activities and open new markets. The San Gabriel Valley strategy has been able to develop a spatially dense, albeit suburban, configuration, in which social and economic networks can develop and in which immigrant cultural needs can be met.

6 Anatomy of an Ethnoburb

As a form of urban settlement, the ethnoburb has been forged from the interplay of economic globalization and political struggles between and within nation-states, major shifts in U.S. immigration policy, and a host of local circumstances and conditions. We have also seen that there are key actors involved in the ethnoburb development process, individuals who deliberately act to establish the foundations for ethnoburban community growth. What results is a distinctive and complex community, an urban mosaic.

This chapter closely examines the rich variety of ethnoburban characteristics in order to integrate them into a theoretical explanation of ethnoburb formation and to provide a general portrait of one ethnoburb's population. The ethnoburb model suggests that the globalization of capital investment, high technology, and personnel flows, as well as important international geopolitical events, are crucial in the timing of ethnoburb formation and an ethnoburb's population mix. Thus, in assessing the economic and occupational structure of the ethnoburban Chinese of Los Angeles and their demographic characteristics, it is possible to discern their connections to the international economy and to make a correlation between that particular immigrant influx and geopolitical events. We will consider a variety of questions. Where did the LA ethnoburb's main immigrant Chinese groups originate? When did they arrive, and were their arrivals linked to important geopolitical events in their countries of origin or major U.S. policy shifts? Since the model suggests that significant socioeconomic polarization can be expected inside the ethnoburb, we need to demonstrate the existence and variations in socioeconomic and demographic stratification by place of birth and by residential and business concentration. Finally, the model predicts that an ethnoburb differs from a traditional ethnic enclave, and indeed, when we compare the San Gabriel Valley ethnoburb with the downtown Los Angeles Chinatown, we can readily see the extent to which these two communities differ.

A multiracial community, the San Gabriel Valley area was home to 35.3 percent non-Hispanic white, 23.3 percent Hispanics, 18.5 percent Asian and

Pacific Islanders, and 4.3 percent African Americans by 1990.[1] Chinese people comprised 9.4 percent of the total population in the San Gabriel Valley in 1990. This percentage was higher than that for Chinese in the total county-wide population, which was 2.8 percent in 1990, and much higher than the national average of 0.66 percent. However, this figure was significantly lower than the 51.5 percent in the four key Chinatown census tracts.[2] The ethnoburb is thus an ethnic community with a larger number but lower density of the ethnic population than the old ethnic enclave had.

Because of economic globalization and geopolitical shifts, the ethnoburb is also an urban ethnic community with extensive external connections. Its residents come from different countries and have different legal status when they arrive. Its economic and occupational structures show strong connections to the mainstream global economy. These factors help to explain the high socio-economic status of much of the ethnoburban Chinese population.

Geopolitical Shifts and Immigration Policy

Residents of the LA ethnoburb come from various regions around the world, and they had immigration status because of global geopolitical changes and shifting U.S. immigration policy. Within the Chinese community, people refer to immigrants who arrived earlier as "old-time overseas Chinese" *(lao qiao)*, and those who came more recently as "new overseas Chinese" *(xin qiao)*. The ethnoburb is mainly a community of new overseas Chinese, mostly from Mainland China, Taiwan, Hong Kong, and Southeast Asia, who arrived after 1965.

From the time the Chinese first began settling in the suburbs, the ethnoburb has been seen as a hub for immigrants, a place where they can make a living and do business mainly through their own networks. The ethnoburb allows them to eat their own types of food, shop in Chinese supermarkets, speak their mother tongue, and keep close ties to their countries of origin by reading newspapers in Chinese and listening to the radio or watching TV in the various Chinese dialects. In other words the ethnoburb makes these new arrivals feel at home. Through word of mouth and promotional propaganda, this ethnoburb has been able to attract more Chinese immigrants as well as Chinese from other parts of the United States to come to live and work. The ethnoburb is, therefore, a suburban ethnic concentration, dominated by immigrants. First-generation immigrants composed over four-fifths of all the Chinese population in the ethnoburb, whereas U.S.-born Chinese comprised less than a fifth in 1990. The proportion of American-born Chinese increased over the 1990s and reached 25.2 percent in 2000, while immigrants counted for 74.8 percent.

Origins

A majority of the ethnoburban Chinese immigrants trace their origins back to China (including both the Mainland and Taiwan), the traditional country of origin for Chinese immigrants to this country. However, a significant number of the immigrants in the ethnoburb have come from other parts of the world, a fact that reflects the global Chinese diaspora and the globalization process. Although census data do not reveal the location of a respondent's last residence before immigrating to the United States, information on the individual's place of birth reflects the diverse geographic origins of these immigrants in general. Therefore, place of birth is used here to represent the country or area of origin for immigrants. In 2000 the ethnoburban Chinese immigrants came from fifty-three countries and areas, representing all the continents in the world. Mainland China (38.3 percent), Taiwan (26.6 percent), Indochina (Vietnam, Cambodia, and Laos, 16.7 percent) and Hong Kong (10.3 percent) were the four primary sources of these Chinese immigrants; the remaining 9 percent came from other countries widely distributed around the world (Map 7). The 1990s witnessed an increasing number of immigrants coming from Mainland China, as their share increased from the 31.3 percent in 1990.

Such diverse geographic origins are partially reflected in languages spoken. In 1990, for all those not speaking English at home, 90 percent spoke Chinese (including Mandarin, Cantonese, Min Nan/Taiwanese, and other unspecified Chinese dialects).[3] Mandarin (the official dialect of both Mainland China and Taiwan) becomes increasingly popular in the ethnoburb. The center of the ethnoburb, Monterey Park, has been referred to as "Mandarin Park" (Horton 1995, 10). Another 5.5 percent spoke the Min Nan dialect, a local dialect originating in southern Fujian Province in Mainland China, which is the mother tongue of most Taiwanese who have lived on Taiwan for generations. Min Nan-speaking Taiwanese Chinese are known as the "people from this province" *(ben sheng ren)* to distinguish them from those who followed the Nationalist government to Taiwan after 1949, who are known as "people from other provinces" *(wai sheng ren)* and speak mostly Mandarin. The other 2.3 percent spoke different Indochinese languages.

Policy Shifts

As the ethnoburb model predicts, waves of Chinese immigration to the United States have mainly followed major U.S. immigration policy changes and significant international geopolitical events. Immigration before 1965 was very limited, with less than 4 percent of all Chinese immigrants coming into the United States during that period. Although the change in government in Mainland China in 1949 caused some immigration to the United States, it did not

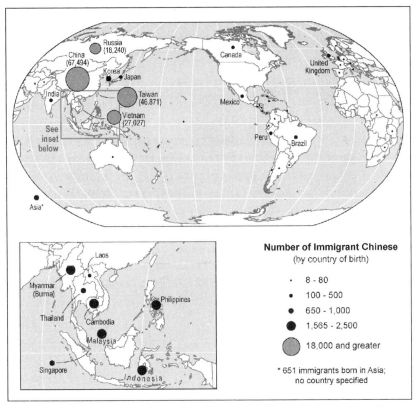

MAP 7. Origins of Immigrant Chinese in San Gabriel Valley, 2000. *Source:* U.S. Census Bureau.

by itself generate a significant wave. It was not until the historic 1965 Immigration Act that large numbers of Chinese arrived: 3.5 percent of all ethnoburban Chinese immigrants came between 1965 and 1969.

Several important international events occurred in the first half of the 1970s, including the ouster of the Republic of China (Taiwan) from the United Nations in 1971, President Richard Nixon's visit to Mainland China in 1972, and the fall of Saigon in 1975. These events prompted Chinese immigrants to pour into the United States, their numbers tripling between 1970–1974 and 1975–1979. These flows have continued to grow ever since.

As Figure 12 reveals, the correlation between geopolitical events, the shift in U.S. immigration policy, and immigrant flows not only involved the years of entry for Chinese immigrants but, more dramatically, shifts in places of origin for different time periods. While immigration from Mainland China has been continuous and increasing from the earliest periods, Chinese immigrants born in Taiwan arrived mainly after 1965. Their numbers almost quadrupled in the

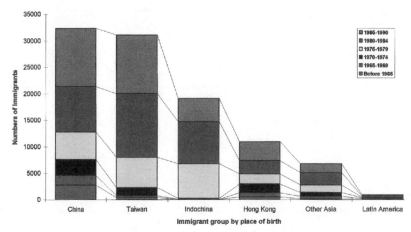

FIGURE 12. Year of Immigration by Immigrant Group in the Ethnoburb, 1990
Source: 1990 Census PUMS

second half of the 1970s and then again more than doubled in the five-year period after the United States and the People's Republic of China established diplomatic relationships in 1979. Immigration of Chinese born in Hong Kong has increased slowly but steadily in the decades before 1985. After the joint declaration by the United Kingdom and the People's Republic of China in 1984 concerning a return of Hong Kong to China, growing numbers of Chinese arrived from Hong Kong.

The most dramatic figures relate to the Chinese born in Indochina. There was almost no immigration from there before 1975, but after the fall of Saigon a massive wave appeared and kept growing until recently. Therefore, we can safely claim that without the Vietnam War and related political turmoil and war in Laos and Cambodia, we would not have witnessed the sudden surge of refugees and immigrants from Indochinese countries.

Internal Mobility

Not all immigrants immediately relocated in the ethnoburb upon arrival in the United States. Many of the Chinese residents in the ethnoburb have made one or more moves since coming to the United States because of job, family, or housing situations. Such moves within the United States can be categorized as internal migration (moving across state or county boundaries) or local residential mobility (moving within the same metropolitan area). These moves show that many ethnoburban Chinese, as relative newcomers, adjust to their new environment by changing their residences and looking for ideal neighborhoods. Thus they are more likely to be recent movers than long-established residents.

About two-thirds of ethnoburban Chinese changed their residences at least once during 1985–1990; this figure includes individuals who came to, or moved within, the ethnoburb during that time. More than 30 percent of them moved in either 1989 or 1990 alone. Less than 10 percent had lived in the same house or apartment since 1970 or earlier, and those longer-time residents were most likely American-born Chinese (ABCs) or earlier immigrants. Immigrant Chinese are more likely to have moved recently than native-born Chinese Americans. Almost three-fourths of all Chinese immigrants moved during 1985–1990. This demonstrates that the ethnoburb, as a Chinese hub, has continued to lure newcomers as well as those from inside the United States as secondary migrants because of the attraction of the ethnoburb's Chinese residential community and the employment and business opportunities available there.

The core area of the ethnoburb in western San Gabriel Valley remained the primary magnet for Chinese during 1985–1990. It not only received 64.3 percent of new immigrants, but also 65.1 percent of internal migrants. At the same time, several thousands of Chinese moved from the core area cities of Monterey Park and Rosemead to other parts of the ethnoburb. This indicates that Monterey Park, the original site of the ethnoburb, had become a redistribution center and a springboard for Chinese making secondary moves inside the ethnoburb. At the same time, it continued to attract both new immigrants, as well as secondary migrants.

Globalization and Economic Status

The economic activities of the ethnoburban Chinese population in the San Gabriel Valley are closely tied to the global economy. Many are involved in international trade and related services and are active players in the local economy, which has undergone restructuring. The ethnoburban economic picture, however, retains some features of an ethnic enclave economy.

The ethnoburb is not simply an ethnic residential neighborhood but also a business center. Many ethnic businesses rely on ethnic resources to supply labor and attract customers. In contrast to Southern California's characteristic distance between home and work, the ethnoburb provides a place to both live and work. It is an integrated business and residential outpost designed to serve globalized capital. The common location of Chinese businesses and residences in the San Gabriel Valley area has served to create a kind of self-contained city-within-a-city. Although not all ethnoburban Chinese hold jobs inside the ethnoburb, a much larger proportion of residents work in the community where they live than is true for most communities. Data reveal the close-knit relationship between home and work and identify the ethnoburb's characteristic integrated residential and business districts. Among all the ethnoburban Chinese residents in 1990, 10.6 percent worked in Monterey Park and Rosemead alone; among immigrants, the percentage was slightly higher (11.0 percent).[4] Clearly the original locus of the ethnoburb, Monterey Park, remains an important employment center for many ethnoburban Chinese residents.

In 1990, the extent of the overall job-housing linkage was dramatic: 40.1 percent of all ethnoburban Chinese who worked in Monterey Park or Rosemead also lived there. A total of 78.4 percent of the entire ethnoburban Chinese civilian workforce of Monterey Park and Rosemead lived in the core area of ethnoburb. This also reveals, yet again, that Monterey Park was a hub that continued to attract Chinese workers from nearby communities. This work-residence linkage was far higher for the Chinese than was true in the general workforce: among all Angelinos who worked in Monterey Park and Rosemead, only 23.6 percent actually lived there. The average percentage of people working and living in the same Public Use Microdata Area (PUMA) in LA County was 28.5 percent. Clearly, ethnoburban Chinese are more likely to work and live in the same communities than are other workers.

As an immigrant-dominated community of homes and jobs, one of the most important characteristics of the ethnoburb is its high level of self-employment, and this in turn is linked to the global economy and supports the community. In 1990, 15 percent of the ethnoburban Chinese labor force were self-employed entrepreneurs, a substantially higher percentage than the Los Angeles County workforce as a whole (10.2 percent). The percentage of employment in self-owned businesses among immigrant Chinese (15.7 percent) was considerably higher than among immigrants as a whole in the county (10.1 percent), which also reflects the active role that the Chinese play in both the local and global economies. Moreover, the rates of unpaid employment in family businesses (1.4 percent) were higher than the county average (0.6 percent), indicating the family-based nature of some Chinese business ventures inside ethnoburb.

The characteristics of the jobs performed by ethnoburban Chinese clearly demonstrate their connection to the global economy and point to the function of the ethnoburb as an outpost of the global economy. Chinese people in the United States historically worked in laundries or restaurants, but their occupational structure has changed dramatically with the changes in the composition of the Chinese population, their demographic profile, and their socioeconomic conditions. Globalization of the economy has helped generate these shifts.

Economic restructuring has been very important at the global, national, and local levels in recent decades. The decline of traditional durable goods manufacturing and unionized blue-collar jobs, the rise of high-tech industries, and the resurgence of labor-intensive craft sectors due to increasing numbers of both highly skilled professionals and low-skilled immigrant workers have changed the economic structure of the Los Angeles area. The ethnoburb reflects this, as its workforce is characterized by both high-wage, high-skill professionals and low-wage, low-skill immigrant laborers. Moreover, the industries that employ both groups show a strong connection due to the global economy. Professional and related services, finance, insurance, and real estate (FIRE) were key industries for ethnoburban Chinese (Table 8 I). Within FIRE, banking and real estate alone claimed 9.4 percent of the ethnoburban labor force, more than twice as high as in the county as a whole (4.5 percent; Table 8 I). Ethnoburban Chinese were over-represented in FIRE and under-represented in personal services sectors compared to overall labor force in Los Angeles County. The differences were more prominent when comparing ethnoburban Chinese immigrants with all immigrants in Los Angeles County. Services, especially producer services with international connections like banking, real estate, and wholesale trade, were very important among ethnoburban Chinese, for a total of 11.9 percent of the workforce was employed in these industrial sectors (Table 8 III).

As the result of reindustrialization and international competitive pressures, labor-intensive manufacturing (apparel, furniture, food processing, and so forth) has become important for immigrants who are subcontractors and have access to cheap labor. These manufacturing activities involve Koreans and Latinos in the Los Angeles area, as well as ethnoburban Chinese. Manufacturing was the second largest industry of employment for ethnoburban Chinese, its percentage being higher than for the county in general (Table 8 I). Within manufacturing, the garment industry (apparel and accessories) was by far the most significant and in fact was the third largest sector for ethnoburban Chinese workers (5 percent of total labor force). Ethnoburban Chinese were more likely to be involved in the garment industry than were other Angelinos. In other major blue-collar job categories (operator and laborer, precision, craft and repair), the percentage of ethnoburban Chinese was much lower than among county residents, but still comprised 13.5 percent.

Regarding job types, the majority of all working ethnoburban Chinese were white-collar workers. More than two-thirds were managers and professionals or held administrative support or sales positions (Table 8 II). For Los Angeles County as a whole, the percentage was much lower (55.3 percent). What is really striking is the high percentage of ethnoburban immigrant Chinese engaging in managerial and professional jobs—31.6 percent, compared with only 16.3 percent for all immigrants in the county. This signals large numbers of highly skilled immigrant workers and reflects the high level of Chinese self-employment as well, since business owners/partners are more likely involved in management and define themselves as managers. At the same time,

TABLE 8. Occupational Structure: Ethnoburb versus Los Angeles County, 1990

	Total Population		Immigrants	
	ETHNOBURB	LA COUNTY	ETHNOBURB	LA COUNTY
I. Type of industry				
Retail trade	19.7%	16.5%	20.0%	18.3%
Manufacturing	19.0	20.3	19.3	26.7
Professional & services	17.7	20.4	16.6	14.6
FIRE	13.0	7.4	13.2	5.7
Wholesale	9.3	4.9	9.9	5.3
Communication & public utilities	6.0	6.6	5.8	4.6
Business & repair	4.0	6.5	3.9	6.9
Agriculture & construction	3.9	7.4	4.1	8.9
Personal services	3.3	3.9	3.3	5.9
Public administration	2.3	2.8	2.0	1.4
Entertainment & recreation	1.8	3.3	1.8	1.7
II. Type of occupation				
Manager & professional	32.9%	25.7%	31.6%	16.3%
Administrative support	18.3	17.6	18.4	12.7
Sales occupations	16.4	12.0	17.0	10.5
Service occupations	10.1	13.2	10.6	17.3
Operator & laborer	6.8	8.5	7.0	15.9
Precision, craft, & repair	6.7	10.8	6.9	13.3
Technician & support	5.7	3.2	5.7	2.7
Transportation & material moving	2.8	7.7	2.5	9.4
Farming, forestry, & fishing	0.3	1.3	0.4	2.1

III. Top ten industries (percent total labor force)

ETHNOBURB		LOS ANGELES COUNTY	
1. Eating & drinking places	7.6	1. Construction	5.9
2. Banking	5.8	2. Eating & drinking places	5.0
3. Apparel & accessories	5.0	3. Elementary & secondary schools	4.5
4. Real estate (inc. insurance)	3.6	4. Hospitals	3.9
5. Construction	3.3	5. Apparel & accessories	2.3
		Real estate (inc. insurance)	2.3
6. Hospitals	2.8	6. Theaters & motion pictures	2.2
7. Grocery stores	2.5	7. Banking	2.0
Not specified wholesale trade	2.5		
8. Colleges & universities	2.4	8. Grocery stores	1.9
9. Elementary & secondary schools	2.3	9. Aircraft and parts	1.8
		Insurance	1.8
10. Service incidental to transportation	1.8	10. Business services	1.7

Source: U.S. Bureau of Census, 1990, Public Use Microdata Samples (5 percent).
Note: Percentages may not add to 100 due to rounding.

the ethnoburb as a Chinese immigrant community also provides a large pool of cheap labor for the restructured garment industry (as do other immigrant communities in the county). In addition, it also has created business opportunities for immigrant Chinese to engage in industries with Asian connections and allows them to become active players in the global economy.

The ethnoburb retains some characteristics of an ethnic enclave in that traditional ethnic economic niches remain important sites of employment for ethnoburban Chinese. Among ethnoburban Chinese workers, 10.1 percent were engaged in traditional Chinese ethnic economic niches. For example, a higher proportion of ethnoburban Chinese worked in eating and drinking establishments (restaurants) or grocery stores than of county residents in general (Table 8 III). And the largest sector of employment for ethnoburban Chinese was the retail trade, a traditional stronghold for ethnic economies.

Ethnoburban Chinese workers are concentrated at both the high and low ends of the skills and wage distributions and have close ties to industrial sectors involved in the global economy. The ethnoburb has the ability simultaneously to support and nourish a diverse and unassimilated immigrant population so that it can form a solid base for further expansion. The combination of global ties and local ethnic service jobs gives the ethnoburb its unique characteristics: it is a fully functioning global economic outpost with a distinctive ethnic signature, formed in part as a result of recent international economic restructuring processes and changing geopolitical situations. It is this that differentiates the ethnoburb from a traditional ethnic enclave, as well as from the mainstream economy.

Globalization and Social Status

The ethnoburb's ties to the world economy, particularly sectors such as banking and international trade, contribute to the overall high socioeconomic status of its residents. In general, ethnoburban Chinese are well educated, speak English well, have high incomes, and enjoy good housing conditions. The differences are more dramatic when the ethnoburban immigrant Chinese are compared with other immigrants in Los Angeles County.

The Chinese value system has always stressed education, which is viewed as an important way to improve a family's economic conditions, raise their social status, and glorify a family's ancestors. Whenever possible, Chinese parents encourage, even force their children to become well educated, and many parents are willing to sacrifice their own career advancement and lifestyles in order to offer their children a brighter future. One important reason why the Chinese have immigrated to the United States is to provide their children with better educational and employment opportunities. Obviously, all Chinese on student visas come here for the purpose of higher education and some for potential career opportunities as well. They are therefore potential immigrants. This traditional valuing of education finds expression within the ethnoburb.

Overall, the ethnoburban Chinese are well educated, with high educational attainment levels.[5] Of all ethnoburban Chinese in the data set who were fifteen years old or over, 29 percent had not completed any type of schooling at all or did not graduate from high school. But at the high end, more than 31 percent held at least a bachelor's degree. All others fell somewhere in between (Figure 13). Among ethnoburban Chinese, the educational attainment of the U.S.-born was higher than that of immigrants. Among the college-educated, immigrant Chinese had higher percentages who earned associate degrees and master degrees than U.S.-born Chinese; but they were less apt to hold a professional degree (in, say, medicine, dentistry, or pharmacy), there the U.S.-born were at 7.3 percent and immigrants at 1.9 percent.

The overall educational attainment level among all ethnoburban Chinese clearly surpassed that of Los Angeles County in general in 1990 (Figure 13). Ethnoburban Chinese had higher percentages in every educational attainment category above the associate degree than did the overall Los Angeles County population. Differences were even more profound among immigrants. While

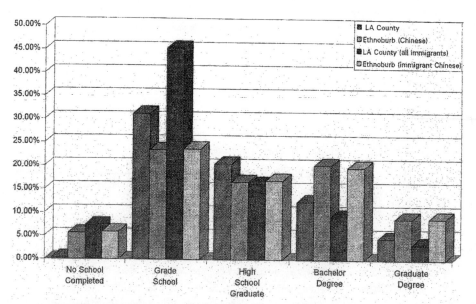

FIGURE 13. Educational Attainment: Ethnoburb versus Los Angeles County, 1990
Source: 1990 Census PUMS

only 29.6 percent of the ethnoburban immigrant Chinese did not have a high school diploma, a majority of all immigrants (52.7 percent) in Los Angeles County were not high school graduates. And while 30.5 percent of ethnoburban immigrant Chinese had at least a bachelor's degree, among all immigrants the percentage was only 13.9 percent.

The high level of education among ethnoburban Chinese immigrants indicates that they are well prepared for, and fit into, the employment trends of the region's globalizing economy. Such preparation can also be demonstrated by their English language ability, measured here by census data on self-evaluated ability in spoken English (Bureau of the Census, 1992, B-24). English language ability is important for immigrants in American society, not only because it is a prerequisite for a decent job in the mainstream job market, but because it is also a symbol of assimilation. Hence, poorly spoken English may not only jeopardize immigrants' chances for betterment in the United States, but may sometimes be used against them as a measure of unwillingness to merge into American society. Overall, ethnoburban Chinese appear to possess good spoken English skills, in spite of the fact that the ethnoburb is an immigrant-dominated community in which one could easily survive without having to speak English. Among all ethnoburban Chinese, those who claimed to speak English very well or well counted for a total of 64.1 percent. Considering the Chinese tradition of humility, such a figure may be an underestimation. Compared with all immigrants in the county, the ethnoburban immigrant Chinese had

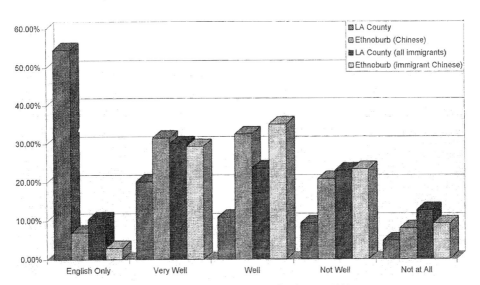

FIGURE 14. Spoken English: Ethnoburb versus Los Angeles County, 1990
Source: 1990 Census PUMS

far superior spoken language skills (Figure 14). A majority (53.3 percent) of immigrant Chinese households did not have language isolation problems.[6]

The overall high socioeconomic status of ethnoburban Chinese population is reflected not only by higher education levels and better spoken English ability than other groups in the county, but also by their household incomes and housing conditions.

Unlike in Chinatown, a traditionally low-income area, income levels among Chinese in the ethnoburb were higher than the county average. Since the ethnoburb is an ethnic community composed primarily of recent immigrants, income data imply that many new Chinese arrivals in the San Gabriel Valley are not poor. Census data only collects information on the money people earn during a given year, and not on their capital resources or total assets (either at home or abroad), so census information does not provide a complete picture of real wealth. However, such data are good indicators of total annual income from diverse sources (including salaries, wages, and rental income received by landlords), and this reflects major economic and job activities by employees, employers, the self-employed, and investors.

Median household income of all Chinese households in the ethnoburb was, at $40,000, $5,035 higher than that of Los Angeles County as a whole. Moreover, a higher percentage of this population had incomes 120 percent or above the county median and a far lower representation in the low income bracket than all county households. The differences between ethnoburban Chinese immigrant households and all immigrant households were even bigger: immigrant Chinese households were over-represented in the higher income bracket of 120 percent or more than the county median income compared with all immigrants in the county (Figure 15).

Higher household incomes may result from the presence of larger numbers of wage earners per Chinese household than in households of other ethnic groups. Thus, household income may not accurately reveal income status. Median personal income among all ethnoburban Chinese who were fifteen years or older and reported their income ($15,000) was $1,000 lower than the county median,[7] but ethnoburban Chinese immigrants' median income was $3,000 more than personal median income of all immigrants in the county ($12,000). Not only was their total personal income higher, their median incomes from different sources, such as salaries, wages, or self-employment income, were higher than those of all immigrants in the county. Income levels of the ethnoburban Chinese varied greatly among those in different occupations. Owners of incorporated businesses had the highest overall personal income. Those who held managerial, professional, or sales jobs, or who were technicians, also had higher incomes than the general population.

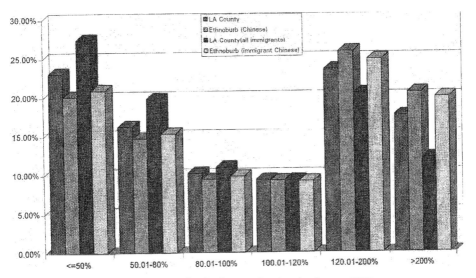

FIGURE 15. Household Income: Ethnoburb versus Los Angeles County, 1989
Source: 1990 Census PUMS

To own property and a home of one's own have always been viewed as important signs of success, especially for immigrants. A majority of ethnoburban Chinese households (two-thirds) owned their own homes, a rate surpassing that of the county and indicating that they had achieved an important element of the American Dream (see Table 9). In addition, a majority of ethnoburban Chinese immigrants were homeowners. In comparison, home ownership among all immigrants in Los Angeles County was almost 28 percentage points lower than among Chinese immigrants in the ethnoburb. Thus ethnoburban Chinese immigrants do not fit the conventional image of immigrants: they arrived with few if any financial resources, but many of them come, rather, with capital to invest. For the Chinese, "real estate is considered a good investment and something to pass down to future generations. Many parents put aside money to buy first homes for their children or help them buy their first homes" (Klein 1997). This is a common practice among Chinese immigrants in the ethnoburb. They, along with other Asian immigrants, are actually driving much of the housing market in the San Gabriel Valley, especially in the eastern district.

There exists a conventional perception that immigrant housing is typically more crowded than average. But a significant proportion of ethnoburban Chinese can be considered well housed, especially with respect to space. In seven-tenths of Chinese households, each person had at least one room (Table 9),

TABLE 9. Housing Characteristics of Ethnoburban Chinese versus Los Angeles County: 1990

	Ethnoburban Chinese Households (%)	LA County Households (%)	Immigrant Chinese Households (%)	LA Co. Immigrant Households (%)
Tenure				
Owner	66.7	48.7	66.0	38.4
Renter	33.3	51.3	34.0	61.6
Owner cost				
Under 30%	49.6	69.6	48.1	60.2
30–49%	25.9	19.7	26.0	23.6
50% and over	24.5	10.8	25.9	16.2
Rent burden				
Under 30%	41.2	51.5	40.1	48.4
30–49%	23.0	25.2	23.5	26.6
50% and over	35.8	23.3	36.4	25.1
Crowding (persons per room)				
Under 0.5	19.8	38.1	17.0	16.4
0.5–1.0	50.7	43.3	51.2	39.6
1.01–1.5	13.8	6.9	14.8	14.1
1.51 and over	15.7	11.6	17.0	30.0

Source: U.S. Bureau of Census, 1990, Public Use Microdata Samples (5 percent).
Note: Percentages may not add to 100 due to rounding.

while only about 15.7 percent of Chinese households faced severe overcrowding, with more than 1.5 persons per room. This was a much lower figure than that for the whole county. The differences were more dramatic when comparing ethnoburban immigrant Chinese households with all immigrant households in the county, for immigrant Chinese had at least one room per person in 68.2 percent of their households, compared with 56 percent among all immigrants in Los Angeles County. Only 17 percent of immigrant Chinese ethnoburban households were extremely overcrowded, compared with 30 percent of all immigrant households in the county.

Housing costs did not present a heavy burden to many ethnoburban Chinese household budgets, especially in comparison with other immigrant groups. This was probably due to the higher income and overall wealth of the

Chinese households, compared with other immigrant households. However, it is true that if we consider the owner cost burden (the mortgage and other housing costs as a percentage of household income), ethnoburban Chinese households were more burdened compared with the county as a whole (see Table 9). This most likely reflects the large share of new immigrants and in-migrants, for new arrival status implies newer mortgages and thus higher mortgage payments. However, renter housing burdens (gross rent as percentage of household income) among ethnoburban Chinese were more polarized than is true for the county as a whole, indicating socioeconomic stratification among the Chinese.

In general, ethnoburban Chinese are better off socioeconomically than the total population in Los Angeles County. The gaps are even more distinct among immigrants, revealing that Chinese immigrants in the ethnoburb do not fit the traditional description of poor and poorly housed new immigrants. Beneath this general picture of well-being and affluence, however, is significant social and economic stratification.

Internal Stratification

As the result of economic globalization and the associated personnel flows, both wealthy and poor Chinese have joined immigrant waves coming to the United States. Thus despite its overall character as an affluent immigrant community and flourishing center of economic activity, the ethnoburb also displays strong internal stratification along the lines of national origins and geographic areas of emigration. Such stratification is driven by the strikingly different conditions in the origin countries, which create immigrant groups with different socioeconomic characteristics. These differences assume geographical expression as these newcomers are sorted spatially by the American urban housing market.

Internal stratification also fits into, and in turn is fed by, economic dynamics at both the global and local levels. The rise of FIRE and other globally linked activities, as well as the need for international investment, has created a concurrent rise in demand for a workforce that is white collar, professionally trained, highly skilled, multilingual, and internationally well connected. Well-educated and wealthy Chinese immigrants are ideal for such positions. At the same time, the restructured, resurgent local craft sectors such as the garment industry and service industries cry out both for managerial personnel (as managers or subcontractors), and for large numbers of low-skill, low-wage immigrant workers to minimize costs and maximize profits. Many of these low-skill workers have no other options but to rely heavily on ethnic networks to survive, and ethnic employers in turn largely rely on ethnic networks for their employees and business transactions. Interestingly all these factors together create the ethno-burb as both a socially and spatially stratified complex. Such class differences within the ethnoburb may be a prerequisite for its growth.

Stratification by Country of Origin

The most significant and obvious stratification exists in the contrasting socioeconomic characteristics of immigrants from different parts of Asia. Chinese born in Taiwan and Hong Kong, those born in Mainland China, and those born in Southeast Asia vary greatly in occupational status, educational attainment, and income.

As two of the Newly Industrialized Countries (NICs), both Taiwan and Hong Kong have developed at a very rapid pace during the last several decades, becoming indispensable components of the global economy. They have produced highly trained professional and skilled workers as well as affluent investors, many of whom have immigrated to the United States. As a former colony, Hong Kong has had a British education system for the last hundred years, while Taiwan adopted an American-style system after World War II. Both also adhere to the traditional Chinese emphasis on the value of education. Many immigrants from these two areas are well educated, with professional training or academic degrees, and have the ability to speak English; some were wealthy people in their countries of origin. Many of them brought portable assets, earn high incomes, purchase expensive homes, hold professional jobs or own businesses, and possess a higher socioeconomic status overall than does the general U.S. population.

At the other end of the immigrant spectrum, the situation of ethnic Chinese born in Southeast Asia is more akin to that of the largest group from Southeast Asia, the Vietnam War refugees who immigrated to the United States after the fall of Saigon. A majority of these refugees did not plan to emigrate until the political situation forced them to do so. Many had personal wealth, but lost it when they left their home countries. Others escaped in boats or fled overland with next to nothing. Least prepared among all major Chinese immigrant groups were those from rural backgrounds, who were poorly educated, poorly trained, and without good spoken English. When they arrived in the United States, many were forced to rely on public assistance or took blue-collar or lower-ranking public sector jobs. They had much lower earnings than other Chinese subgroups.

The situation of Chinese born in Mainland China is much more complicated. Because of census definitions, it is difficult to separate those coming directly from China from those who were born in Mainland China, but who resided for years in Taiwan or Hong Kong before immigrating. This group is more fragmented than the first two in terms of socioeconomic characteristics, educational attainment, occupational structure, and income levels. Their overall situation is better than the Indochinese refugees but not as good as those born in Taiwan or Hong Kong. Mainland Chinese tend to be older than the other three major groups. As economic reforms in Mainland China have accelerated, levels of wealth have risen, and many newly affluent people have begun to participate in the global economy. A growing number have come to the United States as immigrants or business people, beneficiaries of the U.S. immigration law changes in the 1990s.

As Table 10 demonstrates, higher percentages of Taiwan- and Hong Kong–born Chinese immigrants engaged in professional and related services, and FIRE. They also had the highest percentages of managerial or professional jobs. Many came here as investors or entrepreneurs to establish or operate businesses

TABLE 10. Occupational Structure of Ethnoburban Chinese Immigrants by Place of Birth, 1990

	Taiwan	Hong Kong	China	Indochina
Type of industry				
Retail trade	16.7%	17.4%	23.5%	22.9%
Manufacturing	14.9	16.8	22.0	25.8
Professional & services	19.0	22.5	14.9	8.9
FIRE	14.4	13.9	11.0	12.6
Wholesale trade	14.9	7.0	7.8	9.2
Transportation, communication, & public utilities	7.0	7.0	5.0	4.8
Business & repair	2.7	4.6	3.4	5.6
Agriculture, mining, & construction	4.0	2.8	4.9	3.2
Personal services	3.1	1.7	4.5	2.9
Public administration	1.8	3.8	1.4	2.6
Entertainment & recreation	1.6	2.5	1.7	1.7
Type of occupation				
Manager & professional	41.4	36.5	29.6	11.1
Administrative support	17.6	21.4	14.4	23.7
Sales occupations	22.2	13.2	15.0	16.5
Service occupations	7.0	9.4	14.2	11.6
Precision, production, craft, & repair	3.1	3.8	8.8	14.2
Operator & laborer	2.7	2.7	10.3	3.7
Transportation & material moving	1.5	1.6	2.7	5.1
Farming, forestry, & fishing	0.4	0.2	0.4	0.4

Source: U.S. Bureau of Census, 1990, Public Use Microdata Samples (5 percent).
Note: Percentages may not add to 100 due to rounding.

in the ethnoburb. Compared with ethnoburban Chinese immigrants in general, immigrants born in Mainland China were more likely to work in the retail trade and manufacturing, but still, like those born in Taiwan and Hong Kong, the largest job category for China-born immigrants was managerial/professional jobs. Sales was the second largest job category for the Taiwan- and China-born, whereas administrative support was the second for Hong Kong-born. Taiwan- and China-born immigrants were less likely to be technicians than the Hong Kong-born. Although these three groups held similar places in the job ladder, China-born immigrants had lower job prestige than Taiwan- or Hong Kong-born, since they had lower percentages engaged in managerial or professional jobs and higher percentages in service and labor categories. The largest share of Indochina-born Chinese immigrants, in contrast, entered the low-wage labor force and were involved in some type of manufacturing activity. The percentage of Indochinese in blue-collar jobs (precision production/craft/repair and operators/laborers) was the highest among all the major place-of-birth groups, though this group had the largest percentage of administrative support. Among the four major Chinese immigrant groups, Indochina-born immigrants stood on the lowest rung of the occupational ladder.

Different jobs generate different income levels. Not surprisingly, the highest median personal income was earned by immigrants born in Hong Kong ($21,005), followed by Taiwan ($20,000), and then Mainland China ($12,500). The Chinese immigrants born in Indochina had the lowest median income among all groups (Laos: $12,012; Cambodia: $12,000; and Vietnam: $10,619.5). The county median was $16,000. Over 50 percent of those born in Hong Kong or Taiwan had incomes at least 120 percent above the county median, but only 12.3 percent of Indochina-born residents were in that category, and almost 40 percent had less than 50 percent of the county median. The biggest internal polarization existed among the China-born group: a majority (50.4 percent) had incomes 80 percent or below the county median, but the other 35.7 percent had incomes at least 120 percent above it. Immigrants born in Indochina had the highest percentage (15.7 to 27.9 percent) receiving public assistance among all immigrant groups. The rates among all other groups were below 10 percent.

Differences in education and language skills contribute to the dramatic variations in economic status and income levels by place-of-birth group. The Chinese born in Taiwan had the top educational level, with 43.4 percent having at least a bachelor's degree (Figure 16), followed by those born in Hong Kong (39.4 percent) and in Mainland China (27.0 percent). Among those born in Indochina, over half (54.2 percent) did not have high school diplomas. The percentages of Chinese from Mainland China, Hong Kong, and Taiwan without

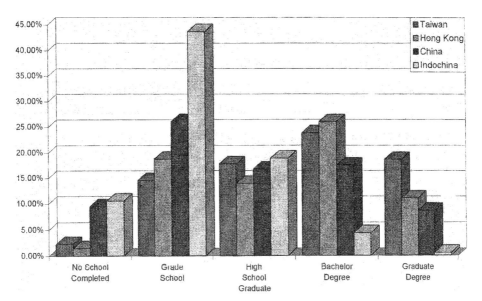

FIGURE 16. Educational Attainment by Immigrant Group in the Ethnoburb, 1990
Source: 1990 Census PUMS

high school diplomas were 33.9 percent, 17.8 percent, and 16.4 percent, respectively. As expected, immigrants born in Mainland China were more stratified with respect to their educational attainment levels. They ranked third with respect to the share with bachelor's or higher degrees, but the group also contained large numbers of people who did not have a high school diploma. Not surprisingly, Hong Kong had the highest levels of spoken English ability (82.1 percent spoke well or very well), followed by the Taiwan-born (74.8 percent). A majority (52.5 percent) of Indochina-born immigrants felt they were linguistically isolated due to their poor English speaking ability.

Stratification by Neighborhood and Workplace

The profoundly different socioeconomic conditions among these groups have strong implications for residential location within the ethnoburb. For instance, in the cities of El Monte, La Puente, Industry, and South El Monte, immigrants of Chinese descent born in Indochina composed the largest group (36.3 to 42.5 percent of all Chinese immigrants). In places like Arcadia, Covina, Hacienda Heights, Rowland Heights, San Marino, Temple City, Walnut, and West Covina, all upscale or upper-middle-class neighborhoods, immigrants born in Taiwan were the largest group. In Diamond Bar, Taiwan-born Chinese immigrants comprised a majority. Immigrants born in Mainland China were the largest group in communities such as Alhambra, Monterey Park, Pasadena, Rosemead, and South Pasadena.

Given the strong socioeconomic and spatial stratification of ethnoburban residents according to country of origin, it is not surprising that the ethnoburb is a complex mosaic of neighborhoods and workplaces marked by social contrast and economic differences. As traditional upscale neighborhoods, Arcadia and San Marino are home to wealthy households and rich single people. The communities attract mainly affluent Chinese and their families. As the result, these areas have not only maintained their high status, but they have even seen it rise. Not counting Arcadia and San Marino, the western San Gabriel Valley comprises long-established and solidly middle-class neighborhoods in the inner suburbs of Los Angeles County. The East San Gabriel Valley area, on the other hand, has a series of more recently developed outer suburbs. These are mainly upper-middle-class neighborhoods that have become new favorites among the ethnoburban Chinese because many prefer brand new houses to older ones; this is evident in Maps 2 and 3. Therefore, ethnoburban Chinese in Arcadia, San Marino, Pasadena, and the East San Gabriel Valley cities and CDPs such as Rowland Heights, Diamond Bar, Hacienda Heights, and Walnut are higher on the socioeconomic scale as indicated by the skills, incomes, education, and housing of their residents. These areas have high percentages of immigrants from Taiwan (in the case of Pasadena, U.S.-born Chinese). About one-fifth or more of all working Chinese here engaged in professional services (varying from 18.9 percent in Hacienda Heights to 44.2 percent in Pasadena). At least three-fourths of these residents had white-collar jobs. Half of all ethnoburban Chinese who were in the highest income bracket ($200,000 and more) lived in the Arcadia and San Marino area alone, and they were all immigrants. Almost one-tenth of the residents in this area had incomes at least three times the county median. The Chinese in Pasadena had the highest education attainment levels (with 59.6 percent having earned at least a bachelor's degree); followed by Diamond Bar and Rowland Heights (54.7 percent); Hacienda Heights (52.8 percent); and Arcadia, San Marino, and Temple City (48.9 percent). In Hacienda Heights, Pasadena, Diamond Bar, Rowland Heights, Covina, West Covina, Arcadia, San Gabriel, San Marino, and Temple City, higher percentages of people spoke English well or very well, compared with the average of ethnoburban Chinese (ranging from 73.4 percent to 68.7 percent).

Regarding housing conditions, in recent-immigrant dominated Hacienda Heights, Rowland Heights, and Diamond Bar, home ownership rates among ethnoburban Chinese were as high as 88.3 percent, a clear sign of relative wealth among the new immigrants. This rate was even higher than that for native-born Pasadena Chinese residents (50.6 percent). Among all Chinese homeowners, more than 45 percent of those households in Arcadia, San Marino, Diamond Bar, Rowland Heights, and Hacienda Heights spent less than 30 percent of their total income on housing. Much of the housing stock in this area is decidedly upscale. This indicates that residents are indeed wealthy people, who came with financial resources. Not only could they afford expensive homes, but some of them were able to buy properties outright in cash or pay off their mortgages rapidly, or spend only a small proportion of their income on housing. In contrast, more than one-third of Chinese owner households in Walnut had to allocate more than 50 percent of their total income for housing expenses. This is probably because those who moved to Walnut and other newer suburbs were likely seeking newer and more spacious housing and willing to increase their housing burden. Renter payment burdens also varied among neighborhoods. While 48.5 percent of Pasadena renters spent less than 30 percent for housing, 58.2 percent renters in Hacienda Heights had to spend more than half of all their income on housing.

These upscale residential neighborhoods also had high percentages of non-Hispanic white people (40 to 50 percent), low proportions of Latinos (less than 20 percent), and even lower percentages of African Americans (usually less than 5 percent). These were neighborhoods of owner-occupied houses, with ownership rates varying from about 60 percent in West San Gabriel Valley to as high as 77 percent in the relatively newly developed East San Gabriel Valley, where up to one-third of the residential buildings were built during the 1980s, and over 70 percent were detached single-family houses. Up to half of these households had incomes that were at least 200 percent the county median, and a majority of households (owner or renter) did not have to spend more than one-third of their total income on housing. More than one-third of all houses in Arcadia and San Marino were valued at more than $400,000. Therefore, upscale Chinese are more likely to live in neighborhoods where other wealthy people live.

On the other hand, the Chinese who live in El Monte, South El Monte, La Puente, and the City of Industry have lower socioeconomic status. As a traditional stronghold of the Latino population, El Monte houses mainly lower- to lower-middle-class Chinese, many of whom were originally from Southeast Asia. Most upper-middle-class Chinese bypassed El Monte, La Puente, and the City of Industry (largely an industrial area as its name indicates). About a quarter of the Chinese workforce in these poorer areas was involved in the retail trade and another fifth in manufacturing activity. Their proportions of white-collar occupations were 10 to 15 percentage points lower than those living in wealthier areas, and one-fifth of the Chinese in these communities worked as blue-collar workers or held services jobs. No Chinese person living in El Monte earned more than $100,000; over 50 percent had incomes less than half the county median. Chinese living in these areas also had the lowest education levels. Over one-third of all in La Puente, South El Monte, and the City of Industry had not graduated from high school. They did not have adequate spoken English skills either; the Chinese in El Monte had the highest percentage (42 percent) of not speaking English well or not speaking it at all. Severe crowding existed in more than one-fifth of Chinese households. In the El Monte area, Hispanics comprised the overwhelming majority, much higher than in other parts of the San Gabriel Valley, accounting for almost half of the total population. Non-Hispanic whites were less than 16 percent. Overall, these communities are lower-middle-class or lower-class neighborhoods. For example, over 30 percent of all households in El Monte had incomes of only 50 percent of the Los Angeles County median or lower, and the city's home ownership rate was the lowest among all San Gabriel Valley communities (41.3 percent).

Ethnoburban Chinese living in other parts of the ethnoburb (Alhambra, Monterey Park, Rosemead, San Gabriel, and Temple City) were in the middle in terms of their overall socioeconomic status. Almost equal proportions of those living in these areas were engaged in professional and related services, retail, and manufacturing (15 to 25 percent). About 60 percent were white-collar workers, while around 10 percent worked as blue-collar workers or held service occupations. Although about 5 percent of these residents had incomes three times or more than the county median, some 40 percent of them had less than half the median. About one-fourth of the Chinese residents had not graduated from high school, whereas another third had at least a bachelor's degree. About one-third did not speak English well or they did not speak it at all, but a majority (about 60 percent) spoke well or very well. The Chinese households here were about equally split between owning and renting their homes, crowding levels were low, and overall housing cost burdens were moderate.

In general, this area—the core and earliest part of the ethnoburb—had highest overall percentages of Asian and Pacific Islander population (from 33.9 percent in Alhambra and South Pasadena to 44.9 percent in Monterey Park and Rosemead). Latinos accounted for about 15 percent, and non-Hispanic whites were the smallest component. In these communities, between one-fifth and one-fourth of all households had incomes of 50 percent or lower of the county median, while another 12 to 13 percent had incomes of 200 percent or more, which suggests great diversity within the area. Households were about equally divided between owner and renter occupied. A large majority of all houses were valued in the middle-range bracket ($100,000–$399,999). These neighborhoods thus appear to be solidly middle class.

As described by the ethnoburb model, the ethnoburb is not only a mosaic of residential areas, but also a complex of business districts. Differentiation of business districts can be identified spatially on the basis of various labor force characteristics and different economic structures, indicating their different roles in the local economy. Table 11 demonstrates some of these spatial variations by using three PUMAs within the ethnoburb, which were identified

TABLE 11. Internal Variation of Chinese Workforce and Economy in the Ethnoburb, 1990

	Monterey Park & Rosemead	El Monte	Pasadena	Ethnoburb
Workforce characteristics				
EDUCATIONAL ATTAINMENT				
No high school diploma	22.2%	20.0%	7.9%	29.0%
High school, some college	44.6	46.8	33.5	39.6
Bachelor's degree or higher	33.2	33.2	58.6	31.4
SPOKEN ENGLISH				
No English spoken	4.8	3.2	1.5	8.0
Speak not well	25.8	26.3	4.9	20.9
Speak well	39.9	35.6	31.3	32.5
Speak very well	27.5	19.3	50.4	31.5
IMMIGRANT BIRTHPLACE				
China	34.4	36.8	27.3	31.2
Taiwan	33.4	26.4	22.2	29.7
Indochina	17.8	21.8	14.5	18.5
Hong Kong	10.7	8.6	21.6	10.6
Place of residence for workforce				
Monterey Park & Rosemead	40.1	17.4	13.7	24.7
El Monte	5.1	13.6	5.5	5.5
Pasadena	1.7	0.0	25.0	3.3
Other parts of ethnoburb core	38.2	33.4	39.4	37.8
All other ethnoburban areas	14.9	35.6	16.4	28.7
Economic structure				
TYPE OF OWNERSHIP				
Private for profit	75.1	64.6	60.7	69.0
Private non profit	2.0	5.7	16.8	4.8
Government	5.3	8.3	12.0	9.8
Own not incorporated	8.9	13.0	6.2	9.1
Own incorporated	7.7	8.5	3.9	5.9
Non-pay family business	1.0	0.0	0.6	1.4

(continued)

TABLE 11. Internal Variation of Chinese Workforce and Economy in the Ethnoburb, 1990 *(cont.)*

	Monterey Park & Rosemead	El Monte	Pasadena
Top five industries			
(percent of total employment)	Retail (25.1)	Manufacturing (34.2)	Professional & services (35.5)
	FIRE (21.1)	Retail (14.4)	FIRE (15.3)
	Professional & services (17.6)	Professional & services (10.9)	Manufacturing (13.9)
	Manufacturing (10.3)	Personal services (7.9)	Retail (13.8)
	Communication (6.0)	Business & repair (7.3)	Communication (4.0)
Top five occupations			
(percentages of people engaged)	Manager & professional (35.8)	Manager & professional (28.2)	Manager & professional (46.2)
	Administrative support (16.8)	Operator & laborer (23.2)	Administrative support (16.4)
	Sales occupations (15.9)	Administrative support (13.4)	Service occupations (9.1)
	Service occupations (12.4)	Sales occupations (12.3)	Technicians & support (9.0)
	Precision & craft (6.7)	Precision & craft (10.1)	Sales occupations (8.9)

Source: U.S. Bureau of Census, 1990, Public Use Microdata Samples (5 percent).
Note: Percentages may not add to 100 due to rounding.

individually by the census as workplaces, and showing how they compare with the ethnoburb as a whole.

Overall, the Chinese workforce in Pasadena had the highest education levels and better spoken English abilities of workers in all three areas; those in El Monte had the lowest, while those who worked in Monterey Park and Rosemead tended to either end of the spectrum in their socioeconomic conditions. Overall the workforce in Monterey Park and Rosemead had higher educational attainment, but lower spoken English ability than ethnoburban Chinese workers as a whole. The Monterey Park area as an employment center, then, offered job opportunities for those Chinese professionals who do not speak English very well and as a result had to work in jobs for which they are educationally overqualified. This demonstrates that the ethnoburb (at least the core of it), continues to exhibit some characteristics of an ethnic enclave, where immigrants can both find ways to survive and become an important force in promoting the growth of the area.

The three areas also had different economic structures. The Chinese ethnic economy in Monterey Park and Rosemead focused on retail, Pasadena on professional and related services, and El Monte on manufacturing. Although managers and professionals were the largest occupational category in all three PUMAs, higher percentages of the workforce in El Monte were operators and laborers due to its manufacturing activity. Monterey Park and El Monte also had higher self-employment rates than the ethnoburb overall.

Contrasts with Chinatown

Compared with the ethnoburb, which has stronger global connections and internal stratification, Chinatown continues to be a typical inner-city ethnic enclave. It is comprised mainly of immigrants of Chinese descent from Mainland China and Southeast Asia; the community has more elderly and its residents have lived longer in the United States than the typical ethnoburban population. Overall the socioeconomic status of Chinatown's residents is lower, and traditional ethnic economic niches and occupations dominate the economy.

Compared with the ethnoburb, Chinatown has more "old-timer overseas Chinese," who came from less diversified origins. In Chinatown, a majority (52.6 percent) of Chinese immigrants was born in China, followed by those born in Indochina (30.8 percent). Only a small proportion came from Hong Kong (8.6 percent) or Taiwan (1.3 percent; Figure 17). Chinatown's immigrants have been in the United States much longer on average than those in the ethnoburb; 10.2 percent came before 1965. Among China-born immigrants, the percentage was even higher (16.1 percent). Many of these immigrants came either during 1965–1969, due to the changes in U.S. immigration law, or in 1980–1984, following the Vietnam War. None of the Indochina-born ethnic Chinese immigrants came to the United States prior to 1970. Therefore, Chinatown is a community primarily comprised of immigrants from two main sources, many of whom are longtime settlers. The community has largely been passed over by the newer waves of immigrants from Asia.

Chinatown is also a neighborhood of mixed age groups, with larger percentages of elderly people. In contrast, the ethnoburb is a young and energetic community with an age structure leaning strongly toward younger age groups. The average age of Chinatown Chinese (36.2) was almost four years more than that of the ethnoburb. The age profile for Chinatown Chinese did not have the sharp contrasts between younger and older age groups, but was more balanced among almost all age groups younger than seventy years old (Figures 18a and 18b).

Chinatown Chinese had low levels of educational attainment and English ability compared with the ethnoburban Chinese and the county population in

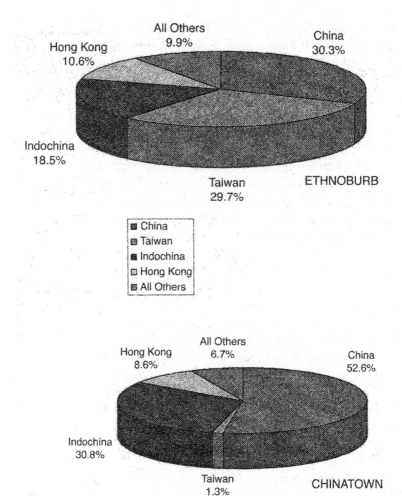

FIGURE 17. Origins of Immigrant Chinese: Ethnoburb versus Chinatown.
Source: U.S. Census 1990 PUMS

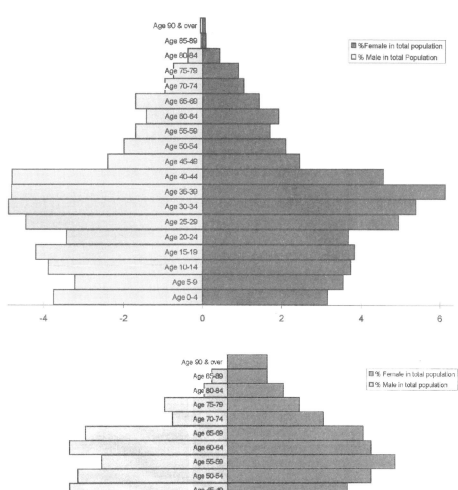

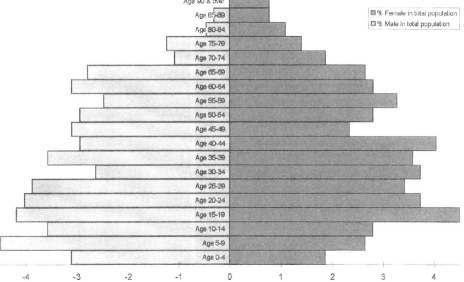

FIGURE 18 a-b. Chinese Population Pyramid: Ethnoburb versus Chinatown, 1990
Source: U.S. Census 1990 PUMS

general (Table 12). The better formal education and superior English language skills of ethnoburban Chinese compared with their Chinatown counterparts were reflected in their higher income levels, occupational structures, and better housing conditions. Such differences were even more dramatic between ethnoburban immigrant Chinese and Chinatown immigrant Chinese; Chinatown immigrant Chinese had the lowest educational levels. Almost 44 percent of them had not graduated from high school, and only about 15.8 percent had a bachelor degree or higher.

Chinatown continues to be a linguistically isolated ethnic island. Almost 45 percent of the Chinatown Chinese did not speak English at all or did not speak it well. Almost two-thirds of China-born immigrants belong to the same two categories. An overwhelming majority (94.5 percent) of all Chinatown Chinese spoke a language other than English at home. The percentage was 97.4 percent for immigrant Chinese and was even as high as 80.4 percent for native-born Chinese. Speaking Chinese is probably the only way that the American-born generation and their non-English-speaking, monolingual parents can communicate. All old-timer "overseas Chinese" (immigrants coming before 1965) spoke Chinese at home.

Not surprisingly, Chinatown Chinese had lower incomes, and more were reliant on public assistance. Median personal income was $6,636, more than $8,300 lower than that of ethnoburban Chinese. Median household income was $23,288 ($16,712 lower than that of ethnoburban Chinese, and also much lower than the county median). Almost 45 percent of Chinatown households had incomes less than 50 percent of the Los Angeles County median, and 14.8

TABLE 12. Educational Attainment: Ethnoburb versus Chinatown (percentages), 1990

Educational Attainment	Ethnoburb	Chinatown
No school completed	5.6	11.5
Grade school	23.3	31.9
High school graduate	16.6	16.3
Some college	14.1	16.0
Associate degree	8.8	0.81
B.A. or B.S.	20.2	11.2
M.A. or M.S.	7.9	2.4
Professional degree	2.3	1.6
Ph.D.	0.9	0.6

Source: U.S. Bureau of Census 1990 Public Use Microdata Samples (5 percent).
Note: Percentages may not add to 100 due to rounding.

percent received some public assistance income. Compared with their ethno-burban counterparts, Chinatown Chinese were also disadvantaged in terms of housing. They were more apt to live in crowded conditions, and they had much lower home ownership rates (30.7 percent). Only about a quarter of Chinatown households lived in single family detached housing, which is as expected given Chinatown's location in downtown Los Angeles. The crowding problems were severe among renter households, with 34 percent having more than 1.5 persons per room. This demonstrates not only the difference between older downtown and newer suburban settings, but also reflects the lower socioeconomic status of the Chinatown Chinese.

In terms of economic structure, Chinatown is still a traditional ethnic enclave with trade as its most important economic activity. Service jobs and laborers continued to be the main occupational categories of residents, which together accounted for 42.4 percent of all workers. Retail trade was more important in Chinatown than in the ethnoburb, engaging 31.6 percent of all working Chinatown Chinese residents, a much higher percentage than in the ethnoburb (Table 13). Manufacturing was more important in Chinatown (26.4 percent) than in the ethnoburb as well. On the other hand, both professional services and FIRE were far less important in Chinatown. Only 17.5 percent of Chinatown residents held managerial and professional jobs, and total white-collar jobs counted for 44.4 percent. The rate of ethnic entrepreneurship among Chinatown Chinese residents (7.2 percent) was also lower than that of the

TABLE 13. Industries Involved: Ethnoburb versus Chinatown (percentages), 1990

Industry	Ethnoburb	Chinatown
Retail trade	19.7	31.6
Manufacturing	19.0	26.4
Professional and services	17.7	15.2
FIRE	13.0	7.4
Wholesale	9.3	4.9
Communication and public utilities	6.0	2.6
Business and repair	4.0	3.1
Agriculture and construction	3.9	2.7
Personal services	3.3	2.7
Public administration	2.3	2.5
Entertainment and recreation	1.8	0.9

Source: U.S. Bureau of Census 1990 Public Use Microdata Samples (5 percent).
Note: Percentages may not add to 100 due to rounding.

ethnoburban Chinese. In fact, many Chinatown business owners or managers live in the ethnoburb. For them, Chinatown is only a place to work, not to live. Again, immigrants were more likely to own their businesses. Businesses owned by Chinatown residents were mostly in retail trade, manufacturing, or FIRE.

Chinatown is more self-contained spatially than the ethnoburb. This is evident in the lower vehicle ownership rates (70.1 percent, compared with the ethnoburb's 93.3 percent) and high reliance on public transportation. About one-fifth of Chinatown residents relied on public transportation to and from work, and another 8.1 percent walked. Such conditions are more likely to restrict the job opportunity among Chinatown residents. These facts again indicate the overall lower socioeconomic status of Chinatown Chinese and their constrained life circumstances and work choices.

Conclusion

The ethnoburb is a global economic outpost characterized by extensive international connections and striking internal stratification. As such, the ethnoburb differs dramatically from a typical ethnic enclave such as Los Angeles' downtown Chinatown. The ethnoburb's demographic and socioeconomic characteristics reflect its role in global economic activities. Internationalization of economic affairs and transnational financial and personnel flows have resulted in internal socioeconomic stratification within the ethnoburban Chinese population. Composed largely of immigrants from a wide variety of origins, the ethnoburban population reflects global geopolitical changes and shifts in U.S. immigration policy.

By and large, the ethnoburban Chinese are generally highly educated, relatively affluent, and well housed. The workforce is concentrated in sectors strongly impacted by economic restructuring and with close ties to international business. But despite its overall affluence, there are clear pockets of poverty, strongly linked to national origin, education, English language skills and labor force characteristics. These create class stratification within the ethnoburb, which was triggered by the influx of immigrant groups with dramatically different levels of financial and human capital. It is, however, a highly functional arrangement from the perspective of developing a spatially contiguous, economically integrated residential and business hub.

The main divisions are among Chinese from Taiwan and Hong Kong, those from China, and those from Indochina. The group from Indochina, who have come to Los Angeles mostly as a result of global geopolitical changes and national political and economic conflicts, have lower educational attainment and incomes. They face a greater likelihood of housing affordability problems.

They are concentrated in low-skill occupations, low-wage manufacturing sectors, and in retail services. This polarization on the basis of national origin and socioeconomic status finds its geographical expression in the spatial differentiation of the ethnoburban landscape. The poorest groups, from Indochina, are predominantly located in El Monte; the most affluent groups from Taiwan and Hong Kong reside in upscale communities. Nonetheless, the ethnoburb forms a stratified sociospatial structure that integrates the most marginalized groups from Indochina into the local immigrant community and the global economy.

The tightly knit character of the ethnoburb, and its relatively self-contained nature, slow the process of immigrant assimilation both for the marginalized groups and the affluent segments of the population. Ultimately, however, the superior educational and economic status of the Taiwan and Hong Kong portion of the Chinese population, and increasingly wealthy Chinese from Mainland China, can be expected to permit these groups to exert substantial control over their rate of assimilation. Their high socioeconomic status gives them more freedom of choice in the assimilation process, but it does not guarantee them a quick integration with the American mainstream. In contrast, the marginalized group from Indochina may be mired in closed ethnic economies and neighborhoods, which reduces their chances for upward mobility in the mainstream society.

7 Portraits of Ethnoburban Chinese

ince 1990 many changes have occurred in the ethnoburb due to shifting immigration policy, the rising economies in some immigrant source countries, and the faster pace of globalization brought about by the establishment and expansion of the World Trade Organization (WTO) and the signing of the North American Free Trade Agreement (NAFTA). As a result the ethnoburban demographic composition has become even more diverse among countries of origin (see Map 7). Socioeconomically, the status of Mainland Chinese residents has risen significantly, the result of both the rapid economic reforms in China and the Immigration Act of 1990, which favored employment-based immigration. Now Chinese residents in the ethnoburb themselves form a mosaic made up of American-born Chinese (ABCs), early suburbanite "old-timer" overseas Chinese, and newly arrived immigrants from different parts of the world. Their stories of survival and achievement resemble some of the traditional immigrant stories, where the individuals have humble beginnings but come to success through hard work. But the new stories have some distinct characteristics that differ from most of the earlier immigrant experiences. This chapter describes the trajectories of certain ethnoburban subgroups and includes a few detailed portraits of individual ethnoburban Chinese in order to personalize the "huddled masses" of the more than the 176,000 Chinese residents and business owners in the San Gabriel Valley in 2000. Through their stories, we can trace the links between their personal lives and the global, national, and local factors and events that have had an important impact on the lives of ethnoburbanites in general.

American-born Chinese: From "Model Minority" to Global Characters

Native-born Americans of Chinese descent, or ABCs, were among the earliest Asian American suburbanites who left inner-city neighborhoods in Los Angeles for Monterey Park. Many of them fit the "model minority" profile; they are well educated and hard working. They attended good schools, obtained good grades, and chose engineering as their careers. Others, including some women, eschewed the traditional stereotypes by making career choices different from their peers. Judy Chu, the three-term Monterey Park City councilwoman, for instance, became a well known and widely respected Chinese American elected official. Betty Tom Chu, a Chinese American lawyer turned banker, is a successful business woman.[1]

Born to Tom Kay Chu, a San Diego grower, and Yee Siu King, an immigrant from Canton (Guangzhou), Betty Chu received her Anglo first name because that was the only English name her mother could pronounce at the time they filled in Betty's birth certificate. As a nine-year old, Betty Chu was stunned to witness some Latino migrant workers being beaten on her father's farm. She later decided to become a lawyer in order to champion the cause of working-class people. After graduation from Grossmont High School, she went to University of Southern California, which she remembered as "the only college that would accept me" at the time; there she earned her law degree. Soon after graduation she became a practicing lawyer and joined a prestigious Los Angeles law firm specializing in immigration. One of the most memorable cases she worked on went all the way to a successful U.S. Supreme Court appeal. This case was considered to have given the impetus for Congress to debate a change in immigration policy and eventually led to the passage of the 1965 Immigration Act, which changed the fates of many Chinese immigrants and their families, along with changing faces of the nation.

Betty Chu was also active in the establishment of the first Chinese American bank in Southern California. In fact, her story is emblematic of the history of Chinese American banking development in Los Angeles County. In the 1950s a group of Chinese Americans, made up of both ABCs and old-timer Chinese immigrants, saw the escalating need for senior housing in Chinatown because the first generation of Chinese immigrants were aging. The group, including Chu, her classmate, attorney Kellogg Chan, another ABC, and his UC Berkeley-educated father, F. Chow Chan, were repeatedly denied loans from mainstream banks, due to persistent discrimination against minorities. They then decided to form their own financial institution by applying to establish a savings and loan association to take advantage of the strong tradition of saving in the Chinese community, but their efforts were repeatedly denied so they tried to establish a commercial bank instead. After a long, painful process of application, evaluation, and approval, Cathay Bank opened its door in the heart of LA Chinatown in 1962, with F. Chow Chan as its chairman of the board. But part of the group did not give up their fight on forming a savings and loan association despite the fact that their requests for approval were again met with total rejection. Then in 1969 Preston Martin (one of Chu's law professors at USC) was named chairman of the Federal Home Loan Bank by President Richard Nixon. Under Martin's leadership the Minority Bank Outreach Program launched a concerted effort to aid minorities. Betty Chu prepared the certificate of application for the first Chinese American saving and loan association in Los Angeles, East West Savings. East West Savings finally got its charter and opened for business in 1972. However, because leadership positions in business sectors were traditionally reserved for men in the largely patriarchal ethnic community of Chinatown, Betty Chu remained carefully in the background, in spite of her prominent role in the establishment of the bank. Chu recalled later, "I knew many persons in Chinatown would never deal with an S&L with a woman in a high-profile post. Things have changed greatly now toward women in business and banking" (NACAB 1992).

In the early 1980s Chu decided the time was right to start her own S&L in Monterey Park, which would capture the financial resources brought by new immigrants. She formed Trust Savings and Loan of San Gabriel Valley in 1981, served as its chairman and CEO, and became one of the first women in the nation to found a bank and serve in a top position. The bank grew at a fast pace in the 1980s. At its peak, Trust Savings and Loan had a total of eleven branches across LA County, most of them located in the San Gabriel Valley. The bank's two-story headquarters at 638 South Atlantic Blvd. in Monterey Park, just across the street from where Chu's family lived, was designed and built in the late 1980s by some of her board members who were architects. But in 1989 economic recession and the real estate depression hurt many businesses, including Trust Savings. Betty Chu had to sell some branches, including the bank headquarters, but she retained three San Gabriel Valley branches in Monterey Park, Arcadia, and West Covina. Chu eventually sold the bank to a group of Chinese investors in the 1990s. Another female Chinese American banker, an immigrant from Taiwan, Marina Wang, served as the president and CEO of the bank in the late 1990s.

Betty Chu was not only a working wife and mother, but also a devoted community activist. She served on many local and national committees, ranging from Monterey Park's Community Relations Commission to the Consumer Advisory Council for the Federal Reserve Board. An American-born Chinese, Chu is a courageous, resilient woman and a firm believer of American ideals, despite the difficulties she faced. Her legal and banking careers also reflect changing gender roles and the development of female leadership in the Chinese American community.

Immigrants from Taiwan: From Dual Citizens to Global Citizens

The overwhelming majority of immigrants from Taiwan or Hong Kong belong to the so-called "new overseas Chinese," who came to the United States after the 1965 Immigration Act. Those from Taiwan have been the key immigrant group in the ethnoburb since the 1970s. The first wave came as international students; they arrived in American universities as undergraduate or graduate students, earned their degrees, and started professional careers or businesses, moving rung by rung up the socioeconomic ladder. Many became professionals and successful business people. After fully establishing themselves in this country and becoming permanent residents or citizens, many sponsored their immediate family members and other relatives to settle in the United States. Other Taiwanese immigrants, however, moved to the United States seeking a safe haven for their investments and their families. They were the first large Chinese immigrant group to deviate from the immigration story of poor and humble beginnings. Instead, they came with financial resources and settled directly in suburban middle-class or upscale neighborhoods. Unlike previous generations, who most frequently settled in inner-city neighborhoods before moving up socioeconomically and moving out spatially, these new immigrants were suburban-bound to begin with; they had neither the desire nor the need to live in downtown Chinatown. Occupationally, many of these wealthy immigrants capitalized on the fast-growing export economy in the Newly Industrializing Countries (NICs) and Los Angeles' economic restructuring to establish flourishing niche industries and businesses of various sizes, ranging from toy manufacturing to business services. Some owned or managed businesses locally, while others specialized in international trade between the United States and other countries.

Many of these Taiwanese immigrants lived initially in the Monterey Park area, but then moved to the wealthier cities of Arcadia and San Marino or to the newer suburban cities in East San Gabriel Valley. Some of the wealthy settled in the latter cities immediately. They were also likely to start their businesses in the western and middle part of the valley, in Alhambra, El Monte, and South El Monte, where small offices and warehouses dominate the business landscape. However, when their businesses grew, and especially after Taiwan relaxed its rigid currency control rules in 1986, causing capital to flow to the United States, those locations could no longer suffice. Many immigrant Chinese businesses started to move to East San Gabriel Valley into places such as the City of Industry, where large warehouses and offices were more common. In fact, the City of Industry has become a high-tech computer assembly and distribution center, later known as the Silicon Valley of Southern California. The trade in computer parts between Taiwan's high-tech areas and the City of Industry was brisk until the Asian financial crisis in the late 1990s. The result of capital inflow from Taiwan also manifested itself in the flourishing Chinese banking sector during the 1980s and early 1990s, when new banks and branches of Taiwanese banks were established and Taiwanese control of local banks increased (bank interview 1999, nos. 8, 20; Flanigan 1998).

Despite many similarities, there are also clear differences between immigrants from Taiwan and Hong Kong. Immigrants from Taiwan were the largest immigrant group among ethnoburban Chinese residents until the 1990s, and their impact can easily been seen all over the valley. Monterey Park, for instance, used to be called Little Taipei and Mandarin Park, due to the large influx of Mandarin-speaking immigrants from Taiwan. Many ethnoburban businesses, especially those in consumer services, adopted famous and familiar Taiwan business names to gain name recognition among immigrants and visitors from Asian countries. Franchised Taiwanese businesses also shared in the ethnoburban consumer market. Many of the immigrants from Taiwan had prior experiences with community involvement or civic duties in Taiwan, and they brought a culture of civic participation with them to the United States. In addition, many immigrants have become American citizens. As a consequence, they have become one of the most active groups among all Chinese immigrants. Their involvement ranges from volunteering in various community events, to participating in their kids' school and PTA activities, serving on community committees, fundraising for political candidates, and running for offices at the local and state levels. Some Taiwanese American candidates have even brought Taiwanese campaign style to local elections. They have wrapped themselves with banners and paraded along the city streets in convertible limousines to attract the support of potential voters. This typical way to gain votes in Taiwan, called *bai piao*, literally means "begging for votes." Such activities raised some eyebrows among Americans unfamiliar with Taiwanese political campaign style.

There are also differences among Taiwanese immigrants themselves, especially between those whose families had lived in Taiwan for generations *(ben sheng ren)*, who are largely Min Nan (Taiwanese) speakers, and those who followed the Nationalist government to Taiwan after 1949 *(wai sheng ren)*, who are mainly Mandarin speakers. Differences between these two groups often show up in disagreements about home-country politics, especially on the future between Taiwan and Mainland China. The Taiwanese government set up the Second Overseas Chinese Cultural Center in the commercial part of El Monte, which caters to the needs and demands of newer Taiwanese immigrants, including *ben sheng ren*. The first cultural center, in Chinatown, caters to old timers, many of whom favor the eventual unification of Taiwan and Mainland China. Many Chinese immigrants from Taiwan hold dual citizenship in both the United States and Taiwan. This is possible because Taiwan (the Republic of China), like some other countries such as Australia, Canada, Great Britain, and

Israel, permits dual or multiple citizenship. The ramifications of this political structure are profound and confer on certain people the legal right to become active players in different parts of the world. Some immigrants with dual citizenship actively participate in electoral politics on both sides of the Pacific. For example, during all four Taiwanese democratic presidential elections—in March 1996, 2000, 2004, and 2008—Taiwanese citizens in the United States organized charter flights from both Los Angeles and San Francisco to carry voters to polling places in Taiwan because Taiwan election rules require voters to cast their votes in person. Their votes helped to oust the Nationalist government led by the Kuomintang (KMT), which had ruled Taiwan for fifty years, in March 2000 (*Chinese Daily News*, March 18–20, 2000). After the election and then the re-election of pro-independence President Chen Shui Bian of the Democratic Progress Party (DPP) in 2000 and 2004 respectively, the pro-independence movement in Taiwan and in the United States was energized. However, pro-Nationalist Taiwanese voters from the United States helped to bring about the victory of the KMT's Ma Ying-jeou, a Harvard-educated JD, who defeated the DPP candidate, Frank Hsieh (Hsieh Chang-ting), in the March 2008 election (Boudreau, 2008). This clearly demonstrates the transnational political involvement cross the Pacific.

Immigrants from Hong Kong: From Reluctant Exiles to Global Capitalists

Chinese immigrants from Hong Kong, on the other hand, face a different situation. As former residents of a colony of the United Kingdom, immigrants from Hong Kong had experienced the freedom to develop enterprises but never enjoyed the full benefits of democracy until the last few years of U.K. rule. They were nation-less people for a long time; they held special certificates issued by the U.K. government, but, with the exception of a few elite residents, they were never allowed to become U.K. citizens. With their legal status in limbo, they were not able to participate in electoral politics in any country. Moreover, residents of Hong Kong are polarized. They range from natives, members of the old-generation traditional Chinese capitalist elite who fled the mainland when the Communist government took over, to illiterate, unskilled workers who managed to escape the hardships on the mainland and seek a living in Hong Kong after 1949. This later group has steadily emigrated to the United States because of their ties to the old-timer Chinese Americans. As immigrants, many who come to the United States from Hong Kong are believed to have a refugee mentality similar to that of Southeast Asian refugees, but for different reasons. When the Chinese and U.K. governments started to negotiate the fate of Hong Kong in the early 1980s, this mentality manifested itself in a full-blown panic. People felt insecure and fled Hong Kong in large numbers. Many of the more well-to-do have been categorized as "reluctant exiles" because they did not want to leave the investment haven that Hong Kong represented, but felt compelled to do so. The old-generation elite, in particular, believed that to save themselves from communist rule they had to go into exile a second time. As a result, recent Hong Kong immigrants include wealthy people seeking a safe haven for their money and family. Actually, most of the really wealthy have resettled in other Commonwealth countries such as Canada and Australia. Vancouver, for instance, has been especially favored by Hong Kong tycoons and their offspring; they have invested heavily in places such as Pacific Place, a large-scale waterfront development in Vancouver.[2]

Nevertheless, many of the Hong Kong immigrants to the San Gabriel Valley are affluent and have a strong business background. They can immediately engage in international trade and other businesses, and they have positioned themselves on arrival as global capitalists. Dominic Ng, the president and CEO of the San Marino-based East West Bank (now with headquarter in Pasadena), for example, came from Hong Kong in 1977.[3] His training and experience helped him run a successful business when he was in his early thirties. Under his management since the early 1990s, the East West Bank was transformed from the first Chinese American savings and loan into LA's largest Chinese American commercial bank, a position it retained until the early 2000s when two other Chinese American banks merged. At the peak of the Asian financial crisis in 1998, an Indonesian Chinese (Syamsul Nursalim) and his family, who owned the bank, had to sell it in order to raise cash to save their other operations. Ng and his Chinese/Indonesian management team were able, within one month, to rally 150 Wall Street institutions, including Merrill Lynch, J. P. Morgan & Co., Oppenheimer and Wellington Fund, and wealthy individual investors, to buy out the bank for $238 million. Soon after, the bank went public and its stock began to be traded on the NASDAQ market. Since that time the East West Bank has become very aggressive in increasing total assets by expanding product lines, establishing new branches, and acquiring other banks.

Immigrants from Mainland China:
From Diverse Immigrants to Global Players

Of all ethnic Chinese immigrants in this country, immigrants from Mainland China have the longest history, but the majority of them actually came after the 1965 immigration law. Until the early 1980s many of these immigrants fit the traditional profile of newcomers who lacked formal education and high-level job skills. Such immigrants were typically sponsored by old-timer Chinese immigrants or their offspring and came for family reunification purposes.

Newer waves of immigrants from the mainland, however, resemble the profiles of those from Taiwan and Hong Kong. After the Cultural Revolution which lasted ten years, Chinese universities reopened in 1977 and admitted the first cohort of freshmen who had passed the reinstated entrance examination. At the end of 1978 the Communist Party adopted an economic reform policy that revived the economy and eventually led to an economic boom in Mainland China. As part of this economic policy package, many Chinese students went abroad to study, either sponsored by the government or on their own. The hope was that they would learn modern science and technology and return to serve the country. In fact, many settled in the Western countries where they studied. Also, the previously tightly controlled emigration policy was loosened, allowing Chinese citizens to migrate legally to other countries. Where it was once a special privilege for a Chinese citizen to hold a passport, it is now relatively easy for people to apply for one. Therefore, while the family-reunification type of immigration into the United States continues, newer waves also include a whole spectrum of people from students to wealthy investors and business people. In many aspects, these new groups from Mainland China repeat the experiences, two decades before, of immigrants from Taiwan and Hong Kong.

Earlier cohorts of Chinese students were likely to arrive in the United States without financial sources, so they had to rely on university assistantships or part-time jobs. By the time of the Tiananmen Square Incident in 1989, many of these students had graduated, held professional jobs, and enjoyed a high socioeconomic status; others were still in school. President George H. Bush signed an Executive Order that permitted all Chinese citizens who had entered the United States by April 11, 1990, to stay. Later President Bill Clinton signed the Chinese Student Protection Act, which allowed those students and other Chinese citizens to apply for permanent residency starting in July 1, 1993. Most people in this group, reportedly more than 100,000, got their green cards late that year and were eligible to apply for citizenship by 1998.

One of the ramifications of their becoming U.S. citizens, however, was the loss of their privileges and rights in the People's Republic of China. Unlike the Taiwanese government, the Mainland Chinese government makes dual citizenship illegal. All naturalized U.S. citizens from Mainland China automatically relinquish their PRC citizenship. One immediate result is that these new U.S. citizens must apply for entry visas when they visit their families and friends or conduct business or professional exchanges in Mainland China. But many of them have already been active players in the economic exchange between the two countries. It will be interesting to see what impact they may have in the political arena in their native land. Mainland Chinese, no less than their Taiwanese counterparts, pay close attention to homeland politics, which includes the relationship across the Taiwan Strait, so sometimes tensions arise between these two groups of Chinese Americans. On the other hand, it may be anticipated that some of these new U.S. citizens, like the earlier immigrants from Taiwan, will actively participate in American electoral politics as voters, as candidates, and increasingly as donors because of their improved financial situation.

Another direct consequence of this new cohort of naturalized U.S. citizens is an anticipated new wave of immigration from Mainland China through chain migration. U.S. citizens can bring their immediate family members on a non-quota basis, while continuing to apply for entry permits for other members of their extended families. This has contributed to continuous growth in the San Gabriel Valley cities, especially of those who do not have a command of English or who lack formal education or the professional credentials recognized by the U.S. government or the professions (such as medicine and dentistry). On the other hand, the economic boom on the mainland has produced a new elite class that has gotten rich via land speculation and other forms of capital accumulation since the late 1980s. Some of them have joined the immigration wave to the United States, while others have invested in U.S. real estate by purchasing houses in upscale residential neighborhoods from Arcadia and San Marino to the coastal cities in Southern California. Reportedly some have completed the deals by cash transactions.

Given these changing economic circumstances, it is not surprising that the immigrants from Mainland China are probably the most stratified subgroup of Chinese immigrants in the ethnoburb. There are undocumented immigrants trapped in the ethnic economy with dead-end jobs and no benefits. Some were professionals in China but cannot find equivalent jobs, because their credentials are unrecognized here in the United States. They take whatever jobs they can find and suffer a loss of status. At the other end of the spectrum, some are active players in the globalized economy who engage in the import/export trade or investment in China. Like their counterparts from Taiwan or Hong Kong, initially they are likely to establish small enterprises in cities in West San Gabriel Valley such as Alhambra, then move eastward when their businesses grow. Similar patterns of eastward movement can also be seen in their residential settlement.

As examples, both Mr. L and Mr. S are native Shanghainese, each married with one daughter. In China they enjoyed professional jobs as a stage director and a stage designer, respectively. Both immigrated to the United States in the

1980s for the sake of their daughters' futures. Although Mr. S came under the category of "professionals with exceptional abilities," his family and Mr. L's had to work hard in jobs outside their professions. Along with a business partner, Mr. and Mrs. L established a small garment shop, finding a niche producing large-sized women clothes for the U.S. domestic market. Mr. S worked in a watch-making factory for many years before getting a job with a Mainland Chinese enterprise. Mrs. S worked in various restaurants and snack shops. The two families lived in one-bedroom apartments in Monterey Park and Alhambra, respectively. Mr. and Mrs. S actually slept on the living room floor for years so that their daughter could live and study in their bedroom. Later, the daughters of both families graduated from the UCLA and found professional jobs. Both families finally settled in West Covina, purchasing their own single-family houses in the mid-1990s. Despite their hardships, these two families never gave up their professions and made tremendous efforts to preserve their contact with the arts. They were actively engaged in local Chinese cultural activities and eventually found success in the cultural exchanges between the United States and China. In addition to their day jobs, Mr. and Mrs. L shot several TV soap operas, including one portraying the lives of Chinese immigrants in Los Angeles that was widely broadcast in China. Mr. S organized several major events, including the visit of Brigham Young University's dance troupe to Shanghai. Their stories of survival and eventual success stand for the many stories of those who suffered a loss of status but never gave up hope.

A Transnational Community

Unlike traditional immigrants of European origin whose move to the United States was mostly unidirectional and who returned to their home countries only as visitors, many of these new Chinese immigrants can be called "transmigrants," individuals whose ties expand across national borders. These truly unconventional migrants include the so-called astronauts who set up households on both coasts of the Pacific and then shuttle between LA and Asia to conduct business activities. Unlike their sojourning predecessors who crossed the Pacific by sea in order to visit their families in China, these Chinese transmigrants jet cross the Pacific to visit their families in Los Angeles. The problems associated with such family patterns include family instability and even divorce.

Another form of the nontraditional transmigrant family is the phenomenon of "parachute kids," those teenage "little overseas students," whose parents are in Asia most the time, while they live alone in houses purchased by their parents or under the guardianship of relatives or family friends in the San

Gabriel Valley. Unlike the astronaut families, families with parachute kids keep the husband-wife relationship largely intact, but there is distancing and sometimes even alienation of the parents from their offspring. Youngsters are left alone to cope with American education and their bicultural identity without daily parental guidance. The social problems associated with this phenomenon are another hot topic among Chinese and mainstream communities alike. The wealthy "home alone" children are often the target of criminals, especially kidnappers. Sometimes these kidnappings and recovery efforts crisscross national boundaries, reflecting the nature of the ethnoburb as a transnational community. In one well-publicized case, a seventeen-year-old student at San Marino High School was kidnapped and held eighteen days before being rescued by FBI agents. Fu Shun Chen, the father of the kidnapped student Johnny Kuan Na Chen, is the owner of the Landwin Corp., which has offices in both Taiwan and Temple City. Their family residence is in San Marino, but the mother reportedly spends a lot of time in Taiwan with the father. The younger Chen was abducted at gunpoint on December 15, 1998, when both of his parents were in Taiwan, and was held in a Temple City house with his hands and feet chained and his eyes and mouth covered by duct tape. The kidnappers called his father in Taiwan and demanded $1.5 million in ransom. The father immediately reported the abduction to San Marino police, then paid one-third of the amount requested in Fuzhou, China, where two of the suspects were arrested after receiving the ransom. Under investigation by the FBI and with the help of police forces in both China and Taiwan, two more suspects from Temple City and New York City were arrested. They were charged with hostage-taking. These suspects had been recruited by a third man who had planned the kidnapping for at least two months. In a similar but unrelated case, six Chinese nationals were arraigned in Pasadena on charges of kidnapping a nine-year-old girl from South Pasadena on December 22, 1998, for a $200,000 ransom. One of the suspects picked up the ransom money and dropped the girl off in Rosemead. Kidnapping children of the rich is a popular crime in Taiwan and appears to be increasing in the ethnoburb, where parachute kids make easy targets (*Los Angeles Times*, January 5, 1999, B1–B2). A related problem associated with parachute kids is that some join gangs and become involved in criminal activities. This problem, depicted in the 2002 Sundance Film Festival winner, *Better Luck Tomorrow*, has also elicited concern among the Chinese American and mainstream communities.

Originally a phenomenon mainly among immigrants from Taiwan and Hong Kong, parachute kids are increasingly common among Mainland Chinese families (*People's Daily Overseas Edition* 2000, 4). Even after the change in 1996 in the immigration law, which prohibits the enrollment of foreign students (F-1 visa holders) in American public elementary and middle schools and severely restricts their enrollment in public high schools, the trend continues as wealthy parents enroll their children in private schools instead. These new parachute kids from Mainland China are mainly concentrated in the Los Angeles area, including the San Gabriel Valley, where there are large numbers of Chinese attorneys and language schools, which make it easier to settle these "little overseas students."

Meanwhile, many of the earlier generations of parachute kids, who came from Taiwan or Hong Kong in the 1970s and 1980s, have graduated from college, inherited their family businesses, or started their own. Known as "second-generation bosses" *(er shi zhu)* in the Chinese business community, some of them were born with silver spoons in their mouths and never experienced financial difficulties (bank 1999, nos. 7, 17). They are the offspring of the generation that profited from the economic prosperity in Taiwan and Hong Kong. Their way of life and business ideals differ from those who came before, and they plunge eagerly into the highly competitive world of American and global businesses. As an example, while many of the current owners or top executives in the Chinese banking sector in Los Angeles are immigrants from Taiwan and Hong Kong, the *er shi zhu* generation are also among the owners of those banks.

From Laundryman to Banker

The story of Henry Hwang, an immigrant and the founder and former president/CEO of Far East National Bank, stands for many successful ethnoburban immigrant stories, but it also illustrates the ways in which racial tensions arise in this new immigrant situation and how they are related not only to the economic cycles of the region, but to the fear of Asia's growing power in the global economy.[4]

Henry Y. Hwang was born and raised in pre-communist China in Shanghai, the capitalist adventurers' haven in the late nineteenth-mid-twentieth centuries, for which it was nicknamed the Paris of the Orient. From an affluent family background, Hwang had opportunities to visit a banker's mansion during his boyhood years and thought he would like to be a banker himself when he grew up. Hwang's path to becoming a banker, however, was not easy.

He attended college in Shanghai, but had to finish his BA degree in political science at Taiwan National University after fleeing the mainland during the revolution. In 1950 he came to the United States as a student and landed in a small town in Oregon, where he majored in international relations at Linfield College. Upon receiving his second BA degree, he drove to Berkeley, CA, hoping to land a job, a goal that proved difficult. By this time his father had lost his fortune, and Hwang was just another penniless immigrant. Eventually he was offered a job, but with the precondition that he relocate to Los Angeles. Hwang's answer was, "I don't know where LA is, but I'm going!" During his first few years in LA, Hwang operated a dry cleaning and laundry store and attended the MBA program in accounting at USC, where he met his future wife, Dorothy Huang, then a music major.

Hwang later became a certified public accountant and started his own practice in Los Angeles in 1960. As the owner of the first Chinese immigrant CPA firm in Southern California, he started off with only one regular client and a billing of $50 per month. He gradually built a clientele largely composed of Caucasian small business owners, who placed their trust in him. Some of these clients became the backers of his own bank in 1973, when there were only two small Chinese American banks in Los Angeles. Both were perceived as mainly catering to old-timer Cantonese-speaking Chinese, and neither could fulfill the needs of the increasing number of newer Mandarin-speaking immigrants. Hwang gathered a group of ten investors and filed an application to establish the nation's first Chinese immigrant-owned federally chartered bank. By October 1973 the group was granted preliminary approval to sell stock for its initial capital, but the stock market crash two months later made raising capital difficult. In addition, Hwang himself had neither large financial resource on his own nor prior banking experiences. He went to Taiwan to seek help and was welcomed by some tycoons who wanted to invest in his bank. The catch was that they required Hwang to hire their children, then studying in the United States, as directors on his bank's board. Hwang refused and came back empty-handed. He was determined to establish a true American enterprise, not one relying on family networks as traditional ethnic Chinese enterprises often do. He had only one option: to raise capital locally. His clients were very supportive of his mission, and the last $50,000 of the initial capital of $1.5 million reached him the day before the deadline. The Far East National Bank (FENB) opened its door in December 1974 in a rented trailer building on the edge of Chinatown. Hwang served as chairman of the board.

The initial years of operation for FENB were not very smooth due to poor management. Hwang was still focused on his CPA firm, and some senior bank personnel allegedly developed disreputable business connections. In 1976 Hwang was kidnapped and released only after a ransom was paid. By 1978 he decided to sell his CPA firm and fully to devote his time and energy to the bank. With Hwang as president, which continued until FENB was acquired by Bank SinoPac of Taiwan in 1997, the bank became strong and profitable and was rated among the highest-performing banks in the nation in the 1980s and 1990s.

Hwang earned many awards for his business acumen, including the 1986 Financial Advocate of the Year from the Small Business Administration, and he was active in a number of bankers' trade associations at the local, state, and national levels. Once among the highest-paid bankers in the nation, Hwang lived with his family in the upscale neighborhood of San Marino for a long time.

Regarding his success, Hwang said:

> What does FENB stand for? Fast, Efficient, Nicest Bank. Our mission—"Fulfilling Your American Dream"—is a reflection of my own hopes and aspiration as an immigrant American. I can never forget how this country enabled me to achieve my greatest ambitions, and I want to help others—immigrants and native-born alike—to realize that same potential. (Author interview, August 1999)

In addition to his business activities, Hwang also gave generous donations and served on the boards of many mainstream nonprofit organizations, such as the YMCA, the Catholic Charities, and the Boy Scouts of America. His commitment to help others not only gained him business success, but public recognition. He was appointed to numerous positions at the local and national levels, including the White House Advisory Committee on Trade Negotiations by President Ronald Reagan in 1984 and the Minority Enterprise Development Advisory Council by the secretary of commerce in 1989.

As a naturalized citizen, Hwang strongly believes in participation in American politics. He has been active in electoral politics and has financially backed candidates who have shared his vision. A lifetime Republican, Hwang has donated money to both major parties. Although it is not uncommon that business people contribute to both political parties, it was a $10,000 contribution to the Democrats during the 1996 presidential campaign, in addition to large deposits from Mainland China to FENB, which brought him problems.

Accused of donating money that might have come from the Chinese government, Hwang's bank became the subject of years of investigation by federal financial regulators and the FBI. The *New York Times* ran a front-page article on May 12, 1999, entitled "China sent cash to U.S. bank, with suspicions slow to rise," that included a photo of Hwang and a long description of his "uncooperative" stance during the investigation. This article was placed side by side with another article, which reported on the guilty plea on May 11, 1999, of former Democratic fundraiser Johnny Chung for campaign-related bank- and tax-fraud allegations. This juxtaposition strongly implied, and in Hwang's opinion was intended to create, the impression that the two cases were actually related.

In early August 1999, when I interviewed Hwang, he had suffered the bad publicity from this *New York Times* article, and other Chinese Americans had also been negatively portrayed in the Cox Report, which alleged that many Chinese students and professionals were working as spies for Mainland China. There was also the Wen Ho Lee case. During Hwang's interview with me, he rebutted point by point the allegations made against him and the bank. His anger and disbelief over the way the reporters treated him, his business associate, and the bank were still very apparent. He had no doubt that he was targeted because of his ethnic background. This incident illustrates that, starting in the 1990s, prominent leaders of the maturing ethnoburb were becoming susceptible to negative political and financial scrutiny on a national level.

That this happened to Hwang can be traced back to his longtime mission of expanding trade across the Pacific Ocean, but it also occurred because of particular international developments, namely, the growing economic power of the Pacific Rim countries. In addition to Hwang's strong commitment to his adopted country, he also had a desire to help his native land. The poor children and bad living conditions he witnessed when he returned, after more than three decades, to visit Mainland China in the early 1980s haunted him and made him determined to contribute to China's modernization. After a failed attempt to set up a mutual fund to help China, he decided to use his position as a businessman to encourage international trade between the United States and China. He wished to help American enterprises enter China's huge market, a development that would help raise the living standards for Chinese people. He went to China several times, but his visits were not fruitful due to his lack of personal connections and the political clout necessary to developing business in China at the time.

His chance came when Ms. X walked into his office in the late 1980s. Unlike some other job seekers, Ms. X did not boast of her credentials or connections, despite the fact that she was the daughter of a high-ranking military official in China. She just asked for an opportunity to try. Hwang did not have high expectations for her—she had no prior banking experience—but he gave her a ninety-day probation period. After all, he pointed out, "neither did I when I started." In fact, it is not uncommon for local Chinese banks to occasionally hire someone without banking experience but with business or political connections, especially in the start-up phase or when dealing with a not-fully-developed market economy like China. To everyone's surprise, the well-connected Ms. X delivered unexpected results, attracting deposits from Chinese firms in Los Angeles to the FENB and helping the bank establish a representative office in Beijing, one of the earliest Mainland China offices among LA's Chinese American banks. Ms. X worked diligently and provided her clients with excellent service, according to Hwang, and he promoted her to a top position at the bank by the mid-1990s.

As the result of Ms. X's work, a total of $92 million was reportedly wire-transferred from various sources in China to FENB, including from a Hong Kong-based investment firm that American officials suspected was associated with Chinese intelligence agencies or controlled by the Chinese government. U.S. officials suspected that the money was intended to pay for Chinese intelligence operations, buy sensitive military technology, make illicit political contributions, launder money, or possibly hide the private fortunes of certain Chinese officials. Such suspicions prompted several extensive investigations by the Office of the Comptroller of the Currency, Federal Reserve Bank, and the FBI, starting in spring 1996. Both Hwang and Ms. X denied any wrongdoing. No charges were brought, and no regulatory actions were taken against the FENB. "We walked out clean after every single investigation," according to Hwang.

Suspicions and allegations, however, continued to haunt Ms. X and Hwang. They and FENB were suspected of involvement in the 1996 presidential election fundraising scandal, largely because Ms. X is a relative by marriage of Liu Chao-ying, who reportedly was the conduit for a $300,000 of Chinese military intelligence money given to the DNC via Johnny Chung. Ms. X categorically denied that she was ever close to Liu Chao-ying. Toward the end of the investigation, two *New York Times* reporters conducted an interview with Hwang and Ms. X. Although the reporters had received a leaked copy of the official investigation report, they pretended to have no prior knowledge about the investigation and just wanted to know the perspective of Hwang and Ms. X. On May 12, their hostile front-page article alluded to a continuing suspicion of FENB, even with regard to allegations that had not been substantiated or that had been cleared by previous government investigations.

The *New York Times'* article had a strongly negative impact on Hwang, Ms. X, and FENB. Hwang, then seventy, retired from the bank two months after the article was published and started a new business, Rock-Asia Capital Group, Ltd. However, business was slow because many potential customers, including some of his long-time clients, were reluctant to deal with him because of the bad publicity. Hwang was frustrated by what happened to him. He said that his son, Tony Award-winning playwright David Henry Hwang, a devoted Democrat, had warned him long ago about racism. David Hwang had asked his dad, "Why do you support these guys [certain Republicans]? They don't like you, they will get you sometime." The elder Hwang, a firm believer of the system and the American Dream, could not believe such things could ever happen to him, a loyal American citizen. He felt betrayed by the reporters who had pretended to be impartial and objective but whom he felt had destroyed the reputations of FENB, Ms. X, and himself. Hwang had since been thinking about how to counter the Chinese-bashing, and he was committed to fighting racism in this country.

What happened to Henry Hwang suggests that he may not only be a victim of vicious partisan politics, a fallout of the 1996 presidential election, but as a Chinese American, he was also subject to "new-fashioned" racism. Racism against racial and ethnic minorities, including Asians, has a long history in America, and fears of the "Yellow Peril" have not died in reference to the competition for jobs and in various racial and political ideologies. But contemporary racism may arise for different reasons and take new forms. The rise of the Asian economy in recent decades has produced an ambivalent reaction, and it has often had the effect of increasing in racist and nativist attitudes and actions against Asian Americans. Economic restructuring and large influx of Japanese cars in the 1980s, for instance, resulted in high unemployment in the traditional auto-manufacturing region. Unemployed workers felt that the Japanese were taking their jobs away. The most extreme expression of this sentiment surfaced when in 1982 two white auto workers who had lost their jobs beat to death Vincent Chin, a Chinese American man they had mistaken for a Japanese.

Anti-Asian American sentiments in general, and anti-Chinese ones in particular, have resurfaced in recent years as part of a fear that economic power may serve the interests of the People's Republic of China in the rivalry between the PRC and the United States in the global economic and political arena. After the 1996 presidential election, Asian Americans were the primary targets of the campaign donation scandal investigations. The heart of the allegations stemmed from a suspicion that donations by Asian Americans were channeling money from the PRC to influence the U.S. election. Despite a lack of concrete evidence, the 1999 Congressional Cox Report alleged that many Chinese students, scholars, and professionals were serving as spies for the PRC, and many Chinese and Chinese American businesses in the United States were simply fronts for the Chinese intelligence agency. The now infamous case of Wen Ho Lee illustrates how, in the minds of many Asian Americans and his supporters, Chinese Americans have been investigated for espionage because of their race. Potentially suspects for espionage and treason based on race and ethnicity alone, Asian Americans have had their constitutional rights denied before. During World War II, Japanese American loyalty to the United States was seriously questioned, which resulted in the internment of Japanese Americans without due process of law.

In light of the persistence of racism in whatever form it may take, is it any wonder that the rise of ethnoburb as a global outpost and the apparent success of Chinese businesses that rely on transnational connections have worked against the Chinese? This development raises some doubts about whether the ethnoburb will have a significant impact on racial power relations in the future. Some ethnoburban Chinese, in spite of their loyalty to America and their investment in its future, will continue to attract scrutiny and suspicion, if not because of their country of origin or heritage, then for their economic acumen. Henry Hwang's case may be just one of many stories, most untold.

Related to Hwang's story is the role of the mass media in American racialized power relations. An analogy between the media coverage of Henry Hwang and its coverage of the Wen Ho Lee case can easily be drawn and raises a number of questions. It is a premise of American political life that any American is presumed innocent until proven guilty, but is this possible when an all-out media blitz is used to heighten hysteria and suspicions, and this in turn results in character assassination? Is it fair to engage in a defamatory trial in the court of public opinion, when official investigations had already cleared the people involved? Or are these tactics only thinly veiled forms of racial profiling?

The experience of Henry Hwang not only shows that as a society, we have a long way to go, but also suggests that while the ethnoburb has undeniably become a unique part of the American urban mosaic, its continuing growth may very likely generate more concerns and even conflicts between different interest groups based on ethnic or class affiliation, national interests, and global geopolitics.

PART 3

Ethnoburbs of North America

8 Opportunities and Challenges for Ethnoburbs

This book has examined the spatial transformation of LA's Chinese community from downtown Chinatown to the San Gabriel Valley. It has proposed a model for this new suburban ethnic settlement—the ethnoburb—which has arisen as the result of changing global geopolitics and economic restructuring; national immigration and trade policies; and local demographic, economic, and political circumstances. It then operationalizes the ethnoburb framework by using secondary demographic and economic data, surveys, and interviews to trace the historical evolution of Chinese settlement; analyzes the formation and manifestation of the San Gabriel Valley ethnoburb; and profiles the demography, socioeconomic features, and microgeography of the Chinese ethnoburb, while briefly comparing the ethnoburb and LA's downtown Chinatown in order to demonstrate that the ethnoburb does indeed stand in sharp contrast to more traditional ethnic enclaves. Finally, it offers portraits of ethnoburban Chinese of different backgrounds to personify the diverse experiences within the ethnoburb.

This final chapter examines once again the primary findings of the book and their implication for the San Gabriel Valley Chinese ethnoburb, followed by descriptions of ethnoburbs in other locales. It will conclude with a review of the opportunities and challenges faced by American society and particular localities in the contexts of suburban ethnic concentrations, immigrants' rights and challenges, and urban racial and ethnic formation.

The New Ethnic Community in Urban America

Ethnoburbs are created by ethnic minority groups. Through a combination of global geopolitics and economic forces, U.S. national policies and local demographics, as well as socioeconomic and political shifts, ethnoburbs have emerged as a new and important form of suburban ethnic settlement.

Ethnoburbs differ in many ways from the traditional types of ethnic settlement, the ghetto and the enclave. They are located in the suburbs, not the central city, occupy larger geographical areas, attract a diverse array of ethnic minority populations, and have lower ethnic densities than ghettos or enclaves. The dynamics of ethnoburb formation also differ from those of ghettos and enclaves. Although ethnoburbs and contemporary ethnic enclaves are both influenced by general trends, such as economic restructuring and social polarization, these trends impact the two types of ethnic community differently. Ethnoburbs have been set up deliberately under the impulse of these broader contexts in order to participate in the new globalized economy and personnel flows, whereas changes inside enclaves are largely passive responses to such social and economic restructuring. The economic activities and business transactions conducted in ethnoburbs are intentionally created as an element within the global economy, whereas enclaves have historically received overseas investment, and continue to do so, mostly because of their existing ethnic business establishment or because of their location within downtown areas targeted for foreign investment and urban renewal. Enclaves like the downtown Chinatown in LA cannot expect to keep pace, match the scale, or play the role that ethnoburbs like the San Gabriel Valley do in the global economy, particularly with respect to international capital flows. And because of these different dynamics, both the economic status and the occupational structure of ethnoburban residents are more highly stratified than they are in ghettos and enclaves. Thus millionaires and the penniless together make up the contemporary wave of immigrants; both settle in the ethnoburb, but they play different roles in economic and community affairs.

The social construction of race and the racialization process differ in ethnoburbs from the way they proceed in enclaves or ghettos. The racialization dynamic is intensified during ethnoburb emergence and growth, due to increased competition between existing residents and businesses and the ethnic newcomers who enter the traditional turf of white Americans—the suburbs. Minority people in ethnoburbs have more interactions with other groups, but continue to manifest ethnic affinity through the establishment of the ethnoburb itself. Despite class differences and conflicts within the ethnic group, common challenges and problems often unite the new residents in struggles to assert their rights and to reinforce group consciousness and identity.

Chinese immigrants have been among the most racialized minorities historically in American society. Constrained economically, legally, and socially, they coped by forming enclaves, such as Chinatown, and created occupational niches that did not directly compete with white Americans. Beginning in the 1960s, the Chinese population suburbanized. However, unlike the scenarios predicted by traditional models, suburbanization of the Chinese in Los Angeles was not accompanied by complete spatial assimilation, nor did only the more affluent segments of the Chinese community move to the suburbs. Instead, there was a spatial transformation of the Chinese community. While downtown Chinatown persisted, suburban areas, characterized by high concentrations of Chinese population, strong contrasts in socioeconomic status, expanding Chinese-owned businesses and industrial districts, and high levels of Chinese participation in local politics emerged.

The San Gabriel Valley ethnoburb has leap-frogged over the traditional multistep migration from urban enclave to suburban living. The ethnoburb expanded eastward between Interstate 10 on the north and State Highway 60 on the south (see Map 2). Its original site—Monterey Park—first experienced a large wave of Chinese residents moving in, followed by Chinese businesses. In other residential areas, like the eastern district communities of Hacienda Heights and Rowland Heights, certain key Chinese businesses and institutions promoted Chinese residential concentrations by establishing business and religious institutions, thus stimulating the growth and expansion of the ethnoburb toward the East San Gabriel Valley.

The ethnic economy not only plays an important role in an ethnoburb's socioeconomic structure, but, depending on its size, type, and function, it contributes importantly to the region's role in the national and global economies. An ethnoburb acts as a global economic outpost through its business transactions, capital circulation, and personnel flows of both entrepreneurs and laborers.

The San Gabriel Valley ethnoburb is not, however, a homogeneous community. Significant socioeconomic differences exist inside it, based primarily on place of origin. People from Hong Kong and Taiwan are most likely to be well educated, speak English well, work in white-collar jobs, and earn a high income; those from Southeast Asian countries are on the opposite end of the spectrum, while those from Mainland China fall somewhere in between. These socioeconomic differences, filtered through American urban housing dynamics, have their geographical expressions in local neighborhoods, which make the ethnoburb an urban mosaic. Affluent Chinese live next to wealthy white Americans in upscale neighborhoods like Arcadia and San Marino, whereas the less affluent mix with largely working- or middle-class Latinos in El Monte and South El Monte.

Unlike ethnic enclaves and ghettos, in which a relatively small ethnic elite population traditionally dominated social life and economic activities and currently jockeys for leadership position with progressive professional organizations, the social hierarchy inside the ethnoburb is more fragmented. Nobody can claim control over the entire multiethnic community, but any individual or organization may potentially play an important role as an agent of social change. This is yet another way in which the ethnoburb demonstrates that it is a new type of ethnic community.

The future of the Chinese ethnoburb depends on many factors beyond the control of the local Chinese American population. As long as globalization continues to generate immigrant inflows and the ethnic economy remains incorporated into the globalized American economy, the San Gabriel Valley ethnoburb will sustain itself and prosper. Therefore, the eastward development path manifested in the 1990s, as illustrated in Map 2, is likely to continue in the twenty-first century. However, the ethnoburb may face limits to its expansion. The San Gabriel Mountains block northward expansion, while downtown and East LA to the west are already saturated. Pomona and San Bernadino to the east are markedly less affluent and lack the kind of residential neighborhoods and good school districts preferred by the more affluent ethnoburban Chinese. But the cheaper land prices in those inland areas may attract savvy Chinese investors to create new centers of ethnic Chinese economic activities. Beyond the San Gabriel Valley, the ethnoburb has already expanded, and is likely expanding further, through a pattern of leap-frog development to areas like Artesia and Cerritos in LA County and Irvine in Orange County. Those areas are ethnically mixed and have many Asian businesses to form the nuclei for further ethnoburb development. Moreover, as a result of heated competition in Southern California, some Chinese businesses and people are also moving northward to the San Francisco Bay Area, eastward toward the Phoenix area, or to altogether different metropolitan areas in the country.

Ethnoburbs in Other North American Cities

The dynamics underlying the formation of an ethnoburb do not just happen in Los Angeles and not even just in the United States. In fact, similar suburban concentrations of minority population and business have occurred in other major North American metropolitan areas and the other major immigrant-receiving countries on the Pacific Rim, Australia and New Zealand (see W. Li 2006). Although the ethnoburb model was developed based on the Chinese community in Los Angeles, it has been surfacing in other localities. This section provides vignettes of ethnoburb development in two metropolitan areas in the United States and Canada respectively.[1] Research on some of these communities is flourishing, and the media report similar patterns involving various ethnic groups in different metropolitan areas. Examples include the Chinese in Houston, the San Francisco Bay Area, Toronto, and Vancouver; the Chinese, Koreans, and Asian Indians in the suburban New York/New Jersey region, and the Vietnamese of Northern Virginia.[2]

Moreover, the ethnoburb itself may take different forms in different localities. Ethnoburbs and other types of ethnic communities exist on a continuum. Some communities may not have become ethnoburbs completely, but function as an intermediate type between the more traditional enclave or ghetto and an ethnoburb. Others may fall closer to an intermediate type between the prototypical ethnoburb and the traditional suburb. A typology can be developed to delineate the characteristics according to which the various forms of ethnic communities differ.

Ethnoburbs in U.S. Cities

"The best examples of the suburbanization of Asian Americans can be seen in areas surrounding Los Angeles, San Francisco, and New York" (T. Fong 1998, 46–47). New York and the San Francisco Bay Area contain even larger numbers of Chinese than the LA area: 537,293 in New York and 518,107 in the Bay Area, compared with 477,075 in Los Angeles as of 2000. The Chinese account for 2.5 percent of total population in New York, 2.9 percent in Los Angeles, and 7.4 percent in San Francisco-Oakland-San Jose Consolidated Metropolitan Statistical Area.[3]

Like Los Angeles, the cities of San Francisco and New York both have Chinatowns that date back to the nineteenth century. What differentiates these two metro areas from Los Angeles is that their Chinatowns continue to house large numbers of Chinese residents, including many new immigrants, and to support vibrant Chinese ethnic business activities, in addition to serving as principal tourist attractions in their areas.[4] As in the case of the San Gabriel Valley, there are also suburban concentrations of Chinese in these two metro areas, and these also include large numbers of new immigrants who settled there directly.

In the New York area, almost 140,000 Chinese people resided in Queens County in 2000, making it the county that housed the third largest Chinese population in the nation after Los Angeles County and San Francisco County. The Chinese are concentrated in the Flushing and Elmhurst-Corona areas. Although, as a borough of New York City, Queens is not technically a suburb, the fact that newly arrived Chinese immigrants have come here directly represents the trend outward, bypassing Chinatown in downtown Manhattan. The growth in the number of Chinese residents and businesses along with the IRT No.7 subway line has caused the line to be nicknamed the Orient Express. Ethnic banks, real estate agents, and business organizations have played important roles in attracting more minority residents and businesses to Queens. In downtown Flushing, for example, some Chinese/Taiwanese Americans bought almost all of the existing businesses along Main Street and revitalized its depressed commercial area. At the same time, large numbers of ethnic realtors promoted concentrations of minority residents in the Flushing area (bank interview 1999, no.18; Smith 1995). These new concentrations have been categorized by academic studies and are known to locals as Satellite Chinatowns. New scholarship, however, questions whether these communities are truly clones of the Manhattan Chinatown, only differentiated by size and location, or whether they represent a transitional form of ethnic community, in sharp contrast to the old Chinatown. H. Chen's *Chinatown No More*, published in 1992, reaches conclusions similar to those in this book. The author found that "such common stereotypes as 'Flushing is a new Chinatown' are not appropriate...[and do] not describe the Queens Chinese communities in the mixed neighborhoods of Flushing and Elmhurst" (H. Chen 1992, x).

San Francisco, known as the "old good mountain" *(jiu jin shan)* among the global Chinese diaspora, has the earliest and largest Chinatown in the United States. It still is home to the highest percentages of Chinese and Asian Americans in the continental United States, at 61.3 percent in 2000.[5] Across the Bay, Oakland also has an old Chinatown, which has recently been undergoing revitalization. In the 1950s and 1960s, however, Asian Americans started to move to other parts of the Bay Area, including the Peninsula, East Bay and South Bay, for better job opportunities and newer, improved living environments. Many of the early suburbanites were American-born Chinese. When Santa Clara Valley, located in the South Bay and formerly known as Valley of the Heart's Delight, became Silicon Valley, the epicenter of American high-tech industries, it drew even more Asian immigrants, Chinese among them, to work and settle in the valley. Just as the valley transformed from a place growing plums to one producing Apple computers, the valley's residents have also changed from a "lily white" to a rainbow population. By 2000, 115,781 Chinese lived in Santa Clara County, a 75.6 percent increase from 1990. These Chinese are largely entrepreneurs, executives, engineers, and professionals, but they are also cheaply paid laborers working in high-tech industries. They came and continue to come primarily for the jobs, but this is followed by the pull of family reunification, so much so that Silicon Valley's integrated circuit (IC) industry has been nicknamed "Indian and Chinese" industry (Saxenian 1999, v). The very presence of Chinese and other Asian American people has also helped to transform Silicon Valley cities such as Cupertino, Fremont, Milpitas, Mountain View, Santa Clara, and Sunnyvale from bedroom suburbs to high-tech agglomerations with multiracial neighborhoods. Asian concentrations, especially in cities such as Cupertino and Fremont, can be primarily attributed to the superior quality of their schools: two of the best high schools in California, Monte Vista High and Mission San Jose High, are located in Cupertino and Fremont, respectively. The relative concentrations of Chinese residents and their businesses in these cities have made a clear imprint on the local commercial landscape in the large shopping centers. These businesses range from Chinese bank branches to chain supermarkets to bakeries and jewelry stores that cater to a mostly Chinese clientele. In the city of Cupertino alone, which has a population of about 50,500, there are three Chinese supermarkets. In the Silicon Valley, there are some large-scale Asian theme malls where Chinese businesses dominate, such as Cupertino Village and Milpitas Square. Both were financed and developed in part through the efforts of Asian Americans and are anchored by 99 Ranch (Tawa) Markets (Akizuki 1999; W. Li and Park 2006).

Among the various forms of ethnic community, including the traditional Chinatown, the LA-type ethnoburb, and the suburbs lacking a distinct minority identity, we find two transitional types: the Queens-style "ethnopolis" and the Silicon Valley "techno/ethnoburb." Although technically not in the suburbs, and bearing many characteristics of inner-city neighborhoods, like high-rise buildings and crowded commercial streets, the ethnopolis nevertheless developed along the same lines as the ethnoburb.[6] A techno/ethnoburb, on the other hand, is a combination of high-tech centers and multiracial neighborhoods. These differing ethnic community types offer a good spectrum for comparative study.

Ethnoburbs in Canadian Cities

Known as MTV, Montreal, Toronto, and Vancouver, the three largest metropolitan areas in Canada, continue to serve as immigrant gateways.[7] Toronto and Vancouver in particular also have large, long-established Chinatowns, which still function as viable ethnic residential neighborhoods and business districts as well as tourist attractions. However, recent spatial patterns of ethnic residential and business districts have mainly been shaped by development in the suburbs.

Toronto continues to house the largest Chinatown in Canada, if not in North America, but its Chinese residents now mainly reside in suburban zones as of a decade ago. Of the 338,265 Chinese residents in the Greater Toronto Area (GTA) in 1996, only 18 percent still lived in the City of Toronto. Its inner suburb zone of East York, Etobicoke, North York, Scarborough, and York accounted for 47 percent of the total Chinese population in the GTA.[8] The outer suburb zone, including Markham, Mississauga, and Richmond Hill, housed the remaining 35 percent. In upscale Markham and Richmond Hill, the Chinese population accounted for 20 percent and 25 percent, respectively, of the total population. Chinese ethnic businesses also demonstrated new concentrations in the suburbs. In 1994 the same three zones already housed 34.2 percent, 44.6 percent, and 21.1 percent of Chinese businesses in the GTA respectively. Furthermore the Chinese economy in Toronto has also experienced structural changes from predominantly restaurants and grocery stores to a whole spectrum of consumer services, and the locations of such businesses have shifted from unplanned retail strips to planned shopping centers. In this shift, suburbs again emerged as favorite locations. Toronto itself had only two shopping centers among all Chinese shopping centers in the GTA in 1996. The inner suburbs had thirty centers, and the outer suburbs had twenty centers, with Scarborough (twenty-seven centers) and Richmond Hill (eleven centers) taking the lead in their respective areas.

As in Los Angeles, Toronto's Chinese population also stratifies along lines of origin and socioeconomic class, which show up in residential patterns. Immigrants from Hong Kong were the largest Chinese subgroup in Toronto. With good education and high job skills, they are primarily concentrated in the upscale outer suburb municipalities of Markham and Richmond Hill. Two large concentrations of Hong Kong Chinese within these two municipalities easily explain the presence of a chain of Hong Kong-style upscale shopping malls. Immigrants from Taiwan are clustered in the northeast part of North York, where their predominance can be attributed to the excellent public schools. This section is also an upscale area, suggesting the affluence of these immigrants. On the other hand, according to the 1996 census, Mainland Chinese immigrants were concentrated in inner-city Chinatowns, which includes the current Chinatown, centered at the intersection of Spadina Avenue and Dundas Street, in addition to the older Chinatown to the east. In the past decade, however, they too increasingly live in suburbs (Lo 2006).

Serving as the Canadian gateway to the Asian Pacific, Vancouver, on Canada's west coast, stands as one of the largest immigrant ports of entry fueled in large part by the contemporary globalization. Vancouver possesses a mild climate and a long tradition of international trade across the Pacific Ocean. Compared with the distance of cities in the east, Vancouver's short physical and psychological distance from Asia makes it feel more like home to Asian transmigrants now settling there. More so than the U.S. government, the Canadian government has actively recruited immigrants of the business/investment type in the past twenty years. Vancouver hosts a disproportionately high percentage of wealthy business immigrants. In 1996, 55 percent of immigrants of this type intended to live in Vancouver, compared with Toronto's 16.8 percent and Montreal's 20.7 percent.

Many of the Hong Kong Chinese immigrants in Vancouver resemble the "reluctant exiles" mentality and emigrated when the prospect of Hong Kong's return to Chinese rule loomed large. These immigrants, from middle class to wealthy families, are likely to own and live in suburban houses. In suburban Richmond, for instance, B. K. Ray and his colleagues observed that "in contrast to the northern suburbs of Metro Toronto, where visible minority immigrants often live in high-rise housing surrounded by single detached dwellings occupied by predominantly white Canadian- and foreign-born residents…in Richmond this pattern is almost reversed" (Ray, Halseth, and Hohnson 1997, 92). One factor has been the presence of Victor Li, son of a Hong Kong tycoon, who was heavily involved in developing and building condominiums in Richmond, and marketing them in Hong Kong. These properties contributed to the concentration of Chinese in this suburban community. Li's father, Li Ka-shing, and his associates bought the former Expo land in the 1980s, a property representing fully one-sixth of downtown Vancouver. The visibility of the economic power of affluent Hong Kong Chinese has raised anti-Hong Kong sentiments among some Canadians. The somewhat overstated nickname "Honcouver" implies that the city is being taken over by wealth from Hong Kong.

Throughout the Vancouver area, rich Hong Kong families have bought single family houses, tore them down, and replaced them with huge mansions that occupy almost the entire lot. As in Arcadia and San Marino in Los Angeles, public outcry has condemned these so-called "monster houses." In Silicon Valley, similar houses are nicknamed "pink palaces" or "pink elephants," due to their Mediterranean building style and color.[9] The phenomenon of large houses owned by Chinese families is common in many urban areas and has resulted in a variety of local responses, ranging from neighborhood public hearings to city council regulations.

The phenomenon of suburban concentrations of minorities does not just exist in the cities discussed here. A study by Rob Paral (2000) has documented the large numbers of immigrants of various ethnic backgrounds who bypass inner-city neighborhoods to settle directly in Chicago's suburbs. Another large Asian mall in the United States, Time Square, was built in the southwest suburb of Houston by the same company that built San Gabriel Square in Los Angeles and modeled after the California prototype. Many famous Southland Chinese businesses had opened their chain or franchised stores in Time Square, including Tawa Supermarket, Harbor Village restaurant, DD's Cafe, and Sing Young Musical World (*Chinese Daily News,* December 14, 1996). These developments demand further scholarly attention as to how they channel immigrants' human and financial resources into the fabric of the receiving societies. The challenge will be to maintain equality and build prosperity for all. The lessons learned from ethnoburbs can shed light on the transformation of suburbs in major North American cities.

Ethnoburb: Opportunities and Challenges

The emergence of the San Gabriel Valley Chinese ethnoburb as a new urban ethnic place has involved an interplay of race and class in international, national, and
local politics; social conditions; cultural heritage; economic structural change;
and demographic shifts. The process of ethnoburb establishment has generated
rapid change, racialized conflicts, and inter-racial group cooperation.

For ethnic minority groups, the ethnoburb offers opportunities that never
existed before, in which their economic strength can play important roles in
the globalized mainstream economy, and their political rights can be exercised
in ethnically mixed neighborhoods and communities. For longtime residents
of other ethnic groups in mainstream society, the ethnoburb provides a window through which to observe and to experience other cultures and traditions.
The establishment of the ethnoburb permits local residents of different ethnic
backgrounds the chance to live and work together and to become integrated
into a functional community while retaining their heritages and developing
ethnic identities. The economic nature of the ethnoburb as a global outpost
also gives localities a chance to better integrate the ethnic economy into mainstream economic affairs, take advantage of immigrants' skills and resources,
adopt alternative strategies during periods of recession, and strengthen their
position in the globalized economy.

But the emergence and manifestation of the ethnoburb generates new challenges. The ethnoburb emerges in particular localities due to shifting large-
scale structural circumstances as well as local conditions. It alters the landscape,
demographic composition, business practices, and social relations of American suburbia at a rapid pace. Lacking state or national policies regarding such
changes, localities where ethnoburbs exist are often left on their own to deal
with the problems associated with the changes. National policy makers usually
do not foresee the impact of legislation on particular localities and thus, unwill-
ingly, create localized problems. As this book has demonstrated, for example,
immigrant waves have been clearly correlated with critical U.S. immigration
policy changes and the shifting international geopolitical map, and these are
linked, directly and indirectly, to U.S. foreign policy. Foreign policy making
in this country tends to consider only U.S. strategic interests, rather than the
impact the policy will have on residents of other countries or on the communities in the United States itself. This is especially evident in those instances where
policy implementation creates refugees or asylum-seekers. The tides of refugees
from Southeast Asia are a good example. Although initially scattered, Southeast
Asian refugees became concentrated, through secondary migration, in several
localities such as Houston, Orange County, San Jose, and the San Gabriel Valley.

Many of them were ill prepared for life in the United States; they have found work only as low-wage manual laborers and live in poverty. And their problems, in turn, impact the local communities where they have settled.

Many new immigrants, however, are eager to learn English and fit into what they regard as an alien society (just as they are considered aliens by American society). Such good intentions deserve to be encouraged and assisted through more government and private sector help. To facilitate a smoother and more rapid transition into U.S. society, there should be a deep re-examination of the challenges faced by immigrant communities, including cultural adjustment, social welfare, immigrants' rights, and business development. However, these issues are often left for localities to deal with, which puts local governments and institutions under great pressure to cope.

Nativism is another challenge facing the ethnoburb. A deep-rooted attitude in this country, the extent of nativism fluctuates with economic cycles. Whenever the economy is booming, the demand for labor surges, jobs are plentiful, and people tend to be more "tolerant" toward immigrants. Such boom times often increase the pressure on government to enact legislation or adopt policies that actively recruit foreign laborers to ease perceived labor shortages. In today's rapidly globalizing labor market, the recruitment of labor has focused more on filling the need for high-tech specialists and workers, as is demonstrated by the demand in increasing H-1B visas. This results in the influx of a completely different type of in-migrant, one who is highly educated and professionally trained, unlike the traditional lower-skilled, less-educated laborer recruited in the past. The reverse is true during economic recessions and the early stages of recovery. Immigrants are more likely to become easy targets and scapegoats, charged with taking jobs away from "real" Americans. During these immigrant-bashing periods, immigrants as a whole group are portrayed as poorly educated, low-skill workers intent upon inundating or even abusing the American welfare system. Such characterizations frequently underlie welfare reform programs, debates over English as an "official" language, and discussions about how to deal with illegal immigration.

Moreover, as American history has demonstrated, economic arguments are not the only basis for attacks on immigrants. In the case of the San Gabriel Valley ethnoburb, many Chinese immigrants are neither poor nor poorly educated, nor are they taking jobs away from non-Chinese. Just the opposite is true: many are well educated and economically better off than the average native-born American, and their economic activities and resources create jobs. As a result, the San Gabriel Valley had one of the lowest unemployment rates and healthiest local economies in Los Angeles County despite the recession in the early 1990s. In this context, ethnoburban Chinese were targeted for a different reason: they had "intruded" into the white Americans' turf and have not behaved according to the "norms" of complete assimilation expected by longtime Anglo residents. Such nativist attitudes have translated into racialized actions against the Chinese.

Many residents of other ethnic backgrounds claim to dislike new Chinese immigrants because of their cultural practices. Such responses raise, once again, questions of who deserves to be "American." Are new immigrants (rich or poor) considered less fit for life in the United States, and should they therefore be barred from the full rights and obligations of citizenship? Cultural differences or lack of understanding of dominant American ways of life should never be the basis for citizenship. Rather, such differences need to be tolerated or where this is not feasible (for example, practices that contravene U.S. laws), education must be the route to conflict resolution and the avenue for full incorporation into U.S. society. At another level, should and will immigrants, rich or poor, laborer or investor, highly or poorly educated, forever be subjects of "tolerance," subject to economic cycles and an uncertain political environment? Or should and will Americans fully embrace and celebrate the diversity brought by immigrants, while addressing the challenges that immigration presents, of rapid change, demographic shift, economic transition, social integration and political participation? These issues are important nationwide, but are particularly pressing in urban and suburban areas where changes are occurring at a faster pace and on a larger scale. The search for solutions must incorporate both top-down and bottom-up approaches.

The arguments used against immigration neglect the fact that immigrants are a heterogeneous group. They contribute to the U.S. economy in different ways—through their financial investments, job creation, technical innovations, and labor. They also contribute to American society by diversifying its culture and bringing different and valuable heritages and traditions. Immigrants and their offspring have made, are making, and will continue to make the United States one of the greatest countries in the world. The very existence of immigrants from different parts of the world offers Americans a chance to observe firsthand and comprehend the diverse cultures and heritages in the globalizing world and strengthens American transnational ties to the world. Not only should the general public share an awareness of the immigrants' role, but policy makers in particular should be sensitized and educated to the challenges and the contributions of new arrivals. It is imperative that we understand changing ethnic attitudes, behavior, and culture; evaluate ethnic minority communities' contributions and challenges; and search for the meaning of suburban ethnic clustering to American society.

The United States is a multiethnic society. The escalating racial and class tensions and conflicts in American urban areas and in the nation as a whole threaten the long-held image of an open, democratic country that has provided opportunities to so many who have come in search of freedom, opportunity, and prosperity.

NOTES

Introduction

1. Calculation based on the U.S. Bureau of the Census, 1990, Census of Population and Housing, STF1a.

2. See Fong 1996 for a complete list of publications from UCLA's Monterey Park Project in the 1980s. Other scholarly work about the San Gabriel Valley Chinese community include Fong 1994; Tseng 1994a, 1994b, 1995; M. Zhou 1998, 2003, 2008; Y. Zhou 1996a, 1996b, 1998a, 1998b.

3. For a partial list of news media coverage in the 1980s and 1990s, see Arax 1987; Deng 1995; Hamilton 1997; Klein 1997; Kotkin 1991; Schoenberger 1993; and Tanzer 1985.

4. See Arax 1987; Fong 1994; and Lai 1988.

5. Author interviews, Judy Chu 1995; Lucia Su 1995.

6. See W. Li 2006. The introductory chapter of that book serves as a basis for Chapter 2.

7. W. Li 1997; see also W. Li 1998a, 1998b, 1998c, 1999; and W. Li et al. 2002. Portions of Chapters 3 through 6 of this book are based in part on these articles. I am grateful for the permission granted by these journals to use these materials here. Part of Li 1998b is reprinted with permission from *Urban Geography* 19(6): 502–517 (©Bellwether Publishing, Ltd., 8640 Guilford Road, Suite 200, Columbia, MD 21046), all rights reserved. A portion of Li 1999 is revised with permission from *Journal of Asian American Studies* 2(1): 1–28. Part of Li et al. 2002 is revised with permission from *Annals of the Association of American Geographers* 94 (2): 777–796, http://www.informaworld.com.

Chapter 1: Ethnicity and Space

1. For examples, see P. S. Li 1998, 2003; Saito 1998; Sanchez 1999; Waters 1999.

2. Hollinger 1995; Jacobson 1998; Lipsitz 1998; Mitchell 2004.

3. See W. Li 2006 for racialized assimilation; and M. Zhou 1997 for segmented assimilation.

4. See, for instance, Bonnett 1997; Kobayashi and Peake 2000; Pulido 2002.

5. Dispersed forms of contemporary immigrant and minority settlements are not the focus of this book. Those interested in that topic may refer to the following publications: Ling 2005; Skop and Li 2003; and Zelinsky and Lee 1998.

6. Numerous case studies appeared in geographical journals and books; examples include Clark (on Milwaukee) 1972; Ernst (on Kinlock) 1976; Morrill (on Seattle) 1965; Rose (on Miami) 1976a; Sanders and Adams (on Cleveland) 1976; Winsberg (on Chicago) 1986. Only a few attempted to address the dynamics of ghetto formation (Harvey 1972); or to treat ghettos as a social phenomenon and process comprehensively (Rose 1970, 1971, 1976b).

7. See, for instance, Aldrich, 1975; Ward 1971.

8. For example, analysis of the residential patterns of different ethnic groups in Philadelphia demonstrates that ethnic groups show a step-wise diffusion pattern. In 1960, the Irish were almost evenly spread out in the whole Philadelphia area; the Polish had a dispersed distribution; the Italians had some recognizable areas of concentration, but were otherwise fairly dispersed; whereas the African Americans had several highly clustered centers (Jakle, Brunn, and Roseman 1976).

9. See, for instance, Farley 1986; Hwang et al. 1985; Jakubs 1986; Lieberson 1961; Miller and Quigley 1990; Stearns and Logan 1986; Torrieri 1982.

10. See, for instance, Hiebert 1993; Light and Bonacich 1988; Light, Bhachu, and Karageorgis 1993; Light and Karageorgis 1994; Light and Rosenstein 1995; Light, Sabahg, Bozorgmehr, and Der-Martirosian 1994; Modell 1977; Portes and Bach 1985; Portes and Jensen 1989; Siu 1987; Tsai 1986; Wilson and Portes 1980.

11. Hiebert 1993, 247; also see Bonacich, Light, and Wong 1977; Light and Bonacich 1988; Portes and Bach 1985.

12. Beauregard 1989; Kotkin 1991; Kwong 1987; Leung 1993; Scott 1988, 1993; Storper and Walker 1989; Thompson 1979, 1989; Wolch and Dear 1993; B. P. Wong 1982, 1988.

13. See Bonacich and Modell 1980; Hiebert 1993; Kwong 1987, 1996; Lin 1998; Min 1994, and M. Zhou 1992.

14. See Garreau 1992; Scott 1988; Soja, Morales, and Wolff 1989.

15. See, for instance, Portes, Guarnizo, and Landolt 1999; Ip et al. 1997.

16. Some examples include Adjei-Barwuah and Rose 1972; Hune et al. 1991; Levin and Leong 1973; Roche 1982; Waldinger and Zseng 1992; M. Zhou and Kim 2003; Y. Zhou 1998a.

Chapter 2: Ethnoburb

1. Congressman Robert T. Matsui (D-Calif.), quoted in the *Washington Post*, November 18, 1993, A-10.

2. See Hing 1994; Hutchinson 1981; Ong and Liu 1994; Sassen 1994.

3. I am using the term here simply for the convenience of representing the three countries mostly affected by the Vietnam War: Vietnam, Laos, and Cambodia.

Chapter 3: Changing Chinese Settlement

1. Part of the discussion of Chinese Americans in the United States was adapted from "Chinese Americans," *Encyclopedia of the World's Minorities*, ed. Carl Skutsch, 296–301 (New York: Routledge (2004). Permission was granted by Routledge to reprint this material.

2. The Bureau of the Census has changed the definition of "Chinese" several times. From the 1920 census through the 1950 census, the category of Chinese meant all the persons born in China, that is, Chinese immigrants from China. In 1960 and 1970, Chinese meant China-born Chinese and their offspring. From the 1980 census through 2000, it has meant all those who identified themselves as being of Chinese ancestry. Unless otherwise noted, the 2000 figures used in this book are people who claim full or partial Chinese heritage in their census form. Since it is impossible to make any adjustment for consistency, all the numbers from census data used here will keep the way they are without adjustment.

3. See Brownstone 1988; Chinese Historical Society of America 1994; Daniels 1988; Fong 1994; Kwong 1996; E. Lee 2003; P. S. Li 1998; Tsai 1986; Tung 1974; L. L. Wang 1994.

4. See H. W. C. Chen 1952; Hsu 2002; Siu 1987; Tsai 1986; Zhao 2002.

5. While Congress and the President sought to reverse the history of injustice for the Chinese in this country, injustice toward another Asian American group was simultaneously being carried out. President Roosevelt signed Executive Order 9066, which led to the unconstitutional internment of over 110,000 west coast Japanese Americans, in remote sections of the U.S. mainland.

6. There were 3,610 Chinese students and scholars enrolled in 454 colleges and universities in the United States in 1949. A high percentage were supported by Nationalist government scholarships and were supposedly to return to China upon graduation. Many of them were stranded after 1949. The United States offered scholarships to these students to finish their study under the China Area Aid Act and provided employment and residence after their graduation. Many among this group were prominent scholars in various fields, including Nobel Physics Prize Laureates T. C. Lee (Li Zhengdao) and C. N. Yang (Yang Zhenning).

7. This figure includes Taiwanese, but does not include people with other racial backgrounds, that is, people of more than one race, who identify themselves as Chinese. Data extracted from http://factfinder.census.gov/servlet/DTTable?_bm=y&-geo _id=01000US&- mt_name=ACS_2006_EST_G2000_C02006

8. See W. H. C. Chen 1952; L. Cheng and S. Cheng 1984; Lou 1982; Mason 1967; Newmark and Newmark 1916; C. C. Wong 1980.

9. See Lou 1982; Pearlstone 1990; Wells Fargo & Co. 1882.

10. See Chan 1986, Tables 10, 11; W. H. C. Chen 1952; Lou 1982.

11. See W. H. C. Chen 1952; Defalla 1960; Lou 1982; Pearlstone 1990.

12. See W. H. C. Chen 1952; L. Cheng and S. Cheng 1984; Lou 1982.

13. See Chen 1938; L. Cheng and S. Cheng 1984; S. Cheng and Kwok 1988; Li, Wong, and Kwan 1974; Quan 1988; B. P. Wong 1988.

14. This map is based entirely on census data. It should be noted, however, that the census did not provide the numbers of Chinese in all cities/CDPs until about 1930. For instance, from 1900 to 1920, only the following cities were reported: Alhambra, Glendale, Long Beach, Los Angeles, Pasadena, and Santa Monica. Therefore, data on the earlier years is incomplete, and the map presents some distortion. For a detailed description of the formula for, and the meaning of, the spatial mean center map, see Fernald 2000, 63–64.

15. See W. H. C. Chen 1952; M. S. Lee 1939; C. C. Wong 1980.

16. See Community Redevelopment Agency, 1985, *Official Statement Relating to Chinatown Redevelopment Project;* Hom and Fong 1988; Li, Wong, and Kwan 1974; Ong 1984.

17. Map 3 depicts Chinese population density change over each decade. Therefore, only negative numbers represent actual population decrease, whereas higher and lower bars represent either faster or slower population growth as compared with the previous decade.

Chapter 4: Building Ethnoburbia

1. Partial displacement is a phenomenon in the migration process described by geographers, see Adams et al. 1973; Roseman 1971.

2. See Barron 1991, 65; Monterey Park Oral History Project 1990; author interview, Ms. M 1992.

3. When it was first established, the City of Monterey Park included the area of what is now Monterey Park and Montebello; Barron 1991; T. Fong 1994, 17.

4. See author interviews, Chu 1995; and Su 1995; T. Fong 1994, 21–23.

5. See Barron 1991; Klein 1997; Knapp 1992.

6. See author interviews, W. Chan 1995 and M. Chang 1996; Monterey Park Oral History Project 1990; Tanzer 1985.

7. See Monterey Park Oral History Project 1990; T. Fong 1994; author interview, Wilbur Woo, August 1999.

8. See Monterey Park Oral History Project 1990; author interviews, Jablonsky 1994 and Su 1995.

9. Hsieh himself, for instance, was actively involved in the Chamber of Commerce and once served as its "Goodwill Ambassador."

10. This was true, for instance, of the author's interviewees Mr. C from Hong Kong, Mr. and Mrs. M from Taiwan, and Mr. and Mrs. Z from Mainland China.

11. Author interviews, Ms. Ryan, director of the Center, 1992; Ms. Chang, music director of the Evergreen Chorus, 1994; Mrs. C 1992.

12. See Barron 1991; T. Fong 1994; Horton 1995, for detailed descriptions.

13. She was elected to the California State Assembly in 2001.

14. The Hsi Lai Temple became associated with a scandal in American politics in 1996, after then Vice President Al Gore attended a fundraising event there for the Democratic National Committee during the 1996 Presidential campaign.

Chapter 5: From Ethnic Service Center to Global Economic Outpost

1. Calculation based on Bureau of the Census 1980 and Asian System Media 1983.

2. A department store with the same name also exists in Taiwan.

3. This restaurant closed in the late 1990s, but the property again houses a Chinese restaurant.

4. Bank interview 1999, no.11; Hamilton 1997; *Los Angeles Times,* April 27, 1997.

5. Its franchised store in Phoenix changed to an independent store in 2006.

6. In Chinese *shun fat* means "smooth, successful, and prosperous," but having "Fat" in the name may discourage some non-Chinese customers.

7. The ownership data used in maps and summary statistics includes only individual, not corporate owners.

8. Usage of the same categories for the total number of Chinese population per tract over census years does not comply with the normal cartographic principles but is based on practical consideration. This serves to provide an effective visual presentation that allows direct comparison across the two decades.

Chapter 6: Anatomy of an Ethnoburb

1. Unless otherwise noted, the data source for this chapter is the 1990 Census 5% Public Use Microdata Sample (PUMS). A statistical software package, Statistical Analysis System (SAS) was used to retrieve and analyze PUMS data. Results presented here are based on weighted data and thus reflect population characteristics with respect to demographic, socioeconomic status, and housing conditions. Eleven Public Use Microdata Areas (PUMAs) within San Gabriel Valley were selected, including twenty-two cities, twelve CDPs, and parts of unincorporated Los Angeles County, which represents the general location of the ethnoburb. The number of Chinese in the 5% sample included all those people who indicated on their 1990 census questionnaire that they were "Chinese" or "Taiwanese." There were a total of 6,540 Chinese people and 1,934 Chinese households in this sample subset, representing 128,624 Chinese people and 37,245 Chinese households in the San Gabriel Valley.

2. Calculation based on U.S. Bureau of Census, 1990.

3. The 1990 census questionnaire lumped Chinese and Cantonese together as one category, so it is impossible to differentiate those who spoke Cantonese only. Thus important data of origins are missing, since the majority of those "old-time overseas Chinese" from Guangdong Province spoke Cantonese only. Such a census categorization may be rooted in the nature of old Chinatowns, where various forms of Cantonese were the "official language." For most Americans, the "Chinese" language was Cantonese.

4. As "place of work," PUMS data listed only a few PUMAs individually and lumped most other PUMAs into groups. Within the ethnoburb, for instance, only Monterey Park and Rosemead (PUMA 05400), El Monte (05800), and Pasadena (06300) were listed as a "place of work"; other PUMAs in San Gabriel Valley were grouped with foothill and Westside areas.

5. The highest level of school completed or the highest degree received among all people who were at least fifteen years old in 1990. Bureau of the Census 1992, B-4.

6. Defined by the Census Bureau as no person of 14 years or older in a household speaks English well or very well.

7. Unlike median household income, however, the median personal income of the county was based on the weighted 5 percent sample instead of the 100 percent count.

Chapter 7: Portraits of Ethnoburban Chinese

1. The story of Betty Tom Chu is largely drawn from National Association of Chinese American Bankers (NACAB) 1992; and bank interview 1999, no. 7. Also see W. Li et al. 2002 for a detailed discussion of the development of Chinese American banks in LA.

2. Mitchell 1993, 2004; Skeldon 1999; Thrift and Olds 1996.

3. The story of Dominic Ng is largely drawn from the following resources: bank interview 1999, nos. 7, 19; Flanigan 1998; Gilley 1998; W. Li et al. 2002; Vrana 1998.

4. The section on Henry Y. Hwang draws heavily from the following sources: author interview, August 4, 1999; David Henry Hwang, June 1994; Hwang 1994a; Hwang 1994b; Golden and Gerth, 1999.

Chapter 8: Opportunities and Challenges for Ethnoburbs

1. This section mainly depicts the ethnoburb phenomenon in the four metropolitan areas in the mid-1990s, which paralleled the San Gabriel Valley development. For more details in the last decade, see, respectively, Smith and Logan 2006 for New York; W. Li and E. Park 2006 for Silicon Valley; Lo 2006 for Toronto and Edgington et al. 2006 for Vancouver.

2. See, for instance, Akizuki 1999; *Chinese Daily News,* December 14, 1996; Chung 1993; Hiebert 1999; Lo and Wang1998; Wood 1997.

3. Calculation based on 2000 Census, SF2. The geographic unit for each of these three areas is "Consolidated Metropolitan Statistical Area," which includes multiple counties.

4. See Kwong 1996; Lin 1998; B. P. Wong 1998, 2005; M. Zhou 1992.

5. Calculation based on 2000 Census SF2.

6. The word "ethnopolis" first appeared in Laguerre 2000. However, Laura Lee-Chin suggested that I use this term to describe Flushing in New York or the Richmond District in San Francisco a dozen years ago.

7. This section on Canadian cities is largely based on the following sources: Citizenship and Immigration Canada 1999, *Facts and Figures: Immigration Overview.* C&I–291-06-99E; Hiebert et al. 1998; Lo and Wang 1998; M. Luk Chiu "The Chinese community in Toronto" (www.ccilm.com/english/features/demograph_e.asp) and "The three Chinese immigrant sub-groups in Toronto" (www.ccilm.com/english/features/immigrant_e.asp); Mitchell 2004; Ray, Halseth, and Hohnson 1997; S. G. Wang 1999.

8. Beginning on January 1, 1998, however, these five inner suburban municipalities in the Toronto Census Metropolitan Area (CMA) joined Toronto, forming the new City of Toronto.

9. See Ley 1995; and P. S. Li 1994 for Vancouver; author interview in Cupertino, no. 2, 14.

References

Adams, J. S. et al. 1973. Interurban migration. Commentary. *Annals of the Association of American Geographers* 63:152–156.

Adjei-Barwuah, B., and H. M. Rose. 1972. Some comparative aspects of the west African Zongo and the black American ghetto. In *Geography of the ghetto: Perceptions, problems, and alternatives*, ed. H. M. Rose, 257–273. DeKalb, IL: Northern Illinois University Press.

Akizuki, D. 1999. Taiwan ties: Immigrants transform Fremont. *San Jose Mercury News*, August 1, 1A.

Alba, R. E. 1985a. *Italian Americans: Into the twilight of ethnicity.* Englewood Cliffs, NJ: Prentice-Hall, Inc.

———. 1985b. *Ethnicity and race in the U.S.A. Toward the twenty-first century.* London: Routledge and Kegan Paul.

———. 1992. Ethnicity. In *Encyclopedia of sociology,* eds. F. Edgar and M. L. Borgatta, vol. 2, 575–584. New York: Macmillan.

Aldrich, H. 1975. Ecological succession in racially changing neighborhoods: A review of the literature. *Urban Affairs Quarterly* 10:327–348.

Allen, J. P., and E. J. Turner. 1989. The most ethnically diverse places in the United States. *Urban Geography* 10 (1989): 523–539.

———. 1996. Ethnic diversity and segregation in the new Los Angeles. In *EthniCity: Geographic perspectives on ethnic change in modern cities,* eds. C. Roseman et al., 1–29. Lanham, MD: Rowman & Littlefield Publishers, Inc.

———. 2002. *Changing faces, changing places: Mapping Southern Californians.* Northridge, CA: California State University, Northridge.

Almaguer, T. 1994. *Racial fault lines: The historical origins of white supremacy in California.* Berkeley, CA: University of California Press.

Anderson, K. J. 1987. The idea of Chinatown: The power of place and institutional practice in the making of a racial category. *Annals of the Association of American Geographers* 77:580–598.

———. 1988. Cultural hegemony and the race-definition process in Chinatown. *Environment and Planning D: Society and Space* 6:127–149.

————1991. *Vancouver's Chinatown: Racial discourse in Canada, 1875–1980*, Montreal, ON: McGill-Queen's University Press.

Arax, M. 1987. Nation's 1st suburban Chinatown. *Los Angeles Times*, April 6.

Asia System Media. 1983. *Chinese Yellow Pages.* Monterey Park, CA.

Barrera, M. 1979. *Race and class in the Southwest: A theory of racial inequality.* Notre Dame, IN: University of Notre Dame Press.

Barron, D. 1991. *Reflections 1916–1991: Monterey Park's past, present and future.* City of Monterey Park, CA.

Basch, L., N. Glick Schiller, and C. Blanc-Szanton. 1994. *Nations unbound: Transnational projects, postcolonial predicaments, and deterritorialized nation-states.* Amsterdam: Gordon and Breach Science Publishers SA.

Beauregard, R. A. 1989. Urban restructuring in comparative perspective. In *Atop the urban hierarchy*, ed. R. A. Beauregard, 239–274. Totowa, NJ: Rowman & Littlefield Publishers, Inc.

Bluestone, B., and B. Harrison. 1982. *The great U-turn: Deindustrialization of America.* New York: Basic Books.

Bonacich, E., E. H. Light, and C. C. Wong. 1977. Koreans in business. *Society* 14:54–59.

Bonacich, E., and J. Modell. 1980. *The economic basis of ethnic solidarity: Small business in the Japanese American community.* Berkeley, CA: University of California Press.

Bonnett, A. 1997. Geography, "race" and whiteness: Invisible traditions and current challenges. *Area* 29:193–199.

Boudreau, J. 2008. Taiwanese in Bay Area return to island for closely fought presidential election. *San Jose Mercury News*, March 30. Accessed March 21, 2008 from http://www.mercurynews.com/news/ci_8635209?nclick_check=1

Brownstone, D. M. 1988. *The Chinese-American heritage.* New York: Facts on File.

Buddhist Light International Association. 1996. *Buddhist Lights Century.* Hacienda Heights, CA, January 16, 1996.

Cater, J., and T. Jones. 1987. Asian ethnicity, home-ownership and social reproduction. In *Race and Racism: Essays in social geography*, ed. P. Jackson, 190–211. London: Allen & Unwin.

Chan, S. 1986. *This bitter-sweet soil: The Chinese in California agriculture, 1860–1910.* Berkeley, CA: University of California Press.

Chen, H. 1992. *Chinatown no more: Taiwan immigrants in contemporary New York.* Ithaca, NY: Cornell University Press.

Chen, W. H. C. 1952. Changing socio-cultural patterns of the Chinese community in Los Angeles. PhD diss. University of Southern California.

Cheng, L., and S. Cheng. 1984. Chinese women of Los Angeles: A social historical survey. In *Linking our lives: Chinese American women of Los Angeles*, ed. Asian American Studies Center & Chinese Historical Society of Southern California, 1–25. Los Angeles: Chinese Historical Society of Southern California.

Cheng, S., and M. Kwok. 1988. The golden years of Los Angeles Chinatown: The beginning. *Los Angeles Chinatown 50th year: The golden years, 1938–1988*, 39–41, 45, 47. Los Angeles, CA: Chinese Chamber of Commerce.

Chinese Historical Society of America. 1994. *The repeal and its legacy: Proceedings of the conference on the 50th anniversary of the repeal of the Exclusion Acts.* San Francisco.

Chinese Yellow Pages, see Asia System Media.

Chiu, M. Luk. 1996. The Chinese community in Toronto. www.ccilm.com/english/features/demograph_e.asp

———. 1996. The three Chinese immigrant sub-groups in Toronto. http://www.ccilm.com/english/features/immigrant_e.asp. Accessed January 10, 2002.

Chou. 1996. Opinion. *Los Angeles Times,* September 28.

Chow, W. T. 1977. *The reemergence of an inner city: The pivot of Chinese settlement in the East Bay region of the San Francisco Bay area.* San Francisco: R & E Research Associates, Inc.

Citizenship and Immigration Canada. 1999. *Facts and figures: Immigration overview.* C&I–291–06–99E Ottawa, ON: CIC.

Clark, W. A. V. 1972. Patterns of black intraurban mobility and restricted relocation opportunities. In *Geography of the ghetto: Perceptions, problems, and alternatives,* eds. H. M. Rose and H. McConnell, 111–126. DeKalb, IL: Northern Illinois University Press.

Clarke, C., D. Ley, and C. Peach. 1984. *Geography and ethnic pluralism.* London: George Allen & Unwin.

Cohen, R. 1978. Ethnicity: Problem and focus in Anthropology. *Annual Review of Anthropology* 7:379–403.

Community Redevelopment Agency. 1985. *Official statement relating to Chinatown Redevelopment Project.* Los Angeles, CA: CRA.

Daniels, R. 1988. *Asian America Chinese and Japanese in the United States since 1850.* Seattle, WA: University of Washington Press.

Davis, M. 1992. Chinatown, revisited? The "internationalization" of downtown Los Angeles. In *Sex, death and God in L.A.,* ed. D. Reid, 19–53. New York: Random House, Inc.

Dear, M. J. 1991. Taking Los Angeles seriously: Time and space in the postmodern city. *Architecture California* 13:36–42.

———, ed. 1996. *Atlas of Southern California.* Southern California Study Center. Los Angeles, CA: University of Southern California.

Defalla, P. M. 1960. Lantern in the western sky. *Historical Society of Southern California* 42:57–88.

Deng, H. 1995. The formation of "New Little Taipei" in east San Gabriel Valley. *Chinese Daily News,* February 13, 1995, B15.

Dunn, K. 2005. A paradigm of transnationalism for migration studies. *New Zealand Population Review* 31:15–31.

Dymski, G. A., and J. M. Vietich. 1996a. Financing the future in Los Angeles: From depression to 21st century. In *Rethinking Los Angeles,* eds. M. J. Dear, H. E. Schockman, and G. Hise, 35–55. Thousand Oaks, CA: SAGE Publications, Inc.

———. 1996b. Financial transformation and the metropolis: Booms, busts, and banking in Los Angeles. *Environment and Planning A.* 287 (July 1996): 1233–1260.

Edgington, D. W., M. A. Goldberg, and T. A. Hutton. 2006. Hong Kong business, money, and migration in Vancouver, Canada. In *From urban enclave to ethnic suburb: New Asian communities in Pacific Rim countries*, ed. Wei Li, 155–183. Honolulu, HI: University of Hawai'i Press.

Ernst, R. T. 1976. Growth, development, and isolation of an all-black city: Kinlock, Missouri. In *Black America geographic perspectives*, eds. R. T. Ernst and L. Hugg, 368–388. Garden City, NY: Anchor Press.

Espiritu, Y. L. 1992. *Asian American panethnicity: Bridging institutions and identities.* Philadelphia, PA: Temple University Press.

Farley, J. E. 1986. Segregated city, segregated suburbs: To what extent are they products of black-white socioeconomic differentials? *Urban Geography* 7:164–171.

Feason, Joe R., and Clairece B. Feason. 1994. Theoretical perspectives in race and ethnic relations. In *Race and Ethnic Conflict*, eds. F. L. Pincus and H. J. Ehrlich, 41–59. Boulder, CO: Westview Press.

Ferguson, C. 1942. Political problems and activities of Oriental residents in Los Angeles and vicinity. MA thesis, University of California Los Angeles.

Fernald, P. 2000. New Gold Mountain: Contrasts in Chinese migration and settlement patterns in Australia. MA thesis, University of Connecticut.

Flanigan, J. 1998. Crisis management: Small banks see opportunity in Southern California's new economy. *Los Angeles Times*, July 22, 1998, D1, D6.

Fong, Timothy. 1994. *The first suburban Chinatown: The remaking of Monterey Park, California.* Philadelphia, PA: Temple University Press.

———. 1996. Transnational newspapers: The making of the post-1965 globalized/localized San Gabriel Valley Chinese community. *Amerasia Journal* 22, no. 3:65–77.

———. 1998. *The contemporary Asian American experience: Beyond the model minority.* Upper Saddle River, NJ: Prentice Hall.

Gans, H. J. 1979. Symbolic ethnicity: The future of ethnic groups and cultures in America. *Ethnic and Racial Studies* 2:1–19.

Garreau, J. 1992. *Edge City: Life on the new frontier.* New York: Doubleday

Gilley, B. 1998. Buyers' market. *Far East Economic Review*, August 27.

Gleason, P. 1992. *Speaking of diversity: Language and ethnicity in twentieth-century America.* Baltimore, MD: Johns Hopkins University Press.

Glick Schiller, N., L. Basch, and C. Blanc–Szanton. 1992. *Towards a transnational perspective on migration: Race, class, ethnicity, and nationalism reconsidered.* New York: The New York Academy of Sciences.

———. 1995. From immigrant to transmigrant: Theorizing transnational migration. *Anthropological Quarterly* 68, no.1:48–63.

Golden, Tim, and Jeff Gerth. 1999. China sent cash to U.S. Bank, with suspicions slow to rise. *New York Times*, A1 May 12.

Gordon, M. M. 1964. *Assimilation in American life: The role of race, religion, and national origins.* New York: Oxford University Press.

Grayson, G. W. 1995. *The North American Free Trade Agreement: Regional community and the new world order.* Lanham, MD: University Press of America.

Hamilton, D. 1997. 99 and counting. *Los Angeles Times,* April 27.

Handelman, D. 1977. The organization of ethnicity. *Ethnic Groups* 1:187–200.

Harvey, David. 1972. Revolutionary and counter-revolutionary theory in geography and the problem of ghetto formation. In *Geography of the ghetto: Perceptions, problems, and alternatives,* eds. H. M. Rose and H. McConnell, 1–26. DeKalb, IL: Northern Illinois University Press.

Hiebert, D. 1993. Jewish immigrants and the garment industry of Toronto, 1901–1931: A study of ethnic and class relations. *Annals of the Association of American Geographer* 83, no. 2:243–271.

———— et al. 1999. Immigration and the changing social geography of greater Vancouver. *BC Studies* 121:35–82.

Hing, B. O. 1994. Reflections on exclusion: We punish boat people. In *The repeal and its legacy: Proceedings of the conference on the 50th anniversary of the repeal of the Exclusion* Acts, 16–18. San Francisco, CA, Chinese Historical Society of America.

Hollinger, D. A. 1995. *Postethnic America: Beyond multiculturalism.* New York: Basic Books.

Hom, B. M., and L. Fong. 1988. Los Angeles Chinatown 1958–1968. In *Los Angeles Chinatown 50th year: The golden years 1938–1988,* 51, 55. Los Angeles: Chinese Chamber of Commerce.

Horton, J. 1995. *The politics of diversity: Immigration, resistance, and change in Monterey Park, California.* Philadelphia, PA: Temple University Press.

Hune, S. et al. 1991. *Asian Americans: Comparative and global perspectives.* Pullman, WA: Washington State University Press.

Hsu, M. Y. 2002. *Dreaming of gold, dreaming of home: Transnationalism and migration between the United States and South China 1882–1943.* Stanford, CA: Stanford University Press.

Hutchinson, E. P. 1981. *Legislative history of American immigration policy 1798–1965.* Philadelphia, PA: University of Pennsylvania Press.

Hwang, D. H. 1994a. The FENB Story. Mimeo (June).

————, 1994b. Biography of Henry Y. Hwang. Mimeo.

Hwang, S. S. et al. 1985. The effects of race and socioeconomic status on residential segregation in Texas, 1970–80. *Social Forces* 63:732–747.

Ignatiev, N. 1995. *How the Irish became white.* New York: Routledge and Kegan Paul.

Ip, D., C. Inglis, C. T. Wu, et al. 1997. Concepts of citizenship and identity among recent Asian immigrants in Australia. *Asian and Pacific Migration Journal* 63, no. 4:363–384.

Jackson, P. 1987. The idea of "race" and the geography of racism. In *Race and racism: Essays in social geography,* ed. P. Jackson, 3–18. London: Allen and Unwin.

Jacobson, M. F. 1998. *Whiteness of a different color: European immigrants and the alchemy of race.* Cambridge, MA: Harvard University Press.

Jakle, J. A., S. Brunn, and C. C. Roseman. 1976. *Human spatial behavior: A social geography.* North Scituate, MA: Duxbury Press.

Jakubs, J. F. 1986. Recent racial segregation in U.S. SMSAs. *Urban Geography* 7:146–163.

Jaret, C. 1991. Recent structural change and US urban ethnic minorities. *Journal of Urban Affairs* 13:307–336.

Johnston, R. J. 1994. Ghetto. In *The dictionary of human geography*, 3rd edition, eds. R. J. Johnston, Derek Gregory, and David M. Smith, 231. Oxford: Blackwell Publishers Ltd.

Kaplan, D. 1998. The spatial structure of ethnic economies. *Urban Geography* 19: 489–501.

King, H., and B. L. Francis. 1980. Chinese in the U.S.: A century of occupational transition. *International Migration Review* 14:15–24.

Klein, K. E. 1997. At home in America. *Los Angeles Times*, April 20.

Kotkin, J. 1991. The Chinese connection. *Los Angeles Times*, December 22.

Knapp, R. 1992. *Chinese landscapes: The village as place.* Honolulu, University of Hawai'i Press.

Kobayashi, A., and L. Peake. 2000. Racism out of place: Thoughts on whiteness and anti-racist geography in the new millennium. *Annals of the Association of American Geographers* 90, no. 2:392–403.

Kwong, P. 1987. *The new Chinatown.* New York: Hill and Wang.

———. 1996. *The new Chinatown.* Revised ed. New York: Hill and Wang.

Laguerre, M. S. 2000. *The global ethnopolis: Chinatown, Japantown and Manilatown in American society.* New York: Palgrave Macmillan.

Lai, D. C. 1988. *Chinatowns: Towns within cities in Canada.* Vancouver, B.C.: University of British Columbia Press.

Lai, H. M. 1994. Unfinished business: The confession program. In *The repeal and its legacy: Proceedings of the conference on the 50th anniversary of the repeal of the Exclusion Acts*, 47–57. San Francisco, CA, Chinese Historical Society of America.

Lee, E. 2003. *At America's gates: Chinese immigration during the Exclusion Era, 1882–1943.* Chapel Hill, NC: University of North Carolina Press.

Lee, M. S. 1939. The recreational interests and participation of a selected group of Chinese boys and girls in Los Angeles, California. MA thesis. University of Southern California.

Leong, K. 1994. Gender, race and the Page Law. In *The repeal and its legacy: Proceedings of the conference on the 50th anniversary of the repeal of the Exclusion Acts*, 33–41. San Francisco: Chinese Historical Society of America.

Leung, C. K. 1993. Personal contacts, subcontracting linkages, and development in the Hong Kong–Zhujiang delta regions. *Annals of the Association of American Geographers* 83, no. 2:272–302.

Levin, J., and W. J. Leong. 1973. Comparative reference group behavior and assimilation. *Phylon* 34:289–294.

Lew, K. 1988. Chinatown: The present. In *Chinatown Los Angeles: The golden years 1938–1988*, 59, 63. Los Angeles, CA: Chinese Chamber of Commerce.

Ley, David. 1995. Between Europe and Asia: The case of the missing sequoias. *Ecumene* 2 (2): 185–210.

Li, P., B. Wong, and F. Kwan. 1974. *Garment industry in Los Angeles Chinatown 1973–1974.* Los Angeles, CA: Asian American Studies Center, UCLA.

Li, P. S. 1994. Unneighbourly houses and unwelcome Chinese: The social construction of race in the battle over "monster houses" in Vancouver, Canada. *International Journal of Comparative Race and Ethnic Studies* 1:14–33.

———. 1998. *Chinese in Canada.* 2nd ed. Toronto: Oxford University Press.

———. 2003. *Destination Canada: Immigration debates and issues.* Don Mills, ON: Oxford University Press.

Li, W. 1990. Downtown-uptown: A geographical study of the Chinese experience in the Washington and Baltimore metropolitan area. Unpublished research proposal. University of Maryland at College Park, College Park, MD.

———. 1998a. Anatomy of a new ethnic settlement: The Chinese *ethnoburb* in Los Angeles. *Urban Studies* 353:479–501.

———. 1998b. Los Angeles' Chinese *ethnoburb*: From ethnic service center to global economy outpost. *Urban Geography* 196:502–517.

———. 1998c. Ethnoburb versus Chinatown: Two types of urban ethnic communities in Los Angeles. *Cybergeo* 10:1–12. http://www.cybergeo.presse.fr/culture/weili/weili.htm

———. 1999. Building ethnoburbia: The emergence and manifestation of the Chinese *ethnoburb* in Los Angeles' San Gabriel Valley. *Journal of Asian American Studies* 21:1–28.

———. 2004. Chinese Americans. In *Encyclopedia of the world's minorities,* ed. Carl Skutsch, 296–301. New York: Routledge and Kegan Paul.

———. 2006. *From urban enclave to ethnic suburb: New Asian communities in Pacific Rim countries.* Honolulu: University of Hawai'i Press.

———, and G. Dymski 2007. Globally connected and locally embedded financial institutions: Analyzing the ethnic Chinese banking sector. In *Chinese ethnic economy: Global and local perspectives,* eds. Eric Fong and L. Chiu, 35–63. London: Routledge.

———, G. Dymski, Y. Zhou, M. Chee, and C. Aldana. 2002. Chinese American banking and community development in Los Angeles County. *Annals of Association of American Geographers* 924, no. 4:777–796.

———, and E. Park. 2006. Asian Americans in Silicon Valley: High technology industry development and community transformation. In *From urban enclave to ethnic suburb: New Asian communities in Pacific Rim countries,* ed. Wei Li, 119–133. Honolulu: University of Hawai'i Press.

Liberson, S. 1961. The impact of residential segregation on ethnic assimilation. *Social Forces* 40:52–57.

Light, I., P. Bhachu, and S. Karageorgis. 1993. Migration networks and immigration entrepreneurship. In *Immigration and entrepreneurship: Culture, capital, and ethnic networks,* eds. I. Light and P. Bhachu, 25–49. New Brunswick, NJ: Transaction Publishers.

———, and E. Bonacich. 1988. *Immigrant entrepreneurs: Koreans in Los Angeles, 1965–1982.* Berkeley, CA: University of California Press.

————, and S. Karageorgis. 1994. Economic saturation and immigrant entrepreneurship. In *Immigration and Absorption: Issues in a multicultural perspective*, eds. Lazin Isralowitz and I. Light, 89–108. Beer-Sheva, Israel: Ben-Gurion University of the Negev.

————, and C. Rosenstein. 1995. *Race, ethnicity, and entrepreneurship in urban America*. New York: Aldine de Gruyter.

————, G. Sabagh, M. Bozorgmehr, and C. Der-Martirosian. 1994. The four Iranian ethnic economies in Los Angeles. In *Immigration and absorption: Issues in a multicultural perspective*, eds. Lazin Isralowitz and I. Light, 109–132. Beer–Sheva, Israel: Ben–Gurion University of the Negev.

Lin, J. 1998. *Reconstructing Chinatown: Ethnic enclave, global change*. Minneapolis: University of Minnesota Press.

Ling, H. 2005. *Chinese St. Louis: From enclave to cultural community*. Philadelphia: Temple University Press.

Lipsitz, G. 1998. *The possessive investment in whiteness: How white people profit from identity politics*. Philadelphia, PA: Temple University Press.

Liu, J. M., and L. Cheng. 1994. Pacific Rim development and the duality of post–1965 Asian immigration to the United States. In *The new Asian immigration in Los Angeles and global restructuring*, eds. P. Ong, E. Bonacich, and L. Cheng, 77–99. Philadelphia, PA: Temple University Press.

Lo, L. 2006. Suburban housing and indoor shopping: The production of the contemporary Chinese landscape in Toronto. In *From urban enclave to ethnic suburb: New Asian communities in Pacific Rim countries*, ed. Wei Li, 134–154. Honolulu: University of Hawai'i Press.

————, and Shuguang Wang. 1998. Settlement patterns of Toronto's Chinese immigrants: Convergence or divergence? *Canadian Journal of Regional Science* 21, no. 2:49–72.

Loo, C., and D. Mar. 1982. Desired residential mobility in a low income ethnic community: A case study of Chinatown. *Journal of Social Issues* 38:95–106.

Lou, M. 1982. The Chinese American community of Los Angeles, 1870–1900: A case of resistance, organization, and participation. PhD diss. University of California, Irvine.

Lowenthal, A., et al. 1996. International linkages. In *Atlas of Southern California*, ed. M. J. Dear, 27–33. Los Angeles, CA: University of Southern California.

Lyman, S. M. 1988. *Chinatown and Little Tokyo*. Millwood, NY: Associated Faculty Press.

Mangiafico, L. 1988. *Contemporary American immigrants. Patterns of Filipino, Korean, and Chinese settlement in the United States*. New York: Praeger.

Mason, W. 1967. The Chinese in Los Angeles. *Museum Alliance Quarterly* 6, no. 2:15–20.

Mathews, J. Asian–Americans in ascendancy. *Washington Post*, November 29, 1983.

Miller, D. W. 2000. The new urban studies: Los Angeles scholars use their region and their ideas to end the dominance of the "Chicago School." *Chronicle of Higher Education*, August 18, A15.

Miller, V. P., and J. M. Quigley. 1990. Segregation by racial and demographic group: Evidence from the San Francisco Bay Area. *Urban Studies* 27:3–21.

Min, P. G. 1994. The economic bases of ethnic solidarity: The New York Korean Community. Paper presented at Department of Sociology seminar. Los Angeles, CA: University of Southern California.

Mitchell, K. 1993. Multiculturalism, or the united colors of capitalism? *Antipode* 254:263–294.

———. 2004. *Crossing the neoliberal line: Pacific Rim migration and the metropolis.* Philadelphia, PA: Temple University Press.

Modell, J. 1977. *The economics and politics of racial accommodation: The Japanese of Los Angeles, 1900–1942.* Urbana, IL: University of Illinois Press.

Monterey Park Oral History Project. 1990. Monterey Park, CA: Monterey Park City library (audio tapes).

Morrill, R. L. 1965. The Negro ghetto: Problems and alternatives. *Geographical Review* 55:339–61.

National Association of Chinese American Bankers (NACAB). 1992. *Bird's-Eye View* 3, no. 2 (May).

———. 2000. *The National Association of Chinese American Bankers 13th Convention 2000.* Los Angeles, CA: NACAB.

Newmark, M. H., and M. R. Newmark. 1916. *Sixty years in Southern California, 1853–1913, containing the reminiscences of Harris Newmark.* New York: Knickerbocker Press.

Omi, Michael, and H. Winant. 1986. *Racial formation in the United States: From the 1960s to the 1980s.* New York: Routledge and Kegan Paul.

———. 1994. *Racial formation in the United States: From the 1960s to the 1990s.* 2nd ed. New York: Routledge and Kegan Paul.

Ong, P. M. 1984. Chinatown unemployment and the ethnic labor market. *The Amerasia Journal* 1:35–54.

———, and John M. Liu. 1994. U.S. immigration policies and Asian migration. In *The New Asian immigration in Los Angeles and global restructuring,* eds. Paul Ong, E. Bonacich, and L. Cheng, 45–73. Philadelphia, PA: Temple University Press.

Padgett, D. 1980. Symbolic ethnicity and patterns of ethnic identity assertion in American-born Serbs. *Ethnic Groups* 3:55–77.

Paral, R. 2000. *Suburban immigrant communities: Assessments by key characteristics and needs.* Chicago: The Fund for Immigrants and Refugees.

Park, R. E. 1950. *Race and Culture.* Glencoe, IL: Free Press.

———, and H. Miller. 1921. *Old World traits transplanted.* New York: Harper and Brothers.

Pearlstone, Z. 1990. *Ethnic L.A.* Beverly Hills, CA: Hillcrest Press.

People's Daily Overseas Edition. 2000. Chinese "little overseas students" in the U.S. June 17, 4.

Peterson, G. E., and W. Vroman. 1992. *Urban labor markets and job opportunity.* Washington, D.C: Urban Institute Press.

Philpott, T. L. (1991). *The slum and the ghetto: Immigrants, Blacks, and reformers in Chicago, 1880–1930*, Belmont, CA: Wadsworth Publishing Co.

Portes, A., and R. L. Bach. 1985. *Latin journey: Cuban immigrants in the United States*. Berkeley: University of California Press.

———, L. E. Guarnizo, and P. Landolt. 1999. The study of transnationalism: Pitfalls and promise of an emergent research field. *Ethnic and Racial Studies* 222:217–237.

———, and L. Jensen. 1987. What's an ethnic enclave? The case for conceptual clarity. *American Sociological Review* 52:768–771.

Pulido, L. 1996. *Environmentalism and economic justice: Two Chicano struggles in the Southwest*. Tucson: The University of Arizona Press.

———. 2002. Reflections on a white discipline. *The Professional Geographer* 541:42–49.

Quan, E. Y. 1988. Pioneer families share their history. In *Chinatown Los Angeles: The golden years 1938–1988*, 29, 31. Los Angeles, CA: Chinese Chamber of Commerce.

Ray, B. K., G. Halseth, and B. Hohnson. 1997. The changing "face" of suburbs: Issues of ethnicity and residential changes in suburban Vancouver. *International Journal of Urban and Regional Research* 21, no. 1:75–99.

Roche, J. P. 1982. Suburban ethnicity: Ethnic attitudes and behavior among Italian Americans in two suburban communities. *Social Science Quarterly* 63:145–153.

Roediger, D. R. 1991. *The wages of whiteness: Race and the making of the American working class*. London: Verso.

Rose, H. M. 1970. The development of an urban subsystem: The case of the Negro ghetto. *Annals of the Association of American Geographers* 60, no. 1:1–17.

———. 1971. *The Black ghetto: A spatial behavioral perspective*. New York: McGraw–Hill Book Company.

———. 1976a. Metropolitan Miami's changing Negro population, 1950–1960. In *Black America geographic perspectives*, eds. R. T. Ernst and L. Hugg, 89–104. Garden City, NY: Anchor Press.

———. 1976b. The origin and pattern of development of urban black social areas. In *Black America geographic perspectives*, eds. R. T. Ernst and L. Hugg, 34–43. Garden City, NY: Anchor Press.

Roseman, C. C. 1971. Migration as a spatial and temporal process. *Annals of the Association of American Geographers* 61:589–598.

Rowe, S., and J. Wolch. 1990. Social networks in time and space: Homeless women in Skid Row Los Angeles. *Annals of the Association of American Geographers* 80:184–204.

Saito, L. T. 1998. *Race and politics: Asian Americans, Latinos, and whites in a Los Angeles suburb*. Urbana: University of Illinois Press.

Sanchez, G. J. 1999. Face the nation: Race, immigration, and the rise of nativism in late-twentieth-century America. In *The handbook of international migration: The American experience*, eds. C. Hirschman, P. Kasinitz, and J. De Wind, 371–382. New York: The Russell Sage Foundation.

Sanders, J., and V. Nee. 1987. On testing the enclave-economy hypothesis, *American Sociological Review* 52:771–773.

Sanders, R. A., and J. S. Adams. 1976. Age structure in expanding ghetto space: Cleveland, Ohio, 1940–1965. In *Black America geographic perspectives*, eds. R. T. Ernst and L. Hugg, 105–113. Garden City, NY: Anchor Press.

Sassen, S. 1994. America's immigration "problem." In *Race and ethnic conflict*, eds. F. L. Pincus and H. J. Ehrlich, 229–236. Boulder, CO: Westview Press.

Satzewich, V. and L. Wong eds. 2006. *Transnational identities and practices in Canada.* Vancouver, BC: University of British Columbia Press.

Saxenian, A. 1999. *Silicon Valley's new immigrant entrepreneurs.* San Francisco, CA: Public Policy Institute of California.

————. 2002. *Local and global networks of immigrant professionals in Silicon Valley.* San Francisco, CA: Public Policy Institute of California.

Saxton, A. 1995. *The indispensable enemy labor and the anti–Chinese movement in California.* Berkeley: University of California Press.

Schoenberger, K. 1993. Chinese: Immigrants boost southland economy. *Los Angeles Times*, October 4, 5.

Scott, A. J. 1988. *Metropolis: From the division of labor to urban form.* Berkeley: University of California Press.

————. 1993. *Technopolis: High-technology industry and regional development in Southern California.* Berkeley: University of California Press.

Seo, D. 1992. Sun down for Chinatown? *Los Angeles Times City Times.* November 1, 24–26.

Singer, A., S. Hardwick, and C. Brettell, eds. 2008. *Suburban immigrant gateways: Immigration and incorporation in new U.S. metropolitan destinations.* Washington, DC: Brookings Institution.

Siu, P. C. P. 1987. *The Chinese laundryman: A study of social isolation.* New York: New York University Press.

Skeldon, R. 1999. Migration of entrepreneurs from Hong Kong: Background, trends and impacts. *New Zealand Geographer* 552:66–71.

Skop, E., and W. Li. 2003. From the ghetto to the invisoburb: Shifting patterns of immigrant settlement in contemporary America. In *Multi-cultural geographies: Persistence and change in U.S. racial/ethnic geography*, eds. John W. Frazier and Florence L. Margai, 113–124. Binghamton, NY: Global Academic Publishing.

Smith, Christopher J. 1995. Asian New York: The geography and politics of diversity. *International Migration Review* 24, no. 1:59–84.

————, and J. Logan. 2006. Flushing 2000: Geographic explorations in Asian New York. In *From urban enclave to ethnic suburb: New Asian communities in Pacific Rim countries*, ed. Wei Li, 41–74. Honolulu: University of Hawai'i Press.

Soja, E. 1989. *Postmodern geographies: The reassertion of space in critical social theory.* London, Verso.

————, R. Morales, and G. Wolff. 1989. Urban restructuring: An analysis of social and spatial changes in Los Angeles. In *Atop the urban hierarchy*, ed. R. A. Beauregard, 87–122. Totowa, NJ: Rowman & Littlefield Publishers, Inc.

Sowell, T. 1981. *Ethnic America: A history.* New York: Basic Books, Inc. Publishers.

Stearns L. B., and J. R. Logan. 1986. The racial structuring of the housing market and segregation in suburban areas. *Social Forces* 65:28–42.

Sterry, N. 1922. Housing conditions in Chinatown Los Angeles. *Journal of Applied Sociology* 7, no. 2:70–75.

———. 1923. Social attitudes of Chinese immigrants. *Journal of Applied Sociology* 7, no. 6:325–333.

Storper, M., and R. Walker. 1989. *The capital imperative: Territory, technology, and industrial growth.* Cambridge, MA: Blackwell Publishers.

Tanzer, A. 1985. Little Taipei. *Forbes,* May 6, 68–71.

Thompson, R. H. 1979. Ethnicity versus class: An analysis of conflict in a North American Chinese community. *Ethnicity* 6:306–326.

———. 1989. *Toronto's Chinatown: The changing social organization of an ethnic community.* New York: AMS Press, Inc.

Thrift, N., and K. Olds. 1996. Refiguring the economic in economic geography. *Progress in Human Geography* 203:311–337.

Torrieri, N. K. 1982. Residential dispersal and the survival of the Italian community in metropolitan Baltimore 1920–1980. PhD diss. University of Maryland at College Park, Department of Geography.

Tsai, S. H. 1986. *The Chinese experience in America.* Bloomington: Indiana University Press.

Tseng, Y. 1994a. Suburban ethnic economy: Chinese business communities in Los Angeles. PhD diss. University of California, Los Angeles

———.1994b. Chinese ethnic economy: San Gabriel Valley, Los Angeles County. *Journal of Urban Affairs* 16, no. 2:169–189.

———. 1995. Beyond "Little Taipei": The development of Taiwanese immigrant businesses in Los Angeles. *International Migration Review* 24, no. 1:33–35.

Tung, W. 1974. *Chinese in America, 1820–1970: A chronology and fact book.* Dobbs Ferry, NY: Oceana Publications Inc.

U.S. Bureau of the Census. Various census reports, by year. Washington, DC: Government Printing Office.

    1860 census year: 1864. *Population of the United States in 1860.*

    1890 census year: 1890. *Eleventh Census of the United States.*

    1910 census year: 1913. *Thirteenth Census of the United States.* Abstract.

    1920 census year: 1923. *Fourteenth Census of the United States.* Abstract.

    1930 census year: 1932. *Fifteenth Census of the United States 1930.*

    1940 census year: 1940. *Sixteenth Census of the United States 1940.*

    1950 census year: 1954. *Census of Population, 1950.*

    1960 census year: 1963. *Census of Population, 1960.* Special Report 1c.

    1970 census year: 1971. *Census of Population, 1970.*

    1980 census year: 1988. *Census of Population, 1980.*

    1990 census year: 1992. *Census of Population, 1990.*

2000 census year: http://factfinder.census.gov/servlet/DTTable. Last accessed: January 7, 2004.

———. 1990. *Census of Population and Housing.* Washington, DC, Government Printing Office.

———. 1992. *Census of Population and Housing,* Summary Tape Files 3a. Washington, DC: Government Printing Office.

U.S. Congress. 1882. *CHAP. 126: An act to execute certain treaty stipulations relating to the Chinese.* Rpt. in Chinese Historical Society of America, 1994. *The repeal and its legacy: Proceedings of the conference on the 50th anniversary of the repeal of the Exclusion Acts.* San Francisco: Chinese Historical Society of America.

———. 1943. *An act to repeal the Chinese Exclusion Acts, to establish quotas, and for other purposes.* Rpt. in Chinese Historical Society of America, 1994. *The repeal and its legacy: Proceedings of the conference on the 50th anniversary of the repeal of the Exclusion Acts.* San Francisco: Chinese Historical Society of America.

———. 1965. Immigration and nationality act: Amendments Public Law 89–236 H.R. 2580. *U.S. Code Congressional & Administrative News, 89th Congress–First Session.* 883–987.

———. 1991. Immigration Act of 1990: Public Law 101–649. *U.S. Code Congressional & Administrative News, 101th Congress–Second Session.* St. Paul, MN: West Publishing Co.

U.S. Immigration and Naturalization Service. 1993. *Statistical yearbook of the Immigration and Naturalization Service.* Washington, DC: Government Publishing Office.

Vertovec, S. 1999. Conceiving and researching transnationalism. *Ethnic and Racial Studies* 222:447–462.

Vrana, D. 1998. East West Bank taking an unusual route to go public. *Los Angeles Times,* December 14.

Waldinger, Roger D., Howard Aldrich, and Robin Ward. 1990. Opportunities, group characteristics, and strategies. In *Ethnic entrepreneurs: Immigrant business in industrial societies,* eds. R. D. Waldinger et al., 13–48. Newbury Park, CA: SAGE Publications, Inc.

———, and Y. Tseng. 1992. Divergent diasporas: The Chinese communities of New York and Los Angeles compared. *Revue Europeénne des Migrations Internationals* 8, no. 3:91–115.

Wang, L. L. 1994. Politics of the repeal of the Chinese Exclusion Laws. In *The repeal and its legacy: Proceedings of the conference on the 50th anniversary of the repeal of the Exclusion Acts,* 66–80. San Francisco: Chinese Historical Society of America.

Wang, S. G. 1999. Chinese commercial activity in the Toronto CMA: New development patterns and impacts. *Canadian Geographer* 431:19–35.

Ward, D. 1971. *Cities and immigrants: A geography of changes in nineteenth-century America.* New York: Oxford University Press.

Waters, M. C. 1999. *Black identities: West Indian immigrant dreams and American realities.* New York: Russell Sage Foundation.

Wells Fargo & Co. 1882. *Directory of principal Chinese business firms in San Francisco.* San Francisco, CA: Wells Fargo & Co.

Wilson, K. L., and A. Portes. 1980. Immigrant enclaves: An analysis of the labor market experiences of Cubans in Miami. *American Journal of Sociology* 86:295–319.

Winsberg, M. D. 1986. Ethnic segregation and concentration in Chicago suburbs. *Urban Geography* 7:135–145.

Wolch, J. R., and M. J. Dear. 1993. *Malign neglect: Homelessness in an American City.* San Francisco, CA: Jossey–Bass Publishers.

Wong, B. P. 1982. *Chinatown, economic adaptation and ethnic identity of the Chinese.* New York: Holt, Rinehart and Winston.

———. 1988. *Patronage, brokerage, entrepreneurship and the Chinese community of New York.* New York: AMS Press.

———. 1998. *Ethnicity and entrepreneurship: The New Chinese immigrants in the San Francisco Bay Area.* Boston, MA: Allyn and Bacon.

———. 2005. *The Chinese in Silicon Valley: Globalization, social networks, and ethnic identity.* Lanham, MD: Rowman and Littlefield.

Wong, Charles C. 1980. The continuity of Chinese grocers in Southern California. *The Journal of Ethnic Studies* 82, no. 2:63–82.

Wood, J. 1997. Vietnamese-American placemaking in northern Virginia. *Geographical Review* 87, no. 2:58–72.

Zelinsky, W., and B. A. Lee. 1998. Heterolocalism: An alternative model of the sociospatial behaviour of immigrant ethnic communities. *International Journal of Population Geography* 4, no. 4:281–298.

Zhao, Xiaojian. 2002. *Remaking Chinese America: Immigration, family, and community, 1940–1965.* New Brunswick, NJ: Rutgers University Press.

Zhou, M. 1992. *Chinatown: The socioeconomic potential of an urban enclave.* Philadelphia, PA: Temple University Press.

———. 1997. Segmented assimilation: Issues, controversies, and recent research on the new second generation. *International Migration Review* 314:975–1008.

———. 1998. "Parachute kids" in Southern California: The educational experience of Chinese Children in transnational families. *Educational Policy* 12, no. 6:682–704.

———, and R. Kim. 2003. A tale of two metropolises: Immigrant Chinese communities in New York and Los Angeles. In *Los Angeles and New York in the new millennium,* ed. David Halle, 124–149. Chicago, IL: University of Chicago Press.

———, Yen-Fen Tseng, and Rebecca Y. Kim. 2008. "Suburbanization and new trends in community development: The case of Chinese ethnoburbs in the San Gabriel Valley, California. In *Contemporary Chinese America: Immigration, ethnicity, and community transformation,* M. Zhou. Philadelphia: Temple University Press.

Zhou, Y. 1996a. Ethnic networks as transactional networks: Chinese networks in the producer service sectors of Los Angeles. PhD diss. University of Minnesota.

———. 1996b. Inter-firm linkages, ethnic networks and territorial agglomeration: Chinese computer firms in Los Angeles. *Papers in Regional Science* 753:265–291.

———. 1998a. How places matter? Comparative study of Chinese immigrant communities in Los Angeles and New York City. *Urban Geography* 196:531–553.

———. 1998b. Beyond ethnic enclaves: Location strategies of Chinese producer service firms in Los Angeles. *Economic Geography* 743:228–251.

Index

Page numbers in **boldface** type indicate figures.

99 Ranch Market, 106
1882 Chinese Exclusion Act, 34. *See also* Chinese Exclusion Act
1892 Geary Law, 56
1907 Gentlemen's Agreement, 34
1917 Immigration Act, 34
1924 National Origins Act, 34
1934 Tydings-McDuffie Act, 34
1964 Civil Rights Act, 34
1965 Immigration and Nationality Act, 34–35, 41, 53
1965 Voting Rights Act, 34
1968 Fair Housing Act, 34
1980 Refugee Act, 37

Acculturation-assimilation, 4, 11, 13, 15, 19–20, 27
Alhambra, 80–81, **82,** 86, 88, 96, 98, 107, 110, 112, 114–116, **114,** 138, 140, 153, 158–159, 188n.14 (chap. 3)
American-born Chinese (ABCs), 56, 58, 68, 119, 123, 150–151, 152, 176
American Competitiveness and Workforce Improvement Act of 1998 (ACWIA), 38
American Indians, 21, 61
Angel Island, 57
Anglo Americans, 12
Anglo-Saxon, 12, 33
anti-miscegenation, 58
Arcadia, 75, **82,** 86, 96, 107, 114–115, **114,** 137–139, 152–153, 158, 173, 179
Arlington, 70

Artesia, 73, 174
Asian Americans, x, 15, 21, 41, 85, 93, 98, 150, 166, 175, 176, 177, 185n.7, 187n.5
Asian Indians, 34, 174
Asian Pacific Economic Cooperation Forum (APEC), 32
Asiatic Barred Zone, 34
Assimilation, 4, 12–14, 16, 19–20, 47–49, 56, 62, 90, 129, 149, 172, 182, 185n.3 (chap. 1)
racialized, 16, 34, 45, 54, 71, 80, 93, 95, 167, 172, 180, 182, 185n.3 (chap. 1); segmented, 16, 185n.3 (chap. 1)
Association of Southeastern Asian Nations (ASEAN), 38
Atlantic Boulevard, 76, 84, 100, 110
Australia, 32, 37, 154, 156, 174

Bank SinoPac of Taiwan, 162
Beijing, 87, 107, 164
Bel Air, 80
ben sheng ren, 120, 154
Broadway, 68, 70, **73**
Buddhist, 68, 76, 95
Burbank, 65
Burlingame Treaty of 1868, 54

Cambodia, 37, 72, 120, 122, 136, 186n.3
Cambodian, 72
Canton (Guangzhou), 151
Cantonese, 2, 61, 72, 120, 162, 189n.3 (chap. 6)

Cathay Bank, 151
Caucasian, 62, 68, 70–71, 162
Census Designated Places (CDPs), 2, 80,
    112, 138, 188n.14 (chap. 3), 189nn.8
    (chap. 5), 1 (chap. 6)
Cerritos, 73, 75, 174
Chan, F. Chow, 151
Chan, Kellogg, 151
Chen, Lily Lee, 93
Chen Shui Bian, President, 155
Chicago, 39, 62, 179, 186n.6
Chicago School of Sociology, 2, 12, 19
China International Trust and Investment
    Corporation (CITIC), 110
Chinatown, 2–3, 5–6, 16, 18, 20, 28, 41,
    45, 47, 58, 62, 64–75, 79–80, 83–85,
    89, 97, 99–100, 107, 111, 118–119, 130,
    143, **144, 145,** 146–148, 151–154, 162,
    171–173, 175–178, 188n.16
Chinatown Gate, 68
Chinatown Plaza, 72
Chinese Air Force, 84
Chinese American, 60–62, 68, 86–87, 93–94,
    96, 98–99, 101, 107, 110, 123, 151–152,
    155–156, 158, 160, 162–164, 166, 174,
    187n.1, 190n.1 (chap. 7)
Chinese Cultural Center, 108, 154
Chinese ethnoburb, vii, 5, 7, 45, 51, 78–80,
    92–93, 96, 117, 144, 171, 174, 180
Chinese Exclusion Act, 56, 58–59, 64
Chinese Student Protection Act, 157
Chineseness, 16
Chu, Betty Tom, 151, 190n.1 (chap. 7)
Chu, Dr. Judy, 94
Chuang, Marshal, 116
CITIC Ka Wah Bank Ltd., 110
City of Industry, 114–115, 139–140, 153
City of Los Angeles, 70, 80–81, 89
City of Monterey Park, 3, 71, 73, 79–80, 91,
    93, 98, 115, 188n.3
City of Toronto, 177, 191n.8
co-ethnic(s), 23–24, 39
College Street, 68
Compton, 85
Confession Program, 60
Covina, **82, 114,** 137–138
Coyote Pass, 84

Cubic Air Ordinance, 67
Cultural Revolution, 157
Cupertino, 176–177, 191n.9
Cupertino Village, 108, 177

Del Mar Avenue, 76
Democratic Progress Party, 155
Diamond Bar, **82,** 87, 114–115, **114,**
    137–139
DiHo Market, 100
downtown versus uptown, 4, 19, 27

East Bay, 176
East Coast, 58
East Los Angeles, 80–81, 84, 94
East West Savings, 152
East York, 177
Eastern District, 80, 87, 106, 115, 117, 131,
    173
EB-5 visa, 38
Echo Park, 83, 89
El Monte, **82,** 86, 114–115, **114,** 137,
    139–140, **141,** 142–143, 149, 153–154,
    173, 189n.4 (chap. 6)
Elmhurst-Corona, 175
enclave economy, 23, 25, 123
er shi zhu, 161
ethnic economic niche, 22–23, 111, 127,
    143
ethnic economy, 5–6, 18, 22–26, 33, 40,
    42–44, 46, 61, 78, 80, 100–101, 106, 111,
    115, 117, 142, 158, 173–174, 180. *See
    also* enclave economy; ethnic economic
    niche
ethnic geography, 1, 11, 13, 18, 28
ethnicity-pluralism, 11–13
ethnoburb, 1, 3–7, 28–30, 33, 41–49, 53,
    73–76, **82,** 85, 87–88, 99–101, **102,**
    103, 106–112, 114–120, 122–125, **126,**
    127–131, 133–134, 136–138, 140–143,
    144, 145, 146, **146,** 147–150, 153, 158,
    160, 164, 166–167, 169, 171–175, 177,
    179–181, 186, 189nn.1, 4 (chap. 6),
    190n.1 (chap. 8)
ethnoburb formation, xi, xiv, 1, 5–7, 39, 42,
    79, 117–118, 172
ethnopolis, 177, 190n.8–6

Etobicoke, 177
Euro-American or European American, 16, 47, 54

Far East National Bank (FENB), 161–162
FCB Taiwan California Bank, 107
FENB (Far East National Bank), 162–165
feng shui, 85
Filipinos, 34
finance, insurance, and real estate (FIRE), 109, 125, 126, 133, 135, 142, 147–148
First Commercial Bank, 107
Flushing, 175–176, 190n.6 (chap. 8)
"forty-niners," 60, 70
Fremont, 176–177
Fu Kuang Shan, 95
Fujian Province, 120
Fuzhou, 160

Garvey Avenue, x
General Agreement of Tariffs & Trade (GATT), 32
Glendale, 188n.14 (chap. 3)
Globalization, 1, 4, 18, 32, 37, 39, 42, 46, 48, 118–120, 123–124, 127, 133, 150, 174, 178
Greater Los Angeles, 5, 110
Greater Toronto Area (GTA), 177–178
Guangdong Province, 54, 61, 72, 189n.3 (chap. 6)

H-1B visa, 38, 41, 181
Hacienda Heights, 76, 80, **82,** 87, 95, 101, 114, 137–139, 173
Hispanic, 62, 80–81, 98, 118, 140
Hong Kong, 2, 31, 37, 61, 80, 85, 88, 90, 107–108, 110, 119–120, 122, 134–137, **141,** 143, 148–149, 152, 154–158, 160–161, 165, 173, 178–179, 188n.10
household income, 130–131, 133, 146, 190n.7 (chap. 6)
Houston, 59, 62, 174, 179–180
Hsi Lai Temple (Coming West Temple), 75–76, **76,** 95, 188n.14 (chap. 4)
Hsieh, Frederick Fukang, 89
Hwang, David Henry, 165, 190n.4 (chap. 7)
Hwang, Henry Y., 161, 190n.4 (chap. 7)

immigrant economy, 22
Immigration Act of 1990, 37–38, 150
income, 20, 23, 33, 67, 112, 127, 130, 132, 134–136, 138–140, 146–148, 173. *See also* household income; personal income
Indian, 24, 176
Indochina, 37, 120, 122, **135,** 136–137, 141, 143, 148–149
Indochinese, 37, 120, 122, 135–136
Indonesia, 108
Inglewood, 85
integrated ethnic economy, 23–24, 40, 44
Invasion-succession, 20, 27
Irvine, 174

Japan Town, 20
Japanese, 20–21, 23, 34, 59, 70, 84–85, 88, 96, 166, 187n.5
Jewish, 22, 25, 95

Kiang, Samuel, 94
Korean, 23, 25, 34, 88, 125, 174
Korean War, 37, 60

L-1 visa, 38
La Puente, **82, 114,** 137, 139–140
Langley Senior Center, 91
lao qiao, 61, 83, 119
Laos, 37, 72, 120, 122, 136, 186n.3
Las Tunas Boulevard, 96
Las Vegas, 107–109
Latin America, 35
Latin American, 31–32
Latino, 21, 41, 84, 87, 116, 125, 139–140, 151, 173
Lee, T. C. (Li Zhengdao), 187n.6
Little Italy, 68
Little Taipei, 90, 154
Little Tokyo, 20, 41, 97
Long Beach, 188n.14 (chap. 3)
Long Beach Freeway, 83
Los Angeles (LA), 1–2, 6–7, 20, 22–23, 25, 28, 33, 39–41, 51, 61–67, 68, 69–74, 79–81, 83–86, 88–91, 94, 98, 103, 106, 110, 117–118, 125, 147–148, 150–153, 155, 159, 161–162, 164, 172, 174–175, 178–179, 188n.14 (chap. 3)

Los Angeles City, 64, 81, **82,** 83, 86, 115
Los Angeles County, 2, 6, 63–65, **63, 69,** 73, 80, **82,** 85–87, **102,** 111, 124–125, **126,** 127–133, 138, 140, 146, 151, 175, 181, 189n.1 (chap. 6)
Los Angeles Times, 3, 65, 94, 97, 160, 189n.4 (chap. 5)
Los Angeles/Southern California, 40

Mainland China, 2, 7, 38, 61, 76, 80, 87, 89, 107, 110, 119–121, 134–137, 143, 149, 154, 156–158, 161, 163–164, 173, 188n.10
Malaysia, 88
Mandarin, 2, 7, 72, 92, 120, 154, 162
Manhattan, 62, 175–176
Markham, 177–178
Mexican American, 93
Mexican Beverly Hills, 84
Midwest, 92
Milpitas, 176
Milpitas Square, 108, 177
Min Nan, 120, 154
Mississauga, 177
Montebello, 80–81, **82,** 106, 109, **114,** 188n.3
Monterey Highlands, 85
Monterey Park, 3, 71–73, 76, 79–81, **82,** 83–86, 88–94, 96–98, 100–101, 106–107, 112, **114,** 115, 117, 120, 123–124, 138, 140, **141,** 142–143, 150–154, 159, 173, 185n.1 (intro), 188n.3, 189n.4 (chap. 6)
Monterey Park Oral History Project 1990, 188nn.2, 6–8
Monterey Pass Road, 84
Montreal, 177–178
Mountain View, 176

Naturalization Law of 1790, 34
nei ren, 88
nei zai mei, 88
New York City, 19, 160, 175
New Zealand, 32, 174
Newly Industrialized Countries (NICs), 38, 134
Ng, Dominic, 156, 190n.3 (chap. 7)
Non-Hispanic white, 4, 16, 21, 40, 139

North America Free Trade Agreement (NAFTA), 32, 150
North American, 5, 7, 32, 174, 179
North York, 177–178
Norwalk, 65

Orange County, 26, 40, 106–108, 174, 180
Oregon, 56, 59, 161

Pacific Coast, 40
Pacific Islanders, 119
Pacific Rim, 3, 32, 40, 87, 110, 164, 174
Page Act (An Act Supplemental to Acts in Relation to Immigration, March 3, 1875), 54
Palos Verdes, 75
panethnicity, 15–16
Pasadena, 65, 80, **82,** 86, **114,** 115, 138–139, **141,** 142, 156, 160, 188n.14 (chap. 3), 189n.4 (chap. 6)
People's Republic of China (PRC), 37, 60, 87, 122, 157, 166
personal income, 130, 136, 146, 190n.7 (chap. 6)
Peter Soo Hoo, 68
Phoenix, 107–108, 174, 189n.5 (chap. 5)
Pomona, 83, 174
Portland, 59
Public Use Microdata Area (PUMA), 124, 141, 143, 189nn.1, 4 (chap. 6)
Public Use Microdata Sample (PUMS), 6, **122,** 126, **128, 129, 131,** 132, 135, **137,** 142, 146–147, 189nn.1, 4 (chap. 6)

Qing Dynasty, 54
Queens, 175–177

Race relation, 12, 15
Racial formation, 15, 17
racialization, 1, 4–5, 11, 15–16, 21, 27, 34, 48, 62, 79, 92–93, 97, 116, 172
Republic of China (Taiwan), 87, 121, 154
Residents Association of Monterey Park (RAMP), 94
Richmond District, 190n.6 (chap. 8)
Richmond Hill, 177–178
Rolling Hills, 75

Rosemead, 80–81, **82,** 86, 107, 112, 114–115, 123–124, 138, 140, **141,** 142, 160, 189n.4 (chap. 6)
Rowland Heights, **77** (figure 10), 80, **82,** 87, 101, 106–109, 114–115, 117, 137–139, 173
Rowland Heights Shopping Plaza, 106

Saigon, 37, 121–122, 134
San Bernadino, 83, 174
San Diego, 151
San Francisco, 20, 24, 39, 56, 59, 61–62, 64, 87–88, 98, 155, 175–176, 190n.6 (chap. 8)
San Francisco Bay Area, 20, 57, 107, 174–175
San Gabriel, 80, **82,** 86, 98, 107, 112, 114, 138, 140
San Gabriel Shopping Plaza, 107
San Gabriel Square, 76, **77** (figure 9), 107–108, 179
San Gabriel Valley, 2–3, 5–6, 28, 41, **45,** 48, 73–76, 78–80, **82,** 83, 86–87, 91, 95–99, 101, 103, 107, 109–112, 114–119, **121,** 123, 130–131, 138, 139, 140, 150, 152, 153, 156, 158, 161, 171–175, 180–181, 185n.2 (intro), 189nn.1, 4 (chap. 6), 190n.1 (chap. 8)
San Gabriel Valley ethnoburb, 15, 23–24, 46, 93, 97, 135–136, 189, 191–192, 199
San Marino, 75, **82,** 86, 96, **114,** 115, 137–139, 153, 156, 158, 160, 163, 173, 179
Santa Clara, 176
Santa Clara County, 176
Santa Clara Valley, 176
Santa Monica, 64, 188n.14 (chap. 3)
Satellite Chinatown, 176
Scarborough, 177–178
Seattle, 59, 107, 186n.6
segregation, 14, 17–20, 45–46, 70
Shanghai, 159, 161
Shanghainese, 158
Silicon Valley, 23, 41, 108, 153, 176–177, 179, 190n.1 (chap. 8)
Singapore, 31
socioeconomic, 2, 29, 36, 43, 48, 62, 133, 150, 153
sojourner, 39, 54, 60, 88
South Bay, 176

South Central Los Angeles, 25
South El Monte, **82, 114,** 137, 139–140, 153, 173
South Korea, 31
South Pasadena, **82,** 86, **114,** 138, 140, 160
South San Gabriel, 80–81, **82, 114**
Southeast Asia, 2, 72, 80, 119, 134, 139, 143, 180
Southeast Asian, 37, 155, 172
Southern California, 64, 66, 68, 70, 84, 88, 90–91, 99, 107, 123, 151, 153, 158, 162, 174
Southland, 76, 107, 179
State of California, 40
structuration, 11
Suburban Chinatown, 2–3
Sunnyvale, 176

tai kong ren, 88
tai tai, 88
Taipei, 87–88, 108
Taiwan, 2, 31, 61, 76, 80, 85, 87–90, 92, 95, 100, 106–110, 119–121, 134–138, **141,** 143, 148–149, 152–155, 157–158, 160–162, 173, 178, 188n.10, 189n.2 (chap. 5)
Tawa, 106–108, 177
Tawa Commercial Property Development Corp., 106
Tawa Investment Inc., 107
Tawa Supermarket, 107–108, 179
techno/ethnoburb, 195
Temple City, **82,** 96, **114,** 137–138, 140, 160
tong, 68
Toronto, 25, 108, 174, 177–179, 190nn.1, 7 (chap. 8), 191n.8
transnational connections, 1, 26–27, 166
Transnationalism, 26–27, 48
Trust Savings and Loan of San Gabriel Valley, 152

United Kingdom, 37, 122, 155
USSR, 36

Valley Boulevard, 76, 110–111
Vancouver, 16, 156, 174, 177–179, 190n.1 (chap. 8), 191n.9

Vernon, 65
Vietnam, 37, 72, 76, 120, 136, 186n.3
Vietnam War, 72, 122, 134, 143, 186n.3
Vietnamese, 72, 174

wai sheng ren, 120, 154
Walnut, 80, **82,** 87, **114,** 137–139
Wang, Marina, 152
War Brides Act (Public Law 713), 60
West Covina, **82,** 115, 137–138, 152, 159
West Los Angeles, 70

Westside, 70–71, 85, 189n.4 (chap. 6)
Woo, Wilbur, 71, 81, 83, 86–87, 100, 188n.7
World Trade Organization (WTO), 32, 150
World War II, 31, 34, 36, 58–59, 80, 84, 87, 134, 166

xin qiao, 61, 119

Yang Zhenning (C. N. Yang), 187n.6
Yokohama Village, 84
York, 177